HOME

COOKERY

YEAR

For Grace, Ivy and Dorothy,
growing up fast.

CLAIRE THOMSON

HOME COOKERY YEAR

**Four Seasons, Over 200 Recipes
for All Possible Occasions**

photography by Sam Folan

Hardie Grant

QUADRILLE

Publishing Director Sarah Lavelle

Copy-editor Judy Barratt

Assistant Editor Stacey Cleworth

Head of Design Claire Rochford

Designer Nicola Ellis

Typesetter Jonathan Baker

Photographer Sam Folan

Cover illustrator Marie Doazan

Prop Stylist Faye Wears

Recipe Development Matthew Williamson

Head of Production Stephen Lang

Production Controller Katie Jarvis

Published in 2020 by Quadrille,
an imprint of Hardie Grant Publishing

Quadrille
52–54 Southwark Street
London SE1 1UN
quadrille.com

Cataloguing in Publication Data: a catalogue record
for this book is available from the British Library.

ISBN 9781787134874

Printed in China

MIX
Paper from
responsible sources
FSC® C020056
FSC
www.fsc.org

CONTENTS

Introduction

This book is for anyone who wants to be able to cook well, with confidence, every day. Understandably this might be viewed with scepticism by some; after all, there are a great many cookbooks out there – what is different about this one, and who says I am the person to enable this?

Home Cookery Year brings together themes that I have previously championed, feeding small children, keeping a well-stocked storecupboard, and how to encourage a new and basic agenda to energize your cooking at home. I am keen on the domesticity the title of this book conjures up. It's not a fashionable title – much more an honest one – and I love it for this. I want to give you a down-to-earth and intuitive framework of how and what to cook all year round. At its heart is an exhortation to shop and cook in tandem with the seasons, which will inevitably give the cook (and keen mealtime recipients) a sense of anticipation and excitement.

The origins of *Home Cookery Year* lie indelibly in a series of notebooks I have kept over the past few years. Disaster struck when my car was broken into and my handbag, complete with current notebook and my wallet, was stolen. It was breaking news locally, with newspaper articles and a radio appearance trying to unearth any information on the whereabouts of my stolen bag. It never materialized and was no doubt launched into a hedge or a black bin, to be collected and turfed into landfill. Panic ensued and I had to do my best to catch up; thankfully, I was able to. Those recipes are in this book; I was able to test and write them again, but sadly the drawings in that particular notebook are lost (the kids have always doodled in my notebooks over the years, peppering the pages, each one a timeline of my work and also their eyes on the world). I recall an especially good one of me drawn by Dorothy, my youngest, then aged 6; in it I have great big bright-red lips, high heels and long, dangly earrings – a case of wishful thinking on her part.

To begin writing this cookbook, and to remind myself of how I have cooked year on year for so many years now, I gathered all my notebooks together and spent a good long while riffling through them all. And sure enough, since the time when I first started out as a chef cooking in restaurants, to now, as a 40-year-old mum of three, there is a rhythm within these books, a beat to how I like to cook.

I am a professional chef and have worked in many different kitchens, under intense pressure – it is a wonderfully enriching and also sometimes stressful job. I will always be glad that I followed it as a career path from the age of 21. Along the way I have met brilliant and extraordinary people working in the field of food; it is an important and ever-changing landscape, one that has a profound impact on everyone, regardless of their occupation.

In more recent years, becoming a parent meant wanting to work less in restaurant kitchens, and trying to recalibrate as someone with a role in food, but one where I could put my children to bed in the evening. Sadly (and I don't think I'm unique in saying this), working as a chef with young children at home is not a combination that dovetails all that well, compounded even more so when your husband is also a chef. Asked what my occupation is these days, my default reply is 'chef', followed by a hastily tacked-on 'food writer'. My role in writing about food is not all that circuitous given that I studied journalism at university. And old student friends delight in telling me that I am now, in fact, exactly who I said I was going to be, back in the days when I would cook vast pots of soup and stews to feed a crowd. My contemporaries all seemed to be on track to becoming doctors, architects and teachers, so my preferred career was certainly viewed as the more leftfield option. Shortly after university I left to go and live in Sydney; fast-track a decade, through more than a few kitchens and quite a few burns, I could call myself a chef. And I still do. Once a week and for occasional events I'll pop on my clogs and button up my whites, lacing an apron tight. Being a chef, being able to cook like one, is an extraordinary skill, and I'm lucky to call it my own. But it is also my objective to encourage others to learn to cook, simpatico as a chef. W

So yes, I think I can show you how – if you would like me to (which, presumably, having bought or borrowed this cookbook, you do). Whilst you don't get the kid's drawings, my shopping lists or indecipherable wine tasting notes, you do get a personal account of what I like to cook, and of how and when I like to cook it. A bit like a chef, a bit like a parent, a bit like me, I suppose.

In *Home Cookery Year* I propose the seasons of spring, summer, autumn and winter are governed, comprehensively, by six different cookery occasions: midweek suppers, on a budget & from the larder, salads as light lunches or side dishes, indulgent or 'treat yourself' cookery, leisurely and weekend cooking, and celebration feasts. Using seasonal plenty with enthusiasm is the cheaper, more rewarding way to cook well. Wait just long enough for the new season to come around, and sure enough, prices drop and opportunity comes thundering along in a shopping basket. A year may have passed, but the sudden influx of broad beans or cherries or Brussels sprouts or radishes always takes me by surprise and fills me with a greedy wonder. The novelty is electric, and I find myself shopping for asparagus or blood oranges like they're going out of fashion. Chefs and those working in food media are mostly quick off the blocks, jostling to be the first to list 'new season' and elusive produce on

their menus or in their magazines. I find it reassuring that, no matter what, when certain ingredients come into season, the dynamic and interested cooks amongst us must then do our best to keep up. It is this style of cooking that I feel is most appropriate to the modern-day diet – leaving nothing to waste, paying acute attention to the food and ingredients we have at our immediate disposal and ensuring we maximize on local bounty. It makes sense, and it always has done, this is not a principle that can or should be swayed by fashion.

The best cooks, to my mind, the thoughtful, savvy ones, will often have many different ways to make use of the one ingredient when in season. Seville oranges are one just example, for marmalade, of course, but also used as a bright citrus seasoning in many of the winter recipes in this book. This habitual attention to food and cooking is a positive one; I want people to return to ingredients and, in turn, recipes, year after year, reminding themselves why this particular dish works so well at a certain point in the season.

*All recipes serve 4 unless otherwise stated. The recipes in the Feast section mostly serve 6–8 people.

**Where parmesan or cheddar is specified, use a good rennet-free alternative if you would prefer to keep the recipe vegetarian.

Midweek Suppers account for a large section of each of the seasons in this book. These are the dishes where you can arrive home from work and have a meal, cooked from scratch, on the table in under 30 minutes. It's this style of cooking that needs to be almost knee-jerk; there is no time for pretension or ego. The food cooked here in this section needs to be quick. Home from work and cooking for your family, feeling a bit stretched, shattered or simply needing to just stop and sit down, I don't imagine there will be many who will want to stand at the stovetop labouring long hours to get dinner on the table in time. It's these meals that are consumed with gusto and eaten at speed; table talk is of the day spent, who, what, where and when, and plans are set for the day ahead. Homework, baths, reading books, uniforms, missing sports socks, spelling tests, there are just a few hours left to get all of this, and more, done and ticked off before bed.

On a Budget & From the Larder:
these are the dishes that use cheaper, stock ingredients and which might warrant a bit more time to create or to eke out flavour. Humble food cooked with care. Dishes where speed is not necessarily the driving force for your cookery, but saving money and being conscientious and careful with the ingredients you do have, are more paramount. Organized storecupboards, knowing what's in your fridge and cultivating a habitual thoughtfulness in home cooking will make you a better cook. The chef in me thrives on paring back my cupboards to a bare minimum, using everything up in an orderly fashion, then replenishing with zeal and beginning again. It's a way of life.

Salads as Light Lunches or Side Dishes:
as categories go, this one is less about cooking and more about gathering flattering ingredients and delivering them in tandem to share amongst your friends and family. These are the plates and bowlfuls to spend a little more time on, adding the finishing touches with a flourish, to prettify and appeal to the people eating them. Some have added protein, fish, cheese or meat, some have grains, potatoes or pulses to bump up and act as bulk, whilst some let the salad, vegetable or fruit ingredients steal the show. This style of cooking (I sometimes feel it is a misnomer even to call it 'cooking'), calls for a certain kind of insouciance that I enjoy in the kitchen. It's about understanding flavour and knowing when to stop, or when to pile in with more herbs, spices, oils and so on.

Treat Yourself
is payday cooking. You're feeling flush, you're in the mood to buy and cook exactly what you feel like. Of course, if we all ate like this on a daily basis, our bank accounts would haemorrhage and our waistlines would swell. These recipes ask you to invest a bit of your budget into a couple of key, more expensive ingredients. This is food you'll want to luxuriate in, perhaps cook with someone special in mind, maybe to give thanks for something in particular, or perhaps to indulge in the fact that, at this point in time, you just can. Cooking is anything but binary. In life, just as in cooking, there are highs, lows and many different middling times, all of which govern how we feel, what we do with our days and with whom we spend our time. This section of the book caters for the times you might need to spoil yourself or celebrate someone else. I cannot think of anything more essential than dedicating some time and care by way of cooking something special when you feel the need to treat yourself and the people you love.

Leisurely and Weekend: these are recipes that will work well at times when you don't feel under pressure of work and general day-to-day busyness. Cooking can be an act of catharsis; there is a certain category of cookery that can indulge the home cook with a more elaborate undertaking, enable a new technique, or simply require more time and absolute concentration. It's a way of giving your brain a break from its normal activity and a chance to follow precise, clear instruction in the form of a succinct recipe with a dedicated and delicious objective. Job done. The cake is baked, the pie is made, the broth is deeply flavoured, the ice cream is churned; these are all recipes that you cannot rush, but you can achieve.

Celebration Feasts: groupings of complementary recipes, menus, sometimes including appropriate drinks or cocktails, to be revelled in as an act of celebration. A feast is no mean feat. It's no-holds-barred cooking, and nothing should be too much trouble. This day has long been anticipated, be it a festive occasion or special event: you've invited your favourite people, the groundwork, by way of sourcing and shopping is done, and all you can do now is get on with the task in hand. It should be a process to enjoy and you'll certainly need some help on the day; assistance in the kitchen with vegetable prep, washing up as you go along to avoid absolute carnage, or laying a table that looks both inviting and breathtaking. Cooking for a feast is more than just the food being cooked; it's about the day itself and the people who come to enjoy it. It's also about the memories that the meal is capable of conjuring for years to come. After all, you want your feasts to go down in history.

This, then, is my *Home Cookery Year.* I'd like for the contents of this book to be evergreen, a little like some of the cookbooks my mum had (and still has) sitting on her kitchen shelf at home. My kitchen is the axis of family life; it's where we pass through the seasons. It's where my children will grow up and we will grow older.

SPRING

Asparagus with Eggs, Wild Garlic & Clotted Cream on Crumpets

300g (10½oz) slim asparagus, trimmed (and cut into 3–5cm/1–2in pieces if on the thick side)

about 60g (2¼oz) wild garlic, spinach, sorrel or watercress, finely shredded

200g (7oz) clotted cream or mascarpone

30g (1oz) unsalted butter, plus more softened for the crumpets

8 eggs, beaten

50g (1¾oz) parmesan or Caerphilly cheese, grated (shredded)

8 crumpets

salt and freshly ground black pepper

Crumpets love butter. You cannot stint them. Which is why I'm suggesting you can go one step further and serve butter and clotted cream together on a crumpet, for supper. Add some asparagus and eggs, throw in some wild garlic (spinach, sorrel or watercress is fine) and some grated (shredded) parmesan. Crumpets – revolutionary in form, but nonetheless reassuringly simple to hurl together at home. This is a super-quick meal. Have warm plates at the ready.

Preheat the oven to 180°C/160°C fan/350°F/ Gas Mark 4. Bring a pan of well-salted water to a boil. Boil the asparagus for 1–2 minutes, until just about tender. Drain well.

Mix half the wild garlic, sorrel or watercress into the clotted cream or mascarpone and season well with salt and pepper.

Melt the butter in a large, ovenproof frying pan (skillet) or oven dish and add the asparagus and remaining wild garlic, spinach, sorrel or watercress. Cook for 2 minutes over a moderate heat.

Season the beaten eggs with salt and pepper and add to the pan, evenly spreading out the asparagus.

Spoon half the creamy wild garlic mixture over the eggs, then sprinkle with the cheese and bake in the oven for 8–10 minutes, until lightly golden on top and barely cooked in the middle.

Toast the crumpets, then butter each generously. Spread them with the remaining clotted-cream mixture.

Remove the eggs from the oven and immediately dollop great spoonfuls onto the top of the hot, buttered crumpets. Serve immediately.

Lemon & Artichoke Meatballs with Tomato Sauce

280g (10oz) artichokes in oil, drained and roughly chopped

1 unwaxed lemon, zested, then cut into quarters

200g (7oz) minced (ground) lamb or beef

1 bunch of spring onions (scallions), thinly sliced

1 small bunch of flat-leaf parsley, leaves picked and finely chopped

100g (3½oz) fresh breadcrumbs

50g (1¾oz) parmesan or other hard cheese, grated (shredded)

3–4 tbsp ras el hanout

1 tsp salt

2 eggs, beaten

plain (all-purpose) flour, for dusting

sunflower oil, for frying

50ml (1¾fl oz) good olive oil, plus more to serve

400g (14oz) tomato passata

salt and freshly ground black pepper

You could prepare fresh artichokes. You could... but given that time is of the essence when under the cosh and cooking midweek, the jarred sort, stored in oil and a stalwart of the storecupboard, works perfectly here. I like to use lamb mince, but you could just as well use beef. The tomato sauce is an aromatic one. Most supermarkets sell the ras-el-hanout spice blend these days, and it is also available online. I would suggest serving the meatballs alongside some couscous, but stuffing them snugly in a baguette or flat bread with some rocket (arugula) or lettuce for company would be equally terrific.

Mix the artichokes with the lemon zest, minced (ground) meat, spring onions (scallions), half the parsley, the breadcrumbs, the parmesan, half the ras el hanout, and the teaspoon of salt. Add the eggs and mix until thoroughly combined. Form into ping-pong-ball-size balls or ovals and dust lightly all over with flour.

Heat a 5mm (¼in) depth of sunflower oil in a deep, cast-iron frying pan (skillet) over a moderately high heat. Fry the meatballs in batches for about 5–8 minutes per batch, turning occasionally, until nicely brown all over. Transfer the cooked meatballs onto paper towels to drain. Keep warm.

While the meatballs are cooking, heat the olive oil in a large saucepan. Add the remaining ras el hanout and cook over a low heat until fragrant (about 10 seconds). Add the passata and simmer over a low heat for about 10 minutes, until the sauce thickens. Season well with salt and pepper.

Place the warm meatballs on top of the tomato sauce and sprinkle with the remaining parsley. A slick more olive oil is good, too. Serve with the lemon wedges on the side.

Cumin-spiked Butter Beans with Chorizo & Padrón Peppers

2 x 400g (14oz) cans butter (lima) beans, drained and rinsed

3 cloves of garlic, roughly chopped

1 tsp ground cumin, plus more to taste

½ tsp salt

juice of 1 lemon

100ml (3½fl oz) olive oil

200g (7oz) chorizo, cut into fat coins

400g (14oz) padrón peppers, whole; or use 2 green (bell) peppers and 2 green chillies, thinly sliced

1 bunch of spring onions (scallions), trimmed and cut into 3cm (1¼in) lengths

1 small bunch of flat-leaf parsley, leaves picked and roughly chopped

salt and freshly ground black pepper, to taste

big pinch of paprika (smoked, sweet or hot, as you like), to serve

good bread, to serve

Padrón peppers come into season in springtime. It's the peppers here, cooked fiercely in the chorizo oil until blistered and wizened, that are stars of the show. If you can't get hold of padrón, use green (bell) peppers with some fresh green chilli fried in the mixture. Omit the chorizo, if you like, but be sure to add a pinch more of the paprika to the peppers once you've cooked them. I like to serve this with good bread on the side to swoop through the oil and white bean purée. Messy, convivial eating – just the ticket.

Blend the beans with the garlic, cumin, salt, half the lemon juice and half the olive oil, 50ml (1¾fl oz) of water and a generous amount of black pepper to a smooth purée. Gently warm in a saucepan over a moderate heat and keep warm to serve while you cook the remaining elements.

Heat 2 tablespoons of the remaining olive oil in a cast-iron frying pan (skillet) over a moderate heat and cook the chorizo for 3–5 minutes, until crisp at edges. Remove from the heat, scoop out the chorizo and put to one side, keeping the oil the pan.

In the chorizo-flavoured oil, fry the padrón (or alternative) peppers and spring onions (scallions), seasoned with salt over a high heat for 2–5 minutes, until golden and blistered. You may need to do this in 2 batches to ensure you get a good fierce heat on the peppers as they cook. Use a little more olive oil, if necessary.

With all the vegetables softened, add the parsley and season to taste with black pepper and the remaining lemon juice. Add an extra pinch of cumin, if you like, and check again for seasoning.

Spread the warm bean purée over a large, warm plate, scatter over the cooked spring onions and peppers and top with the chorizo and any oil leftover from the pan. Top with the paprika and serve with bread.

Smoked Mackerel with Grilled Spring Onions & Jersey Royals with Crème Fraîche & Horseradish

300g (10½oz) Jersey royals or similar small, new-season potatoes

1 bunch of spring onions (scallions), trimmed

olive oil

4 fat fillets of peppered or plain smoked mackerel

3 tsp grated (shredded) fresh horseradish, plus more to serve; or 1 tbsp jarred horseradish

4 tbsp crème fraîche

1 small bunch of flat-leaf parsley, leaves picked and roughly chopped

1 unwaxed lemon, all the zest and a squeeze of the juice

salt and freshly ground black pepper

This isn't really cooking, it's more about intuitively knowing what flavours go with what and how to get the best out of them simply, with maximum effect. Smoked mackerel, the ever-handy packet to have ready and waiting in the fridge, flaked over some warm waxy potatoes, then dressed with a little crème fraîche, pepped as it is here with some horseradish, is alchemy. Grilling (broiling) the spring onions (scallions) until blistered and soft brings out their sweet flavour and adds texture. As potato salads go, this one will take some beating.

Place the potatoes in a saucepan of well-salted water and bring to a boil. Boil until tender – they should take about 20 minutes. Drain and allow to cool until warm.

Meanwhile, heat the grill (broiler) to high. Grill (broil) the spring onions (scallions) with a slick of olive oil for about 3–5 minutes, or until nicely coloured and all soft throughout (or, fry them in a pan over a medium–high heat for about 3–5 minutes). Skin and flake the mackerel, discarding any bones, into a large bowl and add the softened spring onions.

Slice the warm potatoes and add to the bowl with the mackerel and onions. Stir together and check the seasoning.

Mix the horseradish and crème fraîche together with the parsley and add the squeeze of lemon juice to taste. Season with salt and pepper.

Drizzle the crème fraîche dressing over the mackerel and warm potato salad and finish by sprinkling over the lemon zest. Add an extra grating of fresh horseradish, if using. Serve immediately.

Broad Beans Cooked with Eggs, Dill & Cumin & served with Yogurt

400g (7oz) broad (fava) beans, podded (or use frozen)

60g (2¼oz) unsalted butter

1 bunch of spring onions (scallions), trimmed and finely chopped

1 tsp ground turmeric

4 cloves of garlic, finely chopped

1 bunch of dill, finely chopped

60g (2¼oz) crispy fried onions

4 eggs

1 tsp cumin seeds, toasted and lightly crushed in a grinder or mortar

salt and freshly ground black pepper

flat breads, to serve

about 150g (5½oz) natural yogurt, seasoned with a little salt, to serve

The very nature of midweek dishes means that, it's fair to say, eggs feature prominently. They always give good currency. They are quick to cook and what you choose to serve them with is mighty in scope and scale. I've broadly based this recipe on the Turkish dish of menemen – that is to say eggs cooked in a pan on top of some cooked vegetables and served with yogurt. It's traditionally a breakfast dish, but I'd go so far as to say that its versatility makes this dish eminently welcome all day long.

If you're using fresh broad (fava) beans and they are on the large side, blanch them briefly in boiling water and remove the skins before you start. If small, you can cook the beans directly as in the method below.

Melt the butter in a medium saucepan with a tight-fitting lid. Add the spring onions (scallions), turmeric and garlic and cook over a moderate heat for 2 minutes, until fragrant.

Add half the dill and the broad beans to the pan and cook for 1 minute, until the dill is wilted, then add enough water to just cover the broad beans. Bring to a boil, reduce the heat to medium–low and add salt to taste. Cook for 5 minutes, until the beans are tender. Check the seasoning and stir in half the crispy fried onions.

Using the back of a spoon, form 4 wells in the bean mixture. Crack an egg into each well and cover the pan with the lid. Cook for about 3 minutes, until the eggs are just cooked, with the white opaque and the yolk still runny. Sprinkle with the toasted cumin and the remaining dill and crispy onions and serve with the flat breads and seasoned yogurt.

Lemon & Dill Fish Stew

4 tbsp sunflower oil

1 large onion, very finely diced

3 cloves of garlic, thinly sliced

zest and juice of 1 unwaxed lemon

2 tsp ground cumin

2 tsp ground turmeric

1 tsp ground cardamom

4 skinless fish fillets (about 700g/1lb 9oz; the firmer the better)

1 x 400g (14oz) can of chopped tomatoes

1 small bunch of dill, finely chopped (or use flat-leaf parsley)

½ tsp salt, plus more to season

plain (all-purpose) flour, for dusting

freshly ground black pepper

This is a highly flavoured and super-quick-to-cook fish stew. Turmeric, cumin and cardamom are a brilliant trio when matched with lemon and dill. Use any firm fish fillets: I like mackerel – you could use whole sardines, but any inexpensive, sustainable fish will work, although nothing too flaky as the fish will fall apart in the cooking liquid. Some rice or some boiled potatoes are a good accompaniment; equally so, a big, leafy salad with flat breads to mop.

Heat 2 tablespoons of the oil in a pan over a moderate heat. Add the onion and garlic and fry for about 10 minutes, until soft.

Meanwhile, sprinkle half the lemon juice and half the ground spices over the fish. Season with salt and a generous amount of pepper and put to one side.

Add the tomatoes, lemon zest and the remaining spices to the onions and continue to cook for about 5 minutes, until thickened, rich and fragrant. Then add half the dill, the remaining lemon juice and the ½ teaspoon of salt, along with 400ml (14fl oz) of water and bring to a gentle simmer while you continue to prepare the fish.

Dust the fish on both sides with the flour. Heat the remaining oil in a cast-iron frying pan (skillet) and fry the fillets on both sides on a moderate–high heat until golden brown – no need to cook through.

Add the fried fish to the stew, adding a splash of hot water, if needed, to loosen. Cook gently for a few minutes until the fish is just cooked through – if you gently part one of the fillets, the flesh should be opaque and hot throughout. Check the seasoning and serve sprinkled with the remaining dill.

Laksa with Spring Vegetables & Rice Noodles

30g (1oz) tamarind paste with seeds

a little boiling water from a kettle

1–2 red chillies, roughly chopped (use more, if you like)

2 cloves of garlic, roughly chopped

1 tbsp grated (shredded) fresh ginger or galangal

½ bunch of spring onions (scallions), sliced, white and green parts separated

1 small bunch of coriander (cilantro), leaves and stalks separated

2 lemongrass stalks, roughly chopped

2 tsp ground turmeric

1 tsp ground cumin

2 tbsp sunflower oil

500ml (17fl oz) chicken or vegetable stock

1 x 400ml (14fl oz) can of coconut milk

400g (14oz) spring vegetables (purple sprouting broccoli, peas, early green beans or mangetout, asparagus, spinach, radishes, baby carrots)

200g (7oz) thin or fat dried rice noodles, cooked according to the packet instructions

2 tbsp fish sauce, or more to taste

1 tsp caster (superfine) sugar, or more to taste

1 small bunch of mint, leaves picked and roughly chopped, to serve

I first tasted laksa in a pub in Sydney. The pub was a rowdy one and beneath the staircase was a little hatch. One woman (she really did look about 105 years old) was single-handedly serving up bowls of laksa to a queue of revellers snaking on well past the bar and out onto the street. The broth was incredible, skilfully spiced and generous with coconut and fresh herbs; the entire pub, including me, was head down in a bowl of noodles. The pubs back home, pubs I'd been into in any case, certainly weren't like this one – packet of crisps and a pickled egg, at best. This was 20 years ago now, and I can still remember the taste of that bowl of broth. Serve with extra sliced fresh chillies, if you like; likewise, choose a single vegetable – or use a combination.

Bring a pan of salted water to a boil.

Meanwhile, put the tamarind paste in a small bowl and cover with the boiling water from the kettle. Mash with a fork to purée, then pass the purée through a sieve (you should have about 3 tablespoons – by all means add more to taste when instructed below).

Blend the chillies, garlic, ginger, white of the spring onions (scallions), coriander (cilantro) stalks and lemongrass with the turmeric and cumin, adding a tiny splash of water, if required, to form a thick paste.

In a separate pan, fry the paste in the sunflower oil for 2–3 minutes over a medium heat, until the paste begins to stick to the pan. Add the tamarind purée, the stock and the coconut milk and bring the mixture to a boil.

Meanwhile, boil the spring vegetables in the boiling salted water until just tender (no more than 3 minutes), then drain and place in 4 bowls along with the prepared noodles.

Add the fish sauce, sugar and, if necessary, more tamarind, according to taste, to the coconut broth. Pour the broth over the noodles and vegetables and add the chopped mint and green of the spring onions to serve.

Caramelized Coconut Pork Fillet with Roasted Cabbage & Peanuts

1 x 200ml (7fl oz) can or pouch of coconut milk

2 tbsp fish sauce

3 tbsp kecap manis (or use 2 tbsp soy sauce and 1 tbsp caster/superfine sugar)

3 tbsp light brown soft sugar

2 tsp curry powder (mild or hot, as you like)

1 lemongrass stalk, halved and lightly crushed

2 juicy limes

500g (1lb 2oz) pork fillet

4 tbsp sunflower oil

½ green cabbage (or a whole one, if on the small side)

1 bunch of spring onions (scallions), trimmed and cut into 3cm (1¼in) lengths

1 (bell) pepper (any colour), deseeded and roughly chopped

salt and freshly ground black pepper

30g (1oz) roasted peanuts, crushed, to serve

chilli sauce, to serve

cooked rice (basmati or sticky is good), to serve

Again, this dish is pretty quick, all things told. Chilli sauce, up to you which brand you prefer, is a must. I like to use quite a hot one as the sweet coconut sauce can take it. The sauce is split in two here: half to cook and baste the pork fillet, with the remainder used to dress the finished dish. You want the vegetables to be quite charred in places, but still with a bit of crunch for texture. Juicy lime and salty peanuts complete the speedy supper.

Preheat the oven to 210°C/190°C fan/415°F/Gas Mark 6–7.

Put the coconut milk, fish sauce, kecap manis, brown sugar, curry powder and half the lemongrass in a medium pan over a high heat and bring to a boil. Reduce the heat, stirring occasionally, and simmer for 5 minutes, until the sauce is thickened, then stir in the juice of 1 lime. Remove from the heat and put to one side.

While the sauce is cooking, season the pork with salt and pepper. Heat half the sunflower oil in a cast-iron frying pan (skillet) over a high heat and add the pork. Fry for 2 minutes on each side, until nicely browned. Transfer the pork to a suitable baking tray and pour half the sauce over the meat. Cook in the hot oven for about 15 minutes, brushing the pork with a little extra of the sauce mid-way through the cooking time, until nicely caramelized and cooked through. Remove from the oven and rest for at least 5 minutes.

Meanwhile, toss the cabbage, spring onions (scallions) and (bell) pepper with some salt, pepper and the remaining oil and scatter evenly in a baking tray. Roast for about 10 minutes, until nicely charred at the edges and softened.

Slice the pork and serve alongside the roasted vegetables. Sprinkle with the peanuts, drizzle over the remaining sauce and serve with the remaining lime cut into wedges, plus the chilli sauce and rice on the side.

Broad Bean & Green Herb Pilaf

300g (10½oz) basmati rice

3 tbsp good olive oil

1 large onion, thinly sliced

1 big bunch of flat-leaf parsley, stalks and leaves separated, both finely chopped

1 big bunch of dill, stalks and leaves separated, both finely chopped

½ tsp ground turmeric

¼ tsp ground cinnamon

1 tsp salt

200g (7oz) broad (fava) beans, podded, and peeled if large (or use defrosted frozen)

50g (1¾oz) dried sour cherries, or raisins

400ml (14fl oz) boiling water from a kettle

1 lemon, halved

50g (1¾oz) flaked almonds or sunflower seeds, lightly toasted

freshly ground black pepper

about 200g (7oz) natural yogurt, seasoned with salt, to serve

chilli flakes, to serve

A rice dish with Iranian origins that goes by the name of *sabzi polo*. In Persian, *sabz* means green and *polo* is rice cooked using the pilaf method (lidded and cooked in a flavoured liquid). Go big with the herbs. Ideally you want a densely packed fistful each of parsley and dill – you might need two bunches of each if the supermarket is your only option. The rice must taste of the herbs you are using, added as they are in the three stages of cooking: stalks chopped fine and fried with the onions, half of the leaves cooked with the rice, and the remainder giving the final flurry of green. As for broad (fava) beans, a classic spring vegetable and a favourite for me, but no one's going to know if you use the frozen sort. If you're using fresh, pod any that are on the hefty side as the skin can be tough going.

Soak the rice in a bowl of cold water for 10 minutes.

In a large, wide pan that has a lid, heat the oil over a moderate heat and add the onion and the parsley stalks and dill stalks. Cook for about 10 minutes, until soft. Add the spices and salt and cook for 1 minute, until the spices are aromatic.

Drain the rice and add to the pan along with the broad (fava) beans, half the chopped herb leaves and the dried fruit. Stir well for about 30 seconds to coat.

Cover the rice with the 400ml (14fl oz) of boiling water. Cut 2 thin slices from one of the lemon halves and add the slices to the water. Put the lid on the pan and cook for 5 minutes over a moderate heat. Then, turn the heat down to the lowest setting and cook for a further 10 minutes, after which time turn off the heat and leave the lid on for another 5 minutes, until the rice is tender.

To serve, squeeze the juice from the remainder of the sliced lemon half onto the rice and fluff up with a fork. Then, scatter over the remaining herbs and the nuts or seeds, together with a good grinding of black pepper. Cut the remaining lemon half into wedges and have these at the ready with the yogurt and chilli flakes to serve.

Spring Vegetable Noodle Stir-fry

2 tbsp light soy sauce

2 tsp caster (superfine) sugar

2 tbsp oyster sauce

1 tbsp rice wine, sherry or mirin

3 tbsp sunflower oil

300g (10½oz) purple sprouting broccoli, any bigger stalks sliced once or twice through the middle

100g (3½oz) green beans or mangetout; if green beans sliced once down through middle

1 carrot, peeled and cut thinly into rounds, on the diagonal or into sticks

1 red (bell) pepper, deseeded and cut into thin strips

400g (14oz) fresh egg noodles (or use dried noodles, cooked as per packet instructions)

2 tsp sesame oil

1 bunch of spring onions (scallions), trimmed and cut thinly on the diagonal

Not to be confused with authentic chow mein where the noodles are fried until crisp, this is lo mein. It uses egg noodles made with wheat flour that are simply tossed through the stir-fry ingredients to soak up the sauce until hot through. I've kept this meat-free, purely in the interests of speed – you really can have this ready in minutes if you keep things simple. As ever, switch around the vegetables, if you like: thin ribbons of cabbage, as well as peas, radishes, mushrooms and peppers will all work. Just be sure to keep the vegetables all in roughly corresponding size. To really up your game, you could make a quick plain omelette, then shred this into ribbons and add them along with the noodles to heat through.

Make a sauce by mixing together the soy sauce, sugar, oyster sauce and the rice wine, sherry or mirin and set aside.

Heat the sunflower oil in a wok over a high heat until smoking, then stir-fry all the vegetables, apart from the spring onions (scallions), for about 2 minutes, tossing and stirring all the time, so nothing sticks or burns and all get evenly cooked.

Add the noodles and toss everything together until well combined. Add the sauce and continue to cook for another minute or so, until everything is piping hot.

Add the sesame oil and the spring onions to the wok, toss once more and serve immediately.

Kottu Roti

1 large red onion, thinly sliced

2 green chillies, thinly sliced

3 cloves of garlic, roughly chopped

1 tbsp grated (shredded) fresh ginger

1 tbsp Sri Lankan curry powder (or other curry powder, mild or hot)

½ tsp salt, plus more to season

3 tbsp sunflower oil

8 fresh curry leaves (optional)

1 tbsp soy sauce

1 tbsp tomato purée

1 large carrot, peeled and coarsely grated (shredded)

1 spring cabbage or pointed hispi cabbage, cored and finely sliced

3 chapatis or parathas (or use pita or soft tortilla wraps), thinly sliced

3 eggs, beaten

freshly ground black pepper

lime wedges, to serve

This is a Sri Lankan preparation, stir-frying chapati or paratha with beaten egg, curry powder, chilli and vegetables. Frying first the onion, ginger and chilli paste really helps to unlock flavour and gives the rest of the ingredients an almighty head start. Do try to use chapati or paratha here. I especially love how some of the bread soaks up more of the egg mixture than other pieces, leaving some bits deliciously saturated with the egg and spices and some more on the toasted, crunchy spectrum. I like to use a good, juicy spring cabbage in this recipe – a favourite spring vegetable for me, just as this is a favourite of all the spring recipes in the book.

Blend half the onion with half the green chilli, and the garlic, ginger, curry powder and salt to a coarse paste (adding a splash of water, if necessary).

In a cast-iron frying pan (skillet) over a moderate heat, heat the oil and add the paste. Fry with the curry leaves (if using), soy sauce and tomato purée for about 10 minutes, stirring and scraping until the paste is beginning to stick to the bottom of the pan, and it is thickened and intensely fragrant.

Add the remaining onion and all the vegetables and stir-fry over a moderate heat for about 5 minutes, or until the vegetables have softened.

Add the bread and cook for 30 seconds to heat through, scooping and stirring to coat well. Finally, add the beaten eggs and stir-fry for 3–4 minutes, until well scrambled. Check the seasoning, adding a touch more salt if necessary and plenty of black pepper.

Top with the remaining green chilli and wedges of lime. Serve immediately.

Smoked Haddock Brandade on Garlic Toast

FOR THE BRANDADE

250g (9oz) floury potatoes, peeled and cut into large chunks

25g (1oz) unsalted butter

3 cloves of garlic, finely chopped

2 bay leaves, scrunched a little

300g (10½oz) undyed smoked haddock fillets

200ml (7fl oz) whole milk

salt and freshly ground black pepper

FOR THE GARLIC TOAST

unsalted butter, for the spinach and toast

pinch of salt

300g (10½oz) baby spinach

8 slices of sturdy bread, such as sourdough

1 clove of garlic, halved

Brandade is traditionally made using salt cod, but I think smoked haddock is the more accessible ingredient to use if you're in the UK. Floury potatoes beaten with the milk used to cook the fish, piled on hot, buttered and garlic-rubbed toast, this is a smashing midweek meal. Source good, undyed haddock – the dayglo sort is artificially dyed to ape the colour of traditionally smoked haddock, which has a paler yellow hue from the wood it is smoked over. Using the milk to mash the potatoes will give you a deeply flavoured and comforting canvas with which to reintroduce the cooked fish. All in all, clever, though deceptively very easy cooking here. Use cooked chard, green beans or roast tomatoes, seasons withstanding, in lieu of the spinach, if you like.

Put the potatoes into a large pan of salted water, bring to a boil, then reduce the heat and simmer for 15–20 minutes, until tender. Drain well and leave to dry.

In a good-size saucepan over a moderate heat, melt the butter and add the garlic and bay leaves. Cook for about 1 minute, until fragrant, then add the smoked fish fillets in a single layer. Pour over the milk, bring to a boil, reduce the heat and simmer very gently until the fish is cooked and piping hot throughout – anywhere from 5–10 minutes, depending on the thickness of the fillets.

Meanwhile, start the garlic toast. Melt some butter in a separate saucepan over a moderate heat. Add the pinch of salt and the spinach and allow to wilt (about 2 minutes). Remove from the heat, drain and keep to one side somewhere warm.

Drain the fish, reserving the liquid, and keep warm on a plate. Mash the cooked potatoes using enough of the hot, fish-cooking milk until you have a thick purée. Check the seasoning, adding more salt and pepper as necessary.

Discarding the skin and any bones, flake the fish into the mashed potato and mix gently to combine without breaking the fish down too much. Keep warm.

Toast the bread, spread with butter and rub with the halved garlic. Pile the spinach and brandade onto the toast. More black pepper to serve is a good thing.

Orange Blossom & Mascarpone-stuffed Hot Cross Buns

125g (4½oz) mascarpone

zest of 1 small unwaxed orange

½–1 tsp orange blossom water, to taste

2 tbsp runny honey

pinch of flaky salt

4 super-fresh hot cross buns

These are delicious any time of the day, breakfast included. You need super-fresh hot cross buns for this – purchase and use on the day they are baked. (Good brioche would work well, too.) Use your fingers to gently prise the buns apart, as if to leave a pocket in which to squeeze as much of the mascarpone as the bun can take. Bursting at the seams is a good thought when it comes to assembling this quick pudding.

Mix the mascarpone with the orange zest, orange blossom water, honey and salt. Give it a bit of a whisk until voluminous – you want it to have the consistency of Greek yogurt. Use your fingers to open the buns, forming a deep pocket in each one. Spoon the mascarpone cream equally into the buns (or use a piping bag, if you like).

Pan Fried Pineapple with Rum & Brown Sugar & Coconut Yogurt

2 tbsp unsalted butter

4 chunky wedges of fresh, ripe pineapple, cored

2 tbsp light brown soft sugar

2 tbsp dark rum (or brandy, kirsch or Grand Marnier), or use pineapple juice for a non-alcoholic version

1 tsp vanilla extract

400g (14oz) coconut yogurt, to serve

If you're going to bother making a pudding midweek, the recipe needs to be a fast and fairly simple one (you can keep more leisurely baking and pâtisserie work for when you have the time). Choose a good, ripe pineapple: to check, tug one of the leaves to see if it comes easily from the pineapple – if it does, the pineapple is ready to use. That said, given enough heat, I think even the most ordinary pineapple can transcend to something special. I think this recipe is best served with coconut yogurt, because coconut, pineapple and rum are very happy alongside each other, but use natural yogurt or ice cream, if you like.

Melt half the butter in a cast-iron frying pan (skillet) over a moderately hot heat and fry the pineapple wedges for 3–4 minutes each side, until nicely caramelized all over.

Meanwhile in a small saucepan over a low heat, cook the remaining butter, along with the brown sugar, rum (or other spirit or the juice) and vanilla, stirring occasionally, until the sugar is fully dissolved and the sauce is a uniform dark brown (about 3–4 minutes). Keep warm.

Place some pineapple on each plate, spoon the sauce over the pineapple and serve with the coconut yogurt.

Easy Egg Curry

400g (14oz) potatoes, peeled and diced into bite-size (about 2cm/¾in) pieces

6 eggs

4 tbsp sunflower oil

1 onion, finely diced

4 bay leaves, scrunched a little

1–2 dried or fresh red chillies

2 cloves of garlic, finely chopped

1 tbsp grated (shredded) fresh ginger

1 tbsp tomato purée

½ tsp ground turmeric

1–2 tsp chilli powder

3 tsp cumin seeds, toasted and ground

1 tsp coriander seeds, toasted and ground

I love an egg curry. There is something deeply satisfying about the consistency of a hard-boiled egg, solid but tender, with a good, buttery flavour when swathed in a fiery, fragrant curry sauce, the sauce clinging to the eggs, a yin and yang of culinary proportion. If you add potatoes to the curry to bump up quantity, this is an especially thrifty dinner. Be bold with the chilli – the eggs and potatoes can take it. I especially like how some of the toasted and ground cumin is added at the beginning of the cook time, with some reserved as a final seasoning, per dish, at the table.

Bring the potatoes to a boil in a saucepan of well-salted water, then reduce the heat and simmer for about 12 minutes, until just tender, then drain.

Meanwhile, in a saucepan of cold water sufficient in size to hold all the eggs in one layer, bring the eggs to a boil and boil gently for 6 minutes. Remove from the heat and run under cold water until cool enough to peel.

While the eggs are cooking and cooling, heat the oil in a pan over a moderate heat and fry the onion, bay leaves and the whole chillies for 10 minutes, until soft. Add the garlic, ginger, tomato purée, turmeric, chilli powder, 1 teaspoon of the toasted and ground cumin and all the ground coriander. Cook for 1 minute, until fragrant.

Add the peeled eggs, together with 300ml (10½fl oz) of water, and cook for about 10 minutes, until the liquid is almost all but evaporated and a thick sauce coats the eggs. Stir through the potatoes for the last couple of minutes to warm through.

Sprinkle with the remaining toasted cumin and serve immediately. Some naan breads are especially good alongside.

Ham Hock, Pea & Spring Onion Soup

800g (1lb 12oz) uncooked ham hock (smoked or unsmoked, as you like)

2 bay leaves, scrunched a little

8 peppercorns

200g (7oz) peas (fresh or frozen)

100g (3½oz) small pasta shapes, cooked as per the packet instructions

2 tbsp olive oil or a knob of unsalted butter

1 bunch of spring onions (scallions), trimmed and finely sliced

3 cloves of garlic, finely chopped

1 small bunch of flat-leaf parsley, leaves picked and finely chopped

juice of ½ lemon (optional)

salt and freshly ground black pepper

Ham hocks offer unrivalled value for money: you get the slow-cooked meat that falls from the bone and you also get the deeply rich and satisfying stock that you cooked the hock in. By all means add more aromatics to the pot as you cook the hock – a couple of cloves of garlic, an onion, a stick of celery or some coriander seeds are all worthwhile additions. I've kept the ingredient list fairly brief here in the interest of being budget, but what's a few coriander seeds between friends? Make a pot of this when spring still has a nip in the air and a bowl of soup, a couple of lunchtimes on the trot, is best appreciated. Bread and butter on the side, naturally.

Put the ham hock in a deep saucepan with just enough cold water to cover and bring to a boil. Drain, then refill the pan with fresh water, adding the bay leaves and whole peppercorns. Bring the pan back up to a boil again, skim off any of the froth that surfaces, reduce the heat to a simmer and cook for about 1 hour, until the ham is tender throughout when pierced with a sharp skewer.

Remove the ham from the liquor and keep to one side, add the peas to the ham stock and cook for 5 minutes, until tender – or much less if using frozen (1 minute should do). Add the cooked pasta to the stock and leave on the heat.

While the peas are cooking, in a small pan, heat the oil or butter over a moderate heat and fry the spring onions (scallions) and garlic for about 5 minutes, until soft. Add to the stock along with the parsley.

Shred the cooked ham from the bone, removing the skin and any excess fat, and add to the soup. Season to taste with salt and pepper. Likewise, the lemon juice, if you like.

Grilled Sprouting Broccoli with Harissa & Giant Couscous

about 400g (14oz) purple sprouting broccoli, trimmed into bite-size pieces, larger stalks sliced and leaves left attached

1 bunch of spring onions (scallions), trimmed and cut into 2cm (¾in) pieces

4 tbsp good olive oil

½ tsp salt, plus more to season

2 cloves of garlic, finely sliced

200g (7oz) wholewheat Israeli couscous or coarse bulgur wheat

1 small bunch of flat-leaf parsley, leaves picked and roughly chopped

4 tbsp harissa (see page 81)

juice of ½–1 lemon, to taste

50g (1¾oz) hazelnuts or almonds, toasted and chopped

about ½ preserved lemon, flesh finely chopped (optional)

freshly ground black pepper

I think harissa (see page 81) is a must-have ingredient for all year round. Make some and store it in the fridge to give an easy, appetizing boost to many different dishes – it will bump up more day-to-day ingredients, fresh or otherwise, and because it is so flavoursome, a little goes a long way. It is a thrifty friend through and through. I've used purple sprouting broccoli here, but regular broccoli or even cauliflower will work just as well – be sure to use the stalks (peeled, if necessary) and any tender leaves, too. Preserved lemons are, again, a tour de force when it comes to the storecupboard and worth their weight in gold.

Preheat the oven to 220°C/200°C fan/425°F/Gas Mark 7.

Toss the broccoli and spring onions (scallions) on a baking tray with half the olive oil and the salt. Roast for about 10 minutes, until the broccoli is tender and beginning to char in places.

Remove the broccoli from the oven and stir through the sliced garlic, return to the oven for a further 2 minutes to finish off.

While the broccoli is in the oven, bring a medium saucepan of salted water to a boil. Cook the couscous for 10–12 minutes, until al dente (or according to the packet instructions). Drain and transfer to a warm serving dish.

When the broccoli is ready, add it to the couscous with the parsley and spoon on the harissa. Add the lemon juice and the remaining olive oil and stir well to coat. Check the seasoning, adding more salt and seasoning with pepper if appropriate.

Sprinkle with the hazelnuts or almonds, and with the chopped preserved lemon, if using, and serve immediately.

Cauliflower Shawarma with Tahini Dressing

1 whole cauliflower, outer leaves trimmed, pale, smaller ones intact

2 tsp ground cinnamon

2 tsp ground coriander

2 tsp ground cumin

2 tsp ground turmeric

½–1 tsp chilli flakes, or more to taste

½ tsp ground cardamom, nutmeg or allspice

250g (9oz) natural yogurt

1 tsp salt, plus more to season

2 cloves of garlic, finely crushed

juice of 1 large lemon

40g (1½oz) unsalted butter, melted, or use 40ml (1½fl oz) olive oil

1 large red onion, sliced into rounds about 5mm (¼in) thick

2 tsp nigella seeds

1 tbsp olive oil

100g (3½oz) tahini

freshly ground black pepper

TO SERVE

flat breads or pita breads

about 20g (¾oz) pine nuts, or chopped walnuts or almonds, toasted

1 small bunch of coriander (cilantro), mint or flat-leaf parsley, leaves picked and roughly chopped

chilli sauce (optional)

good olive oil

Cauliflowers reign supreme as a vegetable with year-round pedigree. The winter varieties are harvested well into May, when planting then switches to a summer crop for winter pickings. However, peak season – that is to say cheap season – is springtime. A shawarma is a sandwich preparation stuffed in a pita, sometimes with tahini dressing, and is usually made with chicken or lamb. This is the budget, veggie alternative, smothered in spiced yogurt and cooked on top of a tangle of red onions. If you want to simplify the spices, use a ready-made spice blend, such as baharat or ras el hanout.

Preheat the oven to 220°C/200°C fan/425°F/Gas Mark 7.

Bring a large saucepan of well-salted water to a boil and add the cauliflower. Parboil for about 8 minutes, until tender when a knife is inserted in the middle but still intact as a whole cauliflower. Drain well (you want it quite dry).

Meanwhile, mix all of the spices into 100g (3½oz) of the yogurt and add the salt, half the garlic and half the lemon juice.

Rub the drained cauliflower all over with the spiced yogurt, pushing the yogurt into all the crevasses. Brush liberally with the melted butter or olive oil.

In a roasting tray arrange the onions in an even layer, add the nigella seeds and drizzle with the 1 tablespoon of oil. Place the cauliflower on top and roast for 12–15 minutes, until it is nicely coloured all over and the onions are soft and beginning to catch in spots. Use any remaining melted butter to baste the cauliflower a couple of times during cooking. Remove from the oven and keep warm.

In a bowl, whisk the tahini with the remaining yogurt, lemon juice and garlic, along with some salt and pepper to taste, to form a smooth sauce. Add a little water to loosen if necessary.

To serve, cut the cauliflower into good-size slices. Spoon these, together with the onions, any of the cooking juices and the tahini yogurt onto warm or toasted flat breads, to serve. Add a sprinkle of pine nuts, herbs, chilli sauce (if using), and a good slick of olive oil.

Broccoli Soup with Golden Garlic Oil

700g (1lb 9oz) purple sprouting or regular broccoli, cut into bite-size pieces, stalks reserved (peeled, if necessary) and chopped small

6 tbsp good olive oil

big pinch of salt, plus more to season

1 large onion, finely diced

8 cloves of garlic, 4 finely chopped, 4 thinly sliced

1 litre (35fl oz) chicken or vegetable stock (or use water), plus more if necessary

zest and juice of ½ unwaxed lemon

freshly ground black pepper

Sprouting broccoli appears again here because it is the season, but do use regular broccoli if you prefer – some boiled and some roasted, to really ramp up the broccoli flavour. Golden garlic oil sounds like some kind of sorcery, and I suppose it is. You want the garlic to cook crisp and golden with a mellow, enticing flavour – too fierce a heat, too long in the hot oil and the garlic will have an acrid pungency that will be hard to mask.

Preheat the oven to 200°C/180°C fan/400°F/Gas Mark 6.

Toss half of the broccoli florets (no stalks) with 2 tablespoons of the olive oil and a big pinch of salt. Scatter over a baking tray and roast for 15–20 minutes, until tender and beginning to char in places. Remove from the oven and keep warm.

Heat 1 tablespoon of the remaining oil in a saucepan over a moderate heat. Add the onion and cook for about 10 minutes, until soft. Add the chopped garlic and cook for 2 minutes more, then add the broccoli stalks. Stir to coat, then add the stock or water. Bring to a boil, then reduce the heat to a simmer, cooking for about 5 minutes, until the stalks are tender. Then, add the remaining uncooked florets and simmer for about 5 minutes, until tender.

Transfer the soup to a blender and blitz until very, very smooth (work in batches, if necessary). Pour the soup back into the pan, thin with a little extra stock or water, if required, and season with more salt and some pepper to taste. Keep warm.

Heat the remaining oil in a small, cast-iron frying pan (skillet) over a moderate–high heat. Add the sliced garlic and cook for 1–2 minutes, until the slices begin to turn golden brown (don't let them get too dark or the garlic will become bitter). Remove from the heat.

Stir the lemon zest and juice through the soup to taste and serve topped with the roasted broccoli florets and the golden garlic oil.

Slow-cooker Lamb with Carrots, Bay & Thyme

1kg (2lb 4oz) lamb neck chops

2 tbsp sunflower or olive oil

1 onion, finely diced

2 carrots, peeled and diced into 1cm (½in) pieces

3 cloves of garlic, finely chopped

2 tbsp tomato purée

3 bay leaves, scrunched a little

2 thyme sprigs

2 tbsp plain (all-purpose) flour

800ml (28fl oz) chicken, lamb or vegetable stock or water

400g (14oz) small new potatoes, scrubbed

1 small bunch of flat-leaf parsley, leaves picked and roughly chopped

salt and freshly ground black pepper

Use lamb-neck, or bone-in scrag-end neck chops for this recipe – they are considerably cheaper than more premium chops, which are cut from the loin. However, the neck versions will require slow cooking. (If you can't find neck chops you could use other slow-cooking lamb cuts like breast, shanks or diced shoulder.) I've used a slow cooker because I like the steady, hands-off, economical blip of using one. If you don't have a slow cooker, though, use a sturdy casserole with a tight-fitting lid and simmer the chops for about 1½ hours before adding the potatoes and cooking for a further 45 minutes–1 hour, until the lamb is tender and the potatoes are cooked through. Good served with some buttered spring greens.

Season the lamb with salt and pepper. Heat 1 tablespoon of the oil in a large, cast-iron frying pan (skillet) and brown the chops over a high heat in batches until nicely coloured all over, but not cooked through. Remove the chops as you brown them, keeping any fat in the frying pan, and place in a preheated slow cooker or casserole.

Reduce the heat on the pan, add the remaining oil and the onion and carrots. Cook for 10 minutes, until the onion is soft, then add the garlic and cook for 2 minutes more. Add the tomato purée, bay and thyme and cook for a couple of minutes until thick and beginning to stick to the bottom of the pan. Sprinkle the pan with the flour and cook for 1 minute, stirring and scraping all the time.

Stir in the stock and bring the pan to a rapid simmer, remove from the heat and pour the contents over the chops in the slow cooker.

If using a slow cooker, cook on high for 2 hours before adding the potatoes. Reduce the heat to low and cook for a further 5 or so hours, until the lamb is tender and the potatoes are cooked through. Season to taste with salt and plenty of black pepper, stir through the parsley, then serve.

Cherry Bakewell Oven-baked Pudding

200g (7oz) unsalted butter, softened

175g (6oz) caster (superfine) sugar

200g (7oz) ground almonds

4 large eggs, lightly beaten

zest and juice of ½ unwaxed lemon

2 x 425g (15oz) cans of cherries in light syrup, drained (or gooseberries, peaches or apricots)

1 small handful of flaked almonds, to decorate

Ludicrously easy. You could use fresh, in-season rhubarb here, chopped small with a couple of tablespoons of caster (superfine) sugar, but I'm suggesting canned fruit for this recipe – inexpensive and ever-handy to have on the shelf at home in the spring, when fresh fruit suitable for a pudding such as this one is still thin on the ground in the early part of the season.

Preheat the oven to 180°C/160°C fan/350°F/Gas Mark 4.

Using an electric hand whisk or a stand mixer, beat the butter, sugar, almonds, eggs and lemon zest together for 2 minutes to combine.

Mix the cherries with the lemon juice and tip into a shallow, oval baking dish, measuring approximately 20–30cm (8–12in) long.

Distribute the topping over the cherries in the baking dish and scatter the top with flaked almonds, to decorate. Bake for 40–45 minutes, until risen and golden. A skewer should come out clean when inserted into the almond batter topping. Serve warm with cream or ice cream.

Quinoa, Smoked Mackerel & Dill Fritters

200g (7oz) quinoa

1 small bunch of dill, stalks finely chopped, leaves less so

2 cloves of garlic, finely chopped

1 bunch of spring onions (scallions), trimmed and very finely sliced

3 eggs, beaten

zest of 1 unwaxed lemon

25g (1oz) plain (all-purpose) flour

25g (1oz) cornflour (cornstarch)

4 smoked mackerel fillets, skinned, boned and roughly flaked

200g (7oz) sour cream

sunflower oil, for frying

salt and freshly ground black pepper

I've used quinoa in fritter recipes before, admiring how this pleasant, slightly bitter and nutty-flavoured grain makes for a fritter with excellent form: crunchy on the outside, soft and yielding on the inside. The addition of smoked mackerel makes this more a storecupboard-friendly recipe; less so, I suppose, a budget one. Using a mixture of plain (all-purpose) flour and cornflour (cornstarch) gives these fritters an extra-crisp exterior. Sour cream on the side to serve is a must; some good chilli sauce would be welcome. Some salad or spring vegetables and few boiled potatoes are a fine match, too.

Cook the quinoa in 600ml (21fl oz) salted water for 12 minutes, or until the water has been absorbed and the quinoa is tender. Drain, if necessary, and spread out on a large plate or tray to cool sufficiently.

In a bowl, mix the cooled quinoa with the dill, garlic, spring onions (scallions), egg, lemon zest and both flours. Gently mix in the fish and season well with salt and pepper.

Cut the zested lemon into wedges and squeeze a little of the lemon juice into the sour cream to taste, then season with salt and pepper. Set aside any spare lemon wedges to serve.

Heat a large, non-stick frying pan (skillet) over a moderate heat and add a splash of sunflower oil. Use a spoon to add spoonfuls (about the size of a heaped tablespoon) of the fish mixture into the hot oil and fry on one side for about for 2 minutes, until golden and crisp. Then, flip over and cook on the other side. Transfer the cooked fritters to a warm plate lined with paper towels; keep going until you have used up all the mixture, adding a little more oil to the pan as necessary.

Serve the fritters warm with the flavoured sour cream and the lemon wedges on the side.

Gooseberry Slaw with Hispi, Mooli & Little Gems

300g (10½oz) gooseberries, trimmed and sliced or quartered

1 tbsp caster (superfine) sugar or runny honey, or more to taste

½ clove of garlic, finely crushed

1 hispi cabbage, cored, leaves thinly sliced

1 bunch of spring onions (scallions), trimmed and thinly sliced

½ mooli or daikon radish, peeled and cut finely into long, thin strips

1 or 2 small gem lettuces, sliced

3cm (1¼in) piece of fresh ginger, peeled and cut into very thin sticks

zest and juice of 1 unwaxed lemon

1 tbsp sunflower or good olive oil

1 small bunch of mint, leaves picked and roughly chopped

salt and freshly ground black pepper

In late spring you must get your hands on some fresh gooseberries when they come into season. They are absolutely one of my favourite fruits. Related to the blackcurrant, the gooseberry is like a fat grape with sparse, thin hairs all over. Chopped and used in this savoury salad, these pale, translucent berries give a sweet, floral flavour to complement the crunch of the mooli and gem. A good slaw should have an honest mix of salty and sweet, so the sugar here is essential. Serve as a spring salad, or as an accompaniment to grilled (broiled) fish or roast chicken.

Put the gooseberries in a large mixing bowl with the sugar or honey, the garlic and a pinch of salt. Stir gently and set aside for 30 minutes to soften ever-so slightly.

Add all the remaining ingredients (you may not need all the lemon juice) and mix well together. Check the seasoning, adjusting the salt, sugar and lemon juice if necessary, and serve.

Feta with Whole Toasted Spices, Radish, Parsley & Pomegranate

200g (7oz) feta cheese, crumbled

1 tsp cumin seeds, toasted

1 tsp caraway seeds, toasted

1 tsp coriander seeds, toasted

3 tbsp good olive oil

4 pita breads

200g (7oz) radishes, ½ thickly sliced, ½ quartered lengthways

1 small bunch of mint, leaves picked and roughly chopped

1 small bunch of flat-leaf parsley, leaves picked and roughly chopped

seeds of ½ pomegranate

25g (1oz) walnuts, roughly chopped

Toasting the spices, keeping them whole and using them along with some good olive oil to marinate the feta changes this firm, salty cheese into something really terrific. Lots of herbs is also key to the enjoyment of this recipe, then merrily stuff the lot in a warm pita bread and arm yourself with lots of napkins before going in. Cut the radishes two ways for alternating crunch.

Mix the feta with the toasted seeds in the olive oil. Leave to one side.

Lightly toast the pitas and make a cut in one end of each to form a pocket. Stuff each of the pitas equally with the seeded feta, and all the remaining ingredients.

Radishes with Cucumbers, Cream Cheese & Soft Herbs with Toast

2-3 small bunches of soft herbs (tarragon, flat-leaf parsley, chives, dill – any mixture you like), leaves picked

300g (10½oz) cream cheese

zest of 1 unwaxed lemon

250g (9oz) radishes, thinly sliced (multi-coloured, if you like)

1 cucumber (peeled if tough-skinned), thinly sliced

3-4 tbsp good olive oil

salt and freshly ground black pepper

4 slices of sourdough bread, toasted, to serve

Radishes are beautiful. They are a cheerful gift to the kitchen after months of wintry monochrome and I love their juicy, bright crunch. Some varieties are more peppery than others, but however you like your radishes, the more vivid in colour, the more striking this dish. Against the herb-flecked cream cheese, thinly sliced, the radishes radiate. I rather like composing dishes such as this one, taking my time to ensure the composition is as attractive as it can possibly be. Use plenty of herbs as the recipe suggests. Serve with toast on the side, a convivial side dish or light lunch.

Finely chop half the herbs and stir these through the cheese. Add half the lemon zest and season with salt and black pepper to taste.

On a large serving plate, or 4 small ones, smear the cream-cheese mixture over the bottom of the plate and top with slices of the radishes and cucumber.

Chop the remaining herbs, keeping any smaller leaves whole, if you like, and scatter them over. Add the remaining lemon zest and drizzle everything liberally with olive oil. Another grinding of black pepper and scattering of salt is good.

Peas, Spinach & Sunflower Seeds with Brown Rice & Miso Ginger Dressing

FOR THE DRESSING

30ml (1fl oz) light soy sauce

3 tbsp yellow or white miso

1–2 cloves of garlic (to taste), very finely chopped

2 tbsp grated (shredded) fresh ginger

1 tbsp sesame oil

1 tbsp sesame seeds

1 tbsp runny honey

FOR THE SALAD

700g (1lb 9oz) cooked brown rice (about 350g/12oz uncooked)

zest and juice of 2 unwaxed limes (or use rice wine vinegar)

1 bunch of spring onions (scallions), trimmed and finely sliced

80g (2¾oz) sunflower seeds, toasted

400g (14oz) cooked peas

150g (5½oz) baby spinach

salt and freshly ground black pepper

chilli sauce or sliced fresh chilli, to serve (optional)

Sounds virtuous this one, a good thing from time to time. Brown rice, with only the outer inedible husk removed, leaving the grain with its bran and cereal germ intact, truly is a kitchen staple and one I use frequently throughout the year. Because brown rice has more substance to its form, it's often my go-to grain for salads when I want the finished dish to have a bit of ballast, a bit more heft to it. Miso is made with soybeans, fermented with salt and numerous other good bacteria. Protein-rich, it brings a deeply savoury, umami flavour to many different types of soup, dressing and marinade. White or yellow miso is the milder variety to use here, giving a sweet, salty burst to this dish. I've said 1–2 garlic cloves: given that the garlic is raw in the dressing, and raw garlic can be quite persuasive, use your judgement, depending on the size of the cloves.

Make the dressing by combining all of the dressing ingredients in a bowl. Add a splash of cold water to loosen, if required.

In a large serving bowl, mix all the salad ingredients together and add the dressing. Season to taste with salt and pepper, and serve pepped up with some fresh sliced chillies or chilli sauce, too, if you like.

Avocado & Mango with Prawn, Chilli Powder & Mint

2 large ripe avocados

1 large ripe mango

400g (14oz) peeled cooked prawns

1 cucumber, peeled, deseeded and cut into small bite-size pieces

½ red onion, very thinly sliced

1 small bunch of mint, leaves picked and roughly chopped

4 tbsp sunflower oil

juice of 2 limes, to taste

1 clove of garlic, very finely chopped

½–1 tsp chilli powder (mild or hot, as you like) or thinly sliced fresh red or green chilli

salt and freshly ground black pepper

prawn crackers, to serve

Spring brings the best of mangoes. Succulent with intense tropical aromas, they pair beautifully here with the avocados, prawns and mint. The chilli powder permeates the lot to give this mixture a generous, complete seasoning, one that is full of pep. Prawn crackers – got to love them – give good crunch and are a crucial accompaniment for this bright, beautiful salad.

Peel and de-stone the avocados and mango, and cut into bite-size pieces. Place all the ingredients in a big bowl and gently mix together. Season to taste and serve with the prawn crackers for scooping the salad to eat.

Sprouting Broccoli with Peas & Lettuce, with Clotted Cream & English Mustard

400g (14oz) purple sprouting broccoli, trimmed and sliced once or twice through the middle

2 tbsp olive oil

4 spring onions (scallions), trimmed and cut into 2cm (¾in) pieces

150g (5½oz) cooked peas

1 small, soft lettuce, leaves separated

salt and freshly ground black pepper

FOR THE DRESSING

1 tsp English mustard

½–1 clove of garlic, finely crushed

1 tbsp cider vinegar

100g (3½oz) clotted cream

pinch of sugar

Clotted cream seems a decadent option for a dressing, but here with the English mustard and cider vinegar it gives a creaminess that really ramps up flavour for the other ingredients.

Mix all the dressing ingredients together in a small bowl. You may need to add a little water to loosen it – you want the consistency of double cream. Set aside.

Steam or boil the broccoli for 3–5 minutes, until the stems are tender. Drain well and put to one side.

Heat the oil in a small saucepan over a moderate heat. Add the spring onions (scallions) and fry for about 2 minutes, until softened. Add the cooked peas and stir to combine. Season with a little salt and pepper to taste.

Arrange the lettuce leaves on a serving platter and add the broccoli, peas and spring onions; spoon over the dressing to serve.

Rhubarb & Strawberry Salad with Hazelnuts, Mint & Mozzarella

2 long, pink rhubarb stalks, thinly sliced on an angle

2 tbsp caster (superfine) sugar or runny honey

1 small red onion or 2 shallots, very thinly sliced

boiling water from a kettle

2 tsp red wine vinegar, plus more to taste

good pinch of salt

500g (1lb 2oz) strawberries, hulled and quartered

about 200g (7oz) mozzarella, burrata or ricotta cheese

1 small bunch of mint or basil, leaves picked and roughly chopped

60g (2¼oz) blanched hazelnuts or almonds, roughly chopped

freshly ground black pepper

about 2 tbsp good olive oil

Some time in spring there is a magnificent point when the last of the forced rhubarb and the first strawberries of the year collide. Both striking in hue, sharp, crunchy raw rhubarb complements beautifully juicy, sweet strawberry. Mint brings a lingering tingle and the mozzarella in this recipe gives a gorgeous, creamy weight to the finished dish (use burrata or ricotta, if you like). Eat this on its own as a salad or starter, or you could serve it alongside a plate of charcuterie – prosciutto or mortadella would be outstanding.

In a mixing bowl, mix the rhubarb and sugar or honey together. Put to one side for about 15 minutes for the rhubarb to ever-so slightly soften and release some of its juices.

Place the onion or shallot in a small dish and pour over enough boiling water to cover. Leave for at least 2 minutes, then drain well and add the vinegar and a good pinch of salt, then put to one side.

On a large serving platter, arrange the strawberries with the rhubarb and onion, giving everything a gentle mix. Season with further salt, as well as black pepper and extra vinegar to taste. Tear and arrange the mozzarella, burrata or ricotta before finally adding the herbs and nuts and drizzle with a little olive oil, to serve.

New Potatoes with Turmeric, Green Olives, Preserved Lemon & Capers

600g (1lb 5oz) new potatoes, scrubbed clean, skin on

4 tbsp good olive oil

1 bunch of spring onions (scallions), trimmed and thinly sliced, green and white parts separated

2 cloves of garlic, finely chopped

1 tsp ground turmeric

½ preserved lemon, flesh finely chopped

100g (3½oz) green olives, pitted and finely chopped

1 tbsp capers, salted and rinsed, or pickled (as you like)

1 small bunch of coriander (cilantro), leaves picked and roughly chopped

juice of 1 lemon

salt and freshly ground black pepper

Turmeric is an astonishing ingredient. It brings a gorgeous bitterness, earthy pungency and an arresting colour. Use new-season, small, waxy potatoes for this salad with the turmeric turning the potato flesh incandescent. I've said it before, and I'll say it again, preserved lemons (capers, too) are a boon for the storecupboard: intense in flavour, they bring a deeply salty, fragrant burst, and I would not be without them in my cooking at home. This salad is good on its own or served alongside some grilled fish, chicken or even halloumi cheese.

Cook the potatoes in plenty of well-salted boiling water for 15–20 minutes, until tender. Drain and cut into wedges.

While the potatoes are cooking, heat half the oil in a cast-iron frying pan (skillet) over a moderate heat and gently fry the white of the spring onions (scallions), the garlic and the turmeric for 2 minutes, until the onion and garlic are softened.

Thoroughly mix together the potatoes and cooked onion mixture with the remaining ingredients and serve at room temperature, adding salt and pepper to taste.

Whole Poached Chicken & Spring Vegetables & Aioli

FOR THE CHICKEN

1 chicken (about 2kg/4lb 8oz)

1 large carrot, peeled

1 onion

1 celery stick

1 leek, trimmed

2 bay leaves, scrunched a little

2 cloves of garlic, unpeeled, crushed with the back of a knife

1 tsp black peppercorns

1 heaped tbsp salt

FOR THE SPRING VEGETABLES

1kg (2lb 4oz) mixed spring vegetables – new season potatoes, little carrots, turnips or radishes, peas, broad (fava) beans (podded, if large), asparagus, and baby spinach

1 small, mixed bunch of loosely packed soft herbs – use any combination of flat-leaf parsley, tarragon, chervil, chives, dill and basil

salt and freshly ground black pepper

1 lemon, cut into wedges, to serve

FOR THE AIOLI

2 egg yolks

1 clove of garlic, crushed

2 tsp Dijon mustard

1 tsp red wine vinegar

big pinch of salt

200ml (7fl oz) groundnut or sunflower oil

50ml (1¾fl oz) good olive oil

SERVES 4-6

This is the method that British chef Fergus Henderson (and I am sure a good many other disciples, as so many of us are) uses for whole-poaching a chicken. If it seems a bit alarming to simply bring the pan to a boil then turn the whole thing off – be reassured: this technique cooks the chicken tenderly and the flesh remains moist. I find jointing the chicken after resting in the broth for the allotted time helpful. This way you can see that the meat is cooked correctly, and then add the chicken back to the simmering, seasoned broth to serve. Do try to use the best spring vegetables available – a good assortment is nice here. Aioli is a poached chicken's best friend, an egg-based emulsion made with voluptuous wobble, garlic, also some Dijon mustard – there are not many better combinations.

Put all the ingredients for the chicken in a large, heavy-based saucepan with a tight-fitting lid. Cover with cold water, place over a high heat and bring to a boil. As soon as the liquid reaches a fast, rolling boil, turn off the heat, put the lid on and leave for 1½ hours.

Meanwhile prepare all the vegetables accordingly, podding peas and broad (fava) beans, and scrubbing, trimming and washing everything else.

Also prepare the aioli. Put the egg yolks, garlic, mustard, vinegar and the big pinch of salt in a food processor and blitz for 20 seconds to incorporate. With the motor running, add the groundnut or sunflower oil in a thin drizzle, and finish with the olive oil. You should have a nice, thick mayonnaise. If the mayonnaise gets too thick during the process, a splash of cold water can thin it, allowing you to add more oil. Season with salt and pepper to taste. (You can make this by hand using a whisk and bowl if you prefer.) Ensure the mixture does not split, lest you have to start once again in a clean bowl with another egg yolk, slowly and carefully adding the split mixture, bit by bit, to form the mayonnaise.

After the 1½ hours, gently remove the chicken to a large plate, cover with foil and put to one side. Strain the broth, discarding the vegetables and other flavourings.

Return the broth to the pan, skim off any excess fat on the surface of the liquid, season to taste with salt and pepper and bring the broth back to a gentle simmer. Add the spring vegetables to the broth in the order of the time they take to cook: start with potatoes, then the carrots and turnips or radishes, then the peas, broad beans and asparagus, adding the spinach and the herbs right at the end.

Either leave the chicken whole or joint it – I like to joint it for ease of serving. Return the chicken to the pan of hot broth and vegetables to serve with the aioli and lemon wedges (to taste) at the table.

Steak with Shallot Rings, Watercress & Mustard Crème Fraîche

FOR THE STEAK

1 thick-cut steak (about 4cm/1½in), rib eye, rump, onglet, sirloin, picaña or fillet – up to you

1 tbsp cold unsalted butter

coarse or flaky salt and coarsely ground black pepper

1 bunch of watercress, tough stems trimmed, to serve

FOR THE DRESSING

1 tbsp Dijon mustard

juice of ½ lemon

250ml (9fl oz) crème fraîche

salt and freshly ground black pepper

FOR THE POTATOES

800g (1lb 12oz) medium to small potatoes, washed but unpeeled

2 tbsp olive oil

1 sprig of rosemary, leaves finely chopped

FOR THE SHALLOT RINGS

75g (2½oz) self-raising flour

big pinch of salt

100ml (3½fl oz) very cold soda or fizzy water

sunflower oil, for deep frying

2 large shallots, thinly sliced into rounds and teased apart

THIS RECIPE SERVES 2. BECAUSE, YOU KNOW, STEAK NIGHT, DATE NIGHT.

Buy one good-size steak, cook it perfectly, rest it and slice it to share... what could be better? I see little point in buying slimmer, individual steaks to cook at the same time, having to overcrowd the pan in order to cook to order. Or, needing to rest some of them longer while the others cook. By choosing to cook one steak you can really concentrate on the method and time it takes. A larger cut of steak is more forgiving and will rest better, retaining juiciness. There is less room for error, which could be catastrophic when cooking an expensive, prime cut. I've said to go with a steak 4cm (1½in) thick, and I can't stress this enough: the size will mean you have enough time to brown and crust any of the fat while still ensuring you do not overcook it. Timing will depend on the meat, how long it has been hung, how well it has been butchered, and its internal temperature when you do come to cook it, as well as the quality of your pan or grill (broiler). Show caution in the cooking times, and max out on the resting. If you give the cooked steak a quick prod, you should be able to leave a slight indentation on the outside.

Take the steak out of the fridge at least 2 hours before you intend to cook so that it can come up to room temperature.

Make the dressing. Mix the mustard and lemon juice into the crème fraîche and season with salt and pepper. Set aside. Next, cook the potatoes in well-salted boiling water until tender, then drain and leave to cool. (You can do both these things several hours ahead.)

Prepare the batter and the cooking oil for the shallots so that you can work quickly while the steak is resting. For the batter, put the flour in a bowl with the big pinch of salt and then quickly whisk in the cold soda or fizzy water until thick – don't over-whisk it. Set aside, keeping the mixture cold until you're ready to fry.

Half-fill a heavy-based, medium saucepan with sunflower oil and heat to 180°C/350°F (a single shallot ring should take 1 minute to turn golden brown and crisp). While the oil is heating up, cook the steak.

For the steak: first, pat the meat dry just before cooking as it will likely be a bit damp.

Heat a heavy griddle or cast-iron frying pan (skillet) over a medium–high heat until very, very hot (smoking). Season the steak generously with the coarse or flaky salt (use more than you'd think; the steak can take it). If the steak has fat on the edge, start by cooking that edge to render into the hot pan until nicely browned, then turn the steak flesh-side downward.

Cook for about 1½ minutes each side, pressing gently until both sides are nicely browned. Add the butter to the griddle or pan to baste the steak, then turn it every minute until it's done to your liking: 3–5 minutes for rare, 5–7 minutes for medium or 7–10 minutes for well done. The steak, however long you cook it, should have a deep brown caramelization on both sides. Allow to rest somewhere warm for at least 10 minutes.

While the steak is resting, cook the potatoes and shallot rings. Cut the potatoes into thick or thin slices. Heat the olive oil in a large, non-stick frying pan over a high heat and add the potatoes. Fry for 5–10 minutes, until golden and crisp. Sprinkle with rosemary and salt to serve.

For the shallot rings, put the batter right next to the pan of hot oil and have a plate lined with paper towels ready. Tip the shallot rings into the cold batter and, working in batches, drop the coated shallot rings into the hot oil, stirring each time with a slotted spoon to prevent them sticking. Don't overcrowd the pan. Remove each batch when crisp and golden (about 1 minute) and keep warm on the lined plate. Sprinkle with flaky salt.

Slice the rested steak and serve with the watercress, dressing and fried potatoes and shallots on the side.

Elderflower & Sauvignon Blanc Cured Sea Trout

1 whole fillet of sea trout (or use a side of small salmon), pin bones removed

freshly ground black pepper

FOR THE CURE

1 tbsp fennel seeds

1 tbsp cracked peppercorns

400g (14oz) coarse sea salt

250g (9oz) caster (superfine) sugar

100ml (3½fl oz) elderflower cordial

100ml (3½fl oz) sauvignon blanc wine

zest of 1 unwaxed lemon, plus wedges to serve

Sea trout comes into season in the spring and curing a whole side of it, to my mind, counts as something of an immense treat. This is a recipe you can make in advance, then serve later with satisfaction. Cured fish also makes for one of the best and easiest starters. Do use a thin-bladed and flexible sharp knife to slice the fish; you want it to be cut thinly, but with the slices still beautifully intact. It helps if you keep the skin on and hold the skin taut as an anchor. The cured flesh should feel firm, still moist, much like smoked salmon. Elderflower and sauvignon blanc are very happy together – you could use the same wine to cure and then drink with the fish when ready to serve. Look out for some frilly, in-bloom, elderflower blossom and scatter a good tablespoon of the flowers (bug-free) in with the salt cure. A couple of heads of fresh blossom look nice as a garnish when you serve the fish. Stored well, in the fridge, on a clean plate and cut with a clean knife each time, this fish should keep for a couple of weeks.

Mix all the cure ingredients together in a mixing bowl. Spread half this mixture in the bottom of a non-reactive tray that will hold the fish in a single layer. (Do cut the fillet in half if that is easier to fit into the tray or your fridge.)

Place the fish on top of the cure mixture, skin-side upward and cover with the remaining cure mixture. Cover and put in the fridge for 12 hours (by which time the cure will have turned into a liquid brine).

After 12 hours, turn the fish skin-side downward, cover again and return to the fridge for another 12 hours.

Remove the fish from the brine, rinse with cold water and gently pat all over with some paper towel.

To serve, use a very sharp knife with a thin blade and slice the cured fish very finely on the angle starting at the tail end. Arrange the slices on a large serving platter, or use single plates, and season with plenty of freshly ground black pepper. Serve with lemon wedges for squeezing over.

Pint of Prawns with Lemon Mayonnaise & Soda Bread

FOR THE SODA BREAD

1 handful of oats

375g (13oz) plain (all-purpose) white flour (or 50:50 white and wholewheat, if you like)

10g (¼oz) salt

7g (generous ⅛oz) bicarbonate of soda (baking soda)

300ml (10½fl oz) buttermilk

FOR THE LEMON MAYONNAISE

2 egg yolks

pinch of salt

½ tsp Dijon mustard

400ml (14fl oz) sunflower oil

zest and juice of ½–1 unwaxed lemon, plus wedges to serve

freshly ground black pepper

FOR THE PRAWNS

4 litres (135fl oz) iced water

7 tbsp salt

1kg (2lb 4oz) shell-on fresh (preferably) or frozen prawns

bay leaves (optional), scrunched a little

plenty of ice

I have super-happy memories of my time spent cooking in the kitchen of The Gurnard's Head, near Zennor in Cornwall. Every day we would make batches of knobbly soda bread to serve alongside pints of prawns, beady eyes all pointing up and out of the pint glass, and with a wobbly, rich mayonnaise and lemon wedges alongside. Such a simple lunch, such a good lunch. In someone sensible's unwritten rulebook – written by someone eminent and articulated on matters of cooking and the enjoyment of eating – pints of prawns in a pub garden facing the sea with good bread and mayonnaise feature prominently. It is the law. Making some at home is a good second best.

Make the soda bread. Preheat the oven to 180°C/ 160°C fan/350°F/Gas Mark 4. Dust a baking sheet with a few of the oats.

Sift the flour into a wide bowl along with the salt and bicarbonate of soda (baking soda). Make a well in the centre and gradually pour in the buttermilk, very gently turning the mixture over in the bowl with a large metal spoon. The trick to a good soda bread is to not mix it too much, but to mix it enough to form a nice, sticky, cohesive mass in the centre of your bowl. You need to be confident to mix it enough to form a dough, but not too much for it to become stodgy and over-worked.

When you have the dough right, lightly flour your work surface and tip the dough onto it. Shape into a nicely sized round and slash the top with a deep cross. Place the loaf on the oat-dusted baking sheet and sprinkle the top liberally with the remaining oats.

Bake for about 35 minutes, until the loaf is nicely coloured and crisp all over. Tap the underside – the loaf should sound hollow. Remove from the oven and cool on a wire rack while you make the mayonnaise.

Using a whisk, combine the egg yolks, pinch of salt and the mustard in a bowl and season with a little pepper.

cont.

Put the oil in a jug. Then, slowly start adding the oil, a few drops at a time, into the egg mixture, whisking all the time. Very slowly increase the quantity of oil you're adding each time, whisking in each addition so it is properly amalgamated, before adding the next. Once the mayonnaise has started to hold its shape, you can start to add the oil in a thin and steady stream, whisking all the while.

When you have added all the oil, you should have a thick and wobbly mayonnaise that holds its shape.

Add lemon zest and juice to taste, and season again with salt and a generous amount of freshly ground pepper. Set aside until you're ready to serve.

Make the prawns. Pour the iced or chilled water into a bowl and season with 4 tablespoons of the salt.

In a large pan over a high heat, boil 4 litres (135fl oz) of water and add the remaining 3 tablespoons of salt. Add all the prawns together and bring quickly to a boil. Cook for about 2 minutes, until bright pink and just cooked through. Do not let them overcook.

Drain and tip the prawns at once into the iced water. Leave for 10 minutes, until thoroughly chilled. Add more ice if the ice that's there melts before the prawns are properly cold. Drain the prawns from the cold water to serve.

Side of Very Slow-cooked Salmon with Butter & Soft Herbs

1 centre-cut (the thickest section) salmon or large trout fillet (about 600g/1lb 5oz)

good olive oil

2 large shallots, finely chopped

zest and juice of 1 unwaxed lemon

1 big bunch of soft herbs (such as tarragon, chervil or flat-leaf parsley), leaves and stalks separated and roughly chopped

100ml (3½fl oz) white wine

200g (7oz) unsalted butter, diced and chilled

250g (9oz) green beans

100g (3½oz) asparagus tips

150g (5½oz) sugar-snap peas, trimmed

salt and freshly ground black pepper

cooked new potatoes, to serve

SERVES 4-6

The good-size tranche of salmon required for this recipe is something to splash out on and to savour for a special occasion. Fish bought from a sustainable source is pricey – buy it with due environmental care, especially so given the grave situation of certain fish stocks. Wild salmon can be extremely expensive. If you would rather use farmed salmon, buy fish that have been organically farmed, as these will have had immeasurably better living conditions than intensively farmed, chemically dyed and pellet-fed, non-organic alternatives. Here, the cooked salmon is delicate and very delicious – softly, softly – a tribute to the fish.

Preheat the oven to 80°C/60°C fan/175°F/Gas Mark ¼ (or as low as your oven will go) and place a baking dish half filled with boiling water in the bottom of the oven.

Brush the salmon fillet all over with a little olive oil and lay it on a baking tray. Season generously with salt and pepper, then top with half the shallots, the lemon zest and the roughly chopped herb stalks. Bake for about 30–40 minutes, until the fish feels just firm to the touch and the white juices are just starting to break through the surface. Rest for 10 minutes and serve straight away, or let the salmon rest covered in foil for up to 2 hours.

While the salmon is resting, make a butter sauce. Boil the remaining shallots and white wine together over a moderate–high heat in a small saucepan until there is only about 2 tablespoons of liquid left.

Remove from the heat and gradually whisk in the cold butter, a little at a time, waiting until most of the butter has melted before incorporating any more.

When you're ready to serve, boil the beans in salted water for 3 minutes, then add the asparagus tips and sugar-snap peas and cook for 2 minutes more. Drain the vegetables, check the seasoning and keep warm.

Gently brush the herbs and shallots off the cooked salmon and sprinkle with a little lemon juice. Tear the fish into big flakes and arrange on a large platter. Spoon over the vegetables, herb leaves and butter sauce. Serve with any extra butter sauce and the potatoes on the side.

Bagna Cauda with the Best Spring has to Offer

assortment of raw spring vegetables, to serve (radishes, asparagus, carrots, cauliflower, artichoke hearts, celery, fennel, cabbage hearts and lettuce or bitter leaves)

1 large bulb of garlic, cloves separated and peeled

whole milk (enough to cover the garlic in a small pan)

1 x 50g (1¾oz) can of best-quality anchovies

250g (9oz) unsalted butter, diced small

250ml (9fl oz) good olive oil

SERVES 8 AS A CANAPÉ OR 4–6 AS AN APPETIZER

Try to buy the best cured anchovies you can find. I think I love these plump fillets of fish best of all in bagna cauda. Firm but juicy with a good salty thwack, anchovies are unrivalled when it comes to tiny ingredients that pack a tremendous punch. Feel free to blow a bit of budget on some spanking seasonal vegetables and salad to showcase this deeply flavoured anchovy sauce. Be sure not to add the oil and butter too quickly, and also ensure a steady and even temperature when adding the fats. If the sauce splits, you will have to begin again with yet more softened garlic and anchovies, slowly, drop by drop, adding in the split mixture. Serve the bagna cauda in a warm bowl to safeguard against fluctuating temperatures. Take your time, be confident. Bagna cauda is the anchovy's magnum opus.

Prepare as many, or as few raw spring vegetables as you like. Take a good amount of time to prepare them carefully – washing, peeling and trimming to size, then arranging them all on a large serving plate.

To make the bagna cauda, put the garlic in a small saucepan, cover with milk and place over a high heat. Bring to a boil, reduce the heat and simmer for 10 minutes, until the garlic is soft and tender. Discard the milk, reserving the garlic, and clean out the pan.

Add the still-warm garlic back into the pan and mash it with the anchovies and one quarter of the butter, over the lowest heat possible, until you have a smooth paste. As soon as the butter begins to melt, whisk the contents of the pan using a small whisk. When the butter is nearly all melted into the anchovy mixture, add the remainder bit by bit, all the time whisking, and continuing until all the butter is incorporated. Don't let the bagna cauda get too hot, and certainly don't let it boil – I find taking the pan off the heat every now and then helps to temper the heat and ensure the mixture does not get too hot.

With all the butter added, continue whisking and pour in the olive oil very gradually – a steady trickle should do it – until you have a thick, glossy bagna cauda. Remove to a warmed bowl and serve immediately.

Tart Tropézienne with Passionfruit

FOR THE BRIOCHE

125ml (4fl oz) warm water

1 tsp dried yeast

2 tbsp whole milk

25g (1oz) caster (superfine) sugar

250g (8oz) strong white bread flour, plus more for dusting

pinch of salt

30g (1oz) cold unsalted butter, diced

1 egg, beaten

1 egg yolk, beaten

2 tbsp pearled sugar nibs

boiling water from a kettle

FOR THE CRÈME PÂTISSIÈRE FILLING

500ml (17fl oz) whole milk

6 egg yolks

200g (7oz) caster (superfine) sugar

50g (1¾oz) cornflour (cornstarch)

150ml (5fl oz) double (heavy) cream, very chilled

6 passionfruit, pulp removed

This is brioche dough baked as a large round, filled with pastry cream (crème pâtissière) and, in this case, passionfruit. Crème pâtissière differs from custard because of the addition of cornflour (cornstarch), which makes for a thicker, more stable filling. This is a decadent cake, much celebrated in France, and even more so when the phenomenon that was Brigitte Bardot was spotted eating one in St Tropez in the 1950s. I've given a slightly cheaty method here for the brioche – rather than mixing softened butter into the dough, you rub the butter into the flour to begin with, which means you can make this brioche by hand. I've used passionfruit because I love them and they also happen to be in season in early spring. You can, of course, flavour your pastry cream with myriad other ingredients: orange-blossom water, or vanilla or lemon would all be excellent. Pearled sugar nibs on top are traditional – bash up some sugar cubes up if you can't find them.

Make the brioche dough. Mix together the water, yeast, 1 tablespoon of the milk and the sugar in a jug and allow to stand for 5 minutes, until it begins to froth a little.

Sift the flour into a bowl, add the pinch of salt and, using your fingertips or a food processor, rub the butter into the flour until the mixture resembles fine breadcrumbs. Make a well in the centre and add the yeast liquid and the beaten egg. Using your hands, combine to a sticky and wet dough, then scrape this out onto a floured work surface.

Stretch and fold the dough in on itself for at least 5 minutes, adding as little flour as possible, until it feels soft and bouncy. Place in an oiled bowl, cover and set aside to rise somewhere warm for about 1 hour, or until doubled in size.

While the brioche is rising, make the crème pâtissière. Bring the milk to a boil in a medium saucepan set over a moderate heat. In a separate bowl combine the egg yolks, sugar and cornflour (cornstarch) in a bowl. Whisk until pale and frothy. Add the hot milk to the eggs and mix until thoroughly combined, then return the mixture to the pan and stir until thickened, much like custard! Place the crème pâtissière in the bowl and cover the surface with cling film (to stop a skin forming). Place in the fridge to cool.

Once the dough has doubled in size, knock out the air and knead again for 2 minutes. Lightly flour the work surface and roll out the dough into a rough 25cm (10in) circle. Slide the dough onto a baking sheet lined with baking paper and loosely cover with a clean tea towel. Leave to prove for about 1 hour, or until doubled in size again.

Preheat the oven to 200°C/180°C fan/400°F/Gas Mark 6. Place a shallow baking tray in the bottom of the oven. Brush the brioche round with the remaining beaten egg yolk and 1 tablespoon of milk and sprinkle with the pearled sugar nibs.

Fill the baking tray at the bottom of the oven with boiling water to create steam. Place the baking sheet in the oven and bake the brioche for 20–25 minutes, until golden. Remove from the oven and leave to cool on a wire rack.

When you're ready to fill the brioche, in a mixing bowl whip the double (heavy) cream until it holds firm peaks. Stir a large spoon of the whipped cream into the cold crème pâtissière, then fold in the remaining whipped cream. Doing it like this should prevent the mixture from forming lumps.

Use a bread knife to slice the brioche in two. Pipe or spread the filling onto the base of the brioche, add the passionfruit pulp, and top with the other half of brioche. Press gently to seal, and serve.

Morel & Wild Garlic Omelette for One

50g (1¾oz; about 6–10) morel
mushrooms

30g (1oz) unsalted butter

1 small handful (about 30g/1oz) of
wild garlic or spinach, sliced into fat
ribbons (optional)

2 or 3 eggs (or use 2 duck eggs,
if you like)

salt and freshly ground black pepper

SERVES 1

Morels and wild garlic are meant for one another.
Spring mushrooms, morels pop up in woodland
areas where they lie dormant through the winter.
As mushrooms go, these are much vaunted by chefs
and eager cooks – they have an indulgent, nutty
flavour and a striking, corrugated flesh to their hollow,
pointed outsides. The modest omelette is given star
treatment: with egg as canvas, the morels punctuate,
complemented by the wild garlic. I also think there is
a beautiful indulgence in spending a bit of money on
some prime ingredients that you don't have to share
with anyone else. A glass of wine is also essential,
so says Elizabeth David.

I like a 23cm (9in) pan for a two-egg omelette –
well-worn cast iron or non-stick, as you like. And,
of course, you could use a more commonplace
mushroom, but that's not really the point in
this recipe.

Carefully clean the morels and make sure there is no dirt
or grit on them. If they are large, split them in half or
quarters; if not, keep them whole. Melt half the butter
in a small saucepan. Add the morels and cook for about
3 minutes, until softened, then add the wild garlic or
spinach and cook for 30 seconds, until just wilted.
Season to taste with salt and pepper, drain any liquid,
and transfer to a plate. Set aside.

Crack the eggs into a small bowl, season with salt and
pepper and beat well. Over a moderate–high heat, using
your best non-stick frying pan (skillet), add the remaining
butter. Let it melt and foam, then tip in the eggs. Shake
the pan vigorously to disturb the eggs while distributing
them evenly for about 1 minute. (You could use a spatula,
if you like, but don't over mix – you want the omelette
to be barely formed with luscious, creamy folds.) Let the
base of the omelette set in the pan for 20 seconds or so,
then add the morels and wild garlic and very gently fold
or roll the omelette to form, cooking it until just set, with
little or no colour, but still slightly runny within.

Tip the omelette out onto a warmed plate and season
with another quick blast of black pepper, if you like.

Crab Noodle Broth

1 bunch of spring onions (scallions), thinly sliced, green and white parts separated

4 cloves of garlic, finely chopped

1 tbsp grated (shredded) fresh ginger

2 lemongrass stalks, roughly chopped

2 tbsp fish sauce, plus more to taste

1 tsp red chilli flakes

1 tbsp annatto seeds (optional)

3 tbsp sunflower oil

2 tomatoes, roughly chopped

800ml (28fl oz) chicken stock

100g (3½oz) minced (ground) chicken or pork, finely chopped

150g (5½oz) peeled prawns (defrosted if frozen)

½ tsp ground black or white pepper

1 tsp caster (superfine) sugar

150g (5½oz) white crab meat (canned is okay)

juice of 2 limes, or more to taste, plus more lime wedges to serve

TO SERVE

150g (5½oz) dried vermicelli rice noodles, soaked or cooked as per the packet instructions (or enough fresh rice noodles to serve 4)

150g (5½oz) bean sprouts

1 small bunch of mint and/or coriander (cilantro), leaves picked

red chilli, thinly sliced, or more chilli flakes (optional)

Native to tropical regions, from Mexico through to Brazil, bright-red annatto seeds are collected from the achiote tree; you can buy the seeds online. Warmed first in the oil, the seeds impart an arresting colour, but what they also give is an intriguing, peppery aroma, almost nutmeg-like. Here, you're not looking for perfect ping-pong balls of mince mixture – much more interesting are small, rough-hewn spoonfuls.

In a food processor, blitz the white of the spring onions (scallions) with the garlic, ginger, lemongrass and 1 tablespoon of the fish sauce to form a smooth paste (add a splash of water to help, if necessary).

In a medium saucepan over a moderate heat, gently cook the 1 teaspoon of chilli flakes and the annatto (if using) in the oil for about 2 minutes, or until the oil turns red. Remove from the heat and strain, returning the coloured oil to the pan.

Fry the blitzed paste along with the tomatoes in the coloured oil over a moderate heat for about 5 minutes, until the tomatoes have broken down and the contents of the pan smell fragrant and delicious and are beginning to stick a little. Add the chicken stock, bring to a boil, then turn down the heat and simmer for about 10 minutes.

While the stock is simmering, in a food processor blitz the minced (ground) chicken or pork together with the prawns, the remaining 1 tablespoon of fish sauce, the ground pepper and the sugar to form a smooth paste.

Using a couple of tablespoons, drop small measures, each about the size of a walnut, into the broth and simmer for 5 minutes, until cooked and piping hot throughout. Finally, add the crab meat, stir well and remove from the heat.

Divide the cooked vermicelli noodles between 4 bowls.

Add lime juice and fish sauce to the broth to taste. Ladle the broth and the meatballs into the bowls, on top of the vermicelli noodles, to serve. Top with the bean sprouts, green parts of the spring onions and the herbs. Add extra chilli, if you like, and serve lime wedges at the table.

Spring Vegetable & Chicken Paella

50ml (1¾fl oz) olive oil

8 small chicken thighs

8 pork ribs, chopped in half (use a cleaver or heavy knife, or ask your butcher to do it)

2 onions, finely chopped

2 green (bell) peppers, deseeded and finely diced

1 bulb of garlic, cloves separated, peeled and finely chopped

1 tsp sweet paprika

200g (7oz) tomato passata

big pinch of saffron, soaked in a little warm water for about 10 minutes

400g (14oz) mixed spring vegetables (peas, broad/fava beans, small artichokes, green beans, spinach, wild garlic, spring onions/scallions), podded and trimmed as relevant

1.2 litres (40fl oz) hot chicken stock or water

600g (1lb 5oz) bomba or paella rice

2 large rosemary sprigs

lemon wedges (although I like orange), to serve

salt

SERVES 6-8

I like the ritual of making a paella. The sourcing of ingredients, the enormous, wide pan, the pursuit for perfect, tender-cooked rice, which forms a crust, just so. Much praised, and always fought over, this crisp barrier of crunchy cooked rice is called the *socarrat*. Beyond this lies the body of the paella, succulent grains of rice, swollen with good stock. Who best to invite? Which of your friends and family will appreciate the conviviality of paella, served as it must be in the pan in which it is cooked, with everyone then digging deep. Purists, of which there are many, of this famous dish all agree that seafood on paella is an abomination. I'm not entirely sure why paella invokes such fury; channel a bit of Fleetwood Mac and 'go your own way' – your guests will be delighted either way. Use duck legs (cleaved in two), if you prefer duck to chicken. Use seafood too, why the hell not? Squid, prawn, mussels and clams will all flatter the rice and chicken. Just steer clear of chorizo, for some will say here lies utter jabberwock.

Heat the oil in a paella or very large, cast-iron frying pan (skillet) over a moderate heat. Add the chicken and pork ribs and fry for about 15 minutes, until nicely coloured and brown all over (no need to cook through fully), then put to one side on a plate.

Add the onions and peppers and cook for at least 10 minutes over a moderate heat, until softened. Add the garlic and cook for 1 minute more, then add the paprika and passata and the saffron and its soaking water.

Let the mixture cook for about 5 minutes, until rich and thick, then return the meat to the pan, add the spring vegetables and mix well.

Add the stock or water and bring the pan to a fierce boil. Season with salt to taste (the paella should be well seasoned to take into account the fact that the rice will absorb lots of flavour – about 1 tablespoon of salt is ideal).

Add the rice to the pan, shaking the pan violently so that the whole mixture evens out. (You can stir the rice to distribute it at this point, if you don't fancy the pan-shaking method.) Reduce the heat to moderate, and from this moment onward do not to stir so that the all-important crust can start to form.

Let the paella cook for about 20–25 minutes, or until the rice is just cooked and the liquid has all been fully absorbed. Then, increase the heat for about 1 minute, until you hear the rice begin to sizzle – keeping it at a high heat for about 30 seconds more will ensure the crust forms on the base. It can take a bit of practice to not let the bottom burn, but to bronze the crust, just enough.

Remove the paella from the heat, place the rosemary sprigs on top, cover loosely with a clean tea towel and leave the paella for at least 10 minutes to rest.

Serve straight from the pan, being sure to scrape up and serve each portion with some of the crust. Serve with lemon wedges (or orange ones), as you like.

Fried Potato Masala Toastie

1 tbsp sunflower oil

1 tsp unsalted butter, softened, plus more to butter the bread

1 tsp mustard seeds

1 red onion, half finely diced, half thinly sliced

300g (10½oz) new potatoes, peeled and cut into large bite-size pieces

big pinch of salt, plus ½ tsp

1 small bunch of coriander (cilantro), leaves picked and roughly chopped

1 tbsp grated (shredded) fresh ginger

juice of 1 lemon

1 clove of garlic, thinly sliced

1–2 green chillies, finely sliced (remove the seeds if you want less heat)

8 slices of white bread

200g (7oz) cheddar, gloucester or gouda cheese, thinly sliced

½ cucumber, peeled and thinly sliced

4 tomatoes, thinly sliced

2 tbsp chaat masala, plus optional more to serve

There isn't a better toasted cheese sandwich than this one. The combination is irresistible – golden fried bread, creamy, soft, spiced potato, obediently melting cheese, all given a greedy slick of fresh ginger and chilli sauce, green as grass and hot as you can bear. Chaat masala is pretty crucial here and readily available from Indian superstores or online (you could use garam masala, but it won't have the same tang). Sour, salty and hot, chaat masala is the transformative pinch to many different Indian dishes, and here, it is insanely good with the cheese and the chutney. Saturday lunch just got a whole lot better.

Heat the oil and butter in a medium saucepan over a moderate heat. Add the mustard seeds and fry until they just begin to pop and dance around. Add the diced onion and cook for about 5 minutes, until soft and beginning to turn a touch golden.

Add the potatoes, the big pinch of salt and 200ml (7fl oz) of water and cover the pan. Cook for 10 minutes, then uncover and cook for a further 10–15 minutes, until the potatoes are soft and the water has evaporated. Drain well and spread the potatoes out on a plate to cool.

In a food processor, blitz the coriander (cilantro), ginger, lemon juice, garlic, green chilli and the ½ teaspoon of salt to form a smooth chutney (add a splash of water to loosen, if necessary).

Butter the bread slices generously on one side, then turn them over and spread with some of the green chutney on the other side. Build up sandwiches (with the buttered side of the bread facing outward) with cheese, cooked potato, sliced onion, cucumber, tomato, and a big pinch of the chaat masala. Top each filling with another slice of bread, buttered side facing outward.

Fry the sandwiches in a large, dry frying pan (skillet) over a moderate heat, turning occasionally, until golden all over and the cheese is beginning to melt (or you can use a toastie maker if you have one). Remove from the heat and serve the sandwiches with any remaining green chutney, and extra chaat masala to sprinkle, if you like.

Fried Prawn Tacos (taquitos)

200g (7oz) tomatoes, roughly chopped

2-4 green or jalapeño chillies, finely chopped (deseeded if you want less heat)

1 small bunch of coriander (cilantro), roughly chopped

1 clove of garlic, finely chopped

1 small red onion, very thinly sliced

½ spring cabbage, cored and thinly shredded

2 limes

150g (5½oz) sour cream

2 tbsp sunflower oil, plus more for frying the tortillas

300g (10½oz) peeled raw prawns

12 small soft corn tortillas

50g (1¾oz) kikos (roasted corn kernels), blitzed to a rough dust (optional)

salt and freshly ground black pepper

hot chilli sauce, to serve

YOU WILL ALSO NEED

toothpicks, to secure the tortillas

Yes and yes: fried prawn and cabbage tacos dusted with fried corn powder. Try to track down kikos (fried corn kernels). Most large food stores have them in the snacks section and Spanish delis will certainly stock them, too. Blitz them to form a rough dust that will give indispensable crunch and extra seasoning to the finished tacos. If the tortillas are difficult to roll without breaking, warm them a little in the oven to soften. There are numerous hot sauces on the market these days, from hot to super-hot, smoky through to fruity. Choose a hot sauce you like best, all of the above will suit these delicious fried tacos. Serve with cold beers – a meal to share with friends (you'll have many, if you plan on making these).

Mix together the tomatoes, chilli, coriander (cilantro), garlic, red onion and cabbage in a large bowl and add the juice of half a lime. Season with salt and pepper to taste and leave to macerate for a good few minutes.

Squeeze the juice of the remaining half lime into the sour cream and leave to one side.

Heat the oil in a large, cast-iron frying pan (skillet) over a moderate–high heat and fry the prawns for 2 minutes, until just cooked through, then tip into the cabbage mixture and check the seasoning.

Place 2 tablespoons of the mixture on one side of a tortilla and roll it tightly into a tube-like shape. Secure with 1 or 2 toothpicks. Repeat until you have used up all the mixture and tortillas.

Pour a 5mm (¼in) depth of oil into a large, non-stick frying pan over a moderate heat. When hot, fry the tortillas in batches for about 2–3 minutes on each side, until golden and crisp. Remove from the heat and set aside to drain on paper towels. Dust each with the blitzed kikos, if using, then serve with the sour cream, hot chilli sauce and the remaining lime cut into wedges. Lots of napkins, too.

Ricotta Baked Pasta with Minted Peas & Pecorino

300g (10½oz) large conchiglioni or other large pasta shapes

500g (1lb 2oz) ricotta cheese

50g (1¾oz) pecorino (or use parmesan), grated (shredded), plus more to serve

½ nutmeg, grated (shredded)

60g (2¼oz) unsalted butter

600g (1lb 5oz) peas (fresh or frozen)

2 cloves of garlic, thinly sliced

1 small bunch of mint, leaves picked (or you could use basil)

salt and freshly ground black pepper

This is a simple recipe – disarmingly easy, in fact, in the spirit of generous, heartfelt cooking. I have used dried pasta and stuffed the barely cooked shells full with creamy clouds of ricotta to bake until blistered and bubbling. Topping this baked pasta dish with buttery minted peas and yet more pecorino makes it one that I would gladly cook for my family or friends, and especially so when either were in need of a little gentle, restorative care. By all means use broad (fava) beans, podded if on the large size, or a mixture of peas and broad beans – up to you. Likewise, I suggest fresh peas, but you and I both know that frozen peas will work. Be generous with the pecorino.

Preheat the oven to 220°C/200°C fan/425°F/Gas Mark 7.

Bring a large pan of well-salted water to a boil and cook the pasta shells until firmly al dente – about 3 or 4 minutes short of the packet-cooking instructions. Drain and allow to cool slightly.

While the pasta is cooking, beat the ricotta and pecorino or parmesan together. Season with salt and pepper and add the nutmeg. Place spoonfuls of the mixture into each of the cooked pasta shells and arrange the filled shells snugly in a baking dish. Dot with a quarter of the butter and add 2 tablespoons of water. Distribute any remaining ricotta mixture among the pasta shapes in the dish. Cover with foil and bake for 20 minutes, uncovering for the last 5 minutes, until the pasta is cooked through and the top is browned.

While the pasta is baking, boil the peas with the garlic in well-salted water for 3–5 minutes, until cooked and tender. Drain, add the remaining butter and keep warm.

To serve, add the chopped mint to the buttered peas and garlic and spoon over the filled pasta. Top with more grated cheese and serve immediately.

Butterflied Leg of Lamb with Green Olives & Parsley, Tzatziki & Flat Breads

FOR THE LAMB

zest and juice of 1 unwaxed lemon

2 tbsp good olive oil

2 tsp ground coriander, toasted

1 tsp cracked black pepper

2 tsp best-quality dried oregano

3 cloves of garlic, crushed

4 bay leaves, roughly torn

75ml (2¼fl oz) rosé or light red wine

about 1.5kg (3lb 5oz) leg of lamb, boned and butterflied

1 tsp salt

flat breads, to serve

FOR THE TZATZIKI

½ cucumber, peeled, deseeded and coarsely grated (shredded)

300ml (10½fl oz) plain or Greek yogurt

juice of ½ lemon

½ clove of garlic, crushed

salt and freshly ground black pepper

FOR THE DRESSING

about 50g (1¾oz) green olives, pitted and roughly chopped

zest and juice of ½ lemon

1 small bunch of flat-leaf parsley, leaves picked and roughly chopped

SERVES 6-8

Ask your butcher to bone and butterfly your leg of lamb for you. If that isn't possible, use a sharp knife and do it yourself. First, cut down the length of the lamb leg to expose the bone. Keep your knife as close to the bone as possible as you cut along one side to completely reveal it, then cut around the bone and remove it. Lay the lamb skin-side downward on a chopping board. Carefully slash the thicker sections with your knife to open it out like a book, partly cutting any sections until you have a flat piece of lamb of more-or-less even 4cm (1½in) thickness. Greek flavours are some of my favourites when it comes to cooking lamb.

Combine all the lamb ingredients except the lamb itself and the salt to create a marinade. Place the lamb in a roasting tray and pour over the marinade. Cover and leave in the fridge for at least 2 hours, or overnight is best. Remove from the fridge to bring it back to approximate room temperature before cooking, adding the salt to the marinade.

Make the tzatziki. Squeeze as much moisture from the grated (shredded) cucumber as possible. Mix it in a bowl with the yogurt, lemon juice and garlic, seasoning with salt and pepper to taste. Set aside.

Set your grill (broiler) to high, and cook the lamb for about 12–15 minutes on each side, turning often, until nicely charred all over but still pink within. By all means cook the lamb longer if you prefer to eat it well done (18–20 minutes each side).

While the lamb is cooking, make the dressing. Mix all the dressing ingredients together and set aside.

Once the lamb is cooked to your liking, remove from the grill (broiler) and spoon over the dressing, leaving the meat to rest for at least 10 minutes under some loose foil before serving.

To serve, warm the flat breads, toasting them slightly under the grill (broiler). Slice the lamb and pile it with cooking juices, dressing and tzatziki.

Porchetta Roll with Rhubarb Ketchup

800g (1lb 12oz) piece of skin-on, boneless pork belly, skin scored all over in lines 1cm (½in) deep

at least 1 tsp salt

freshly ground black pepper

200g (7oz) plain pork sausages, skinned (or use minced/ground pork or sausagemeat)

6 cloves of garlic, crushed

2 tsp fennel seeds, toasted and lightly crushed

½ tsp chilli flakes

2 tbsp chopped fresh rosemary

200ml (7fl oz) white wine or water

FOR THE KETCHUP

400g (14oz) rhubarb, roughly chopped into 2.5cm (1in) batons

1 small onion, diced

1 tbsp grated (shredded) fresh ginger

80g (2½oz) caster (superfine) sugar

80ml (2½fl oz) red-wine, white-wine or cider vinegar

1 tsp salt

¼ tsp freshly ground black pepper

TO SERVE

bread rolls or baps

watercress

SERVES ABOUT 6-8

If you have a ready-rolled pork belly, do try to stuff the pork mince or sausagemeat deep within from both ends of the cavity. Plenty of salt will help with the crackling, as will cooking it low and slow until tender, then cranking up the heat to blast the skin.

Preheat the oven to 160°C/140°C fan/315°F/Gas Mark 2–3. Season the pork belly generously all over with the teaspoon of salt and some black pepper. Make four slashes in the flesh side, each about 2cm (1in) deep.

Mix the sausagemeat or minced (ground) pork with the garlic, fennel, chilli flakes and rosemary, and smear this thick paste all over the pork-belly flesh, pushing deep into the slashes.

Roll up the pork belly tightly and secure with string, tying at 5cm (2in) intervals. Pat dry the outside of the pork and place on a rack in a roasting tray. Roast for 3–4 hours, until a sharp knife easily inserts into the meat.

While the pork cooks, make the ketchup. Put the rhubarb, onion, ginger, sugar and vinegar in a saucepan over a moderate heat. Season with the salt and pepper and cook for about 5 minutes, until the mixture comes to a boil, then reduce the heat and simmer gently, stirring frequently, for 20–30 minutes, until thick and rich. You can blend it or leave the sauce chunky. Remove from the heat, check the seasoning and set aside.

When the pork is cooked and soft, turn up the oven to 220°C/200°C fan/425°F/Gas 7 and roast for another 20 minutes, or until the crackling is golden brown. Keep a watchful eye – the pork must not scorch. Remove from the oven and also from the pan. Transfer the pork to a plate and allow it to rest, uncovered, somewhere warm for at least 30 minutes.

Meanwhile, add the wine or water to the roasting pan and place it over a moderate–high heat, scraping and simmering until the pan juices are thick. Season to taste.

To serve, carve the pork into thick slices, and dip each in the pan juices. Stuff the pork into a bread roll with some watercress and a spoonful of the rhubarb ketchup.

Harissa

200g (7oz) long red chillies

2 ripe tomatoes

1 red (bell) pepper, halved and deseeded

3 cloves of garlic, unpeeled

50ml (1¾fl oz) good olive oil, plus more to seal

2 tsp cumin seeds, toasted and ground

1 tsp caraway seeds, toasted and ground

1 tsp sweet mild paprika

1 tbsp red wine vinegar or sherry vinegar

salt and freshly ground black pepper

This is a north African chilli paste, and, to me, pretty much indispensable throughout the year. Stored under oil and in the fridge, harissa will keep well enough for up to a month. Making your own is a must: use it as a fiery condiment on the table to finish a dish or add a fierce spoonful to jazz up a cooking sauce; stir it through cooked grains or vegetables, or use it as a punchy marinade for meat, poultry and fish. Cooking the peppers, tomatoes and chillies until they blister and blacken sweetens the cooked flesh and makes for a silky-smooth harissa paste. You can use dried chillies, rehydrated in hot water until soft, to blitz if you would rather.

Preheat the grill (broiler) to hot.

Grill (broil) the chillies, tomatoes and halved (bell) pepper (skin-side upward) for about 5 minutes, then turn the chillies and add the garlic. Grill for a further 5 minutes, until everything is blistered and soft. Put to one side to cool slightly.

Remove the skin from the pepper halves, tomatoes and garlic, and skin and deseed the chillies.

Blitz the grilled vegetables with the remaining ingredients to form a smooth sauce, seasoning with salt and pepper to taste. Transfer to a clean container and top with a layer of oil to seal. Store in the fridge.

Focaccia with Wild Garlic & Green Olives

350ml (12fl oz) warm water

5g (⅛oz) dried yeast

500g (1lb 2oz) strong white bread flour

75ml (2¼fl oz) good olive oil, plus more for kneading and rising

1 tsp salt

50g (1¾oz) wild garlic, cut into ribbons

100g (3½oz) green olives, pitted and roughly chopped

freshly ground black pepper

flaky salt, for sprinkling

When you're making focaccia, two crucial rules apply: first, add the salt to the dough after you've mixed it with the yeast and given it all a little rest. Yeast does not like exposure to salt from the off. And, second, give the scalding-hot, just-out-of-the-oven dough a thirsty slurp of good olive oil. The hot crust will drink up the oil, which will make for a springy, chewy focaccia that is full of flavour. If you can't get hold of wild garlic, use rocket (arugula) or baby spinach.

Put the water in a small bowl and mix in the yeast to dissolve.

Place the flour in a large mixing bowl and make a well in the centre. Add 1 tablespoon of the olive oil and the yeast and water mixture. Mix vigorously with a metal spoon to form a soft and sticky dough. Cover and rest for 15 minutes.

Turn out the dough onto an oiled worktop. Add the salt, kneading the dough assertively for about 5 minutes, until it is smooth and elastic. Then, add one quarter of the wild garlic, kneading the greens into the dough for a minute. Place the dough in an oiled bowl, somewhere warm, for about 1 hour, until not quite doubled in size.

Line a rectangular baking tin, about 32 x 22cm (13 x 8½in), with baking paper and preheat the oven to 200°C/180°C fan/400°F/Gas Mark 6. Gently tip the dough into the tin, shaping to fit, but not knocking too much air out. Try to get some nice, deep dimples in the surface of the dough, pressing firmly with well-oiled fingers, but not puncturing all the way through. Put to one side, somewhere warm, for 15 minutes more.

In a small mixing bowl, mix the remaining wild garlic with the olives, 2 tablespoons of the olive oil and plenty of black pepper. Spoon over the top of the dough, gently pushing it deep into the dimples.

Bake for 20–25 minutes, until golden-brown and hollow-sounding when tapped from beneath. Remove from the oven and immediately spoon over the remaining olive oil. Sprinkle generously with flaky salt. Leave in the tin for at least 5 minutes before serving.

Rhubarb & Oat Milk Bircher
with Ginger Syrup & Toasted Oats

200g (7oz) rolled oats

400ml (14fl oz) oat, almond or rice milk

4 rhubarb sticks, trimmed and cut into 3cm (1¼in) lengths

75g (2½oz) caster (superfine) sugar

1 cinnamon stick

2 pieces of stem ginger in syrup, finely chopped

2 tbsp stem ginger syrup, from the jar

These three flavours work remarkably well together. Sharp, roasted rhubarb and warming stem ginger flatter the creamy oats, soaked overnight. Toasting a quarter of the oats makes for a good and crunchy blast to scatter on top of each bowlful. You could serve this for breakfast, but I would just as happily eat this at any time of the day. I have done, in fact.

Preheat the oven to 190°C/170°C fan/375°F/Gas Mark 5.

Place 150g (5½oz) of the oats and all the milk in a bowl and stir to combine. Cover and leave to soak in the fridge. Overnight is ideal.

Combine the rhubarb with 50g (1¾oz) of the sugar, a splash of water and the cinnamon stick. Arrange in a snug-fitting ovenproof dish, cover with foil and bake for about 10 minutes, until the rhubarb is soft but holds some of its shape.

Mix the remaining sugar with the remaining oats and toss in a dry frying pan (skillet) over a medium heat for 3–5 minutes, until golden brown and toasted.

When you're ready to serve, add the cooking juices from the rhubarb, along with the chopped ginger, to the soaked oats and stir to combine. Top with the rhubarb and toasted oats and spoon over some of the ginger syrup.

Lemon, Yogurt & Pistachio Cake with Basil

250g (9oz) caster (superfine) sugar

zest and juice of 1 unwaxed lemon

2 eggs

150g (5½oz) ground almonds or crushed amaretti biscuits

100g (3½oz) self-raising flour, sifted

1 tsp baking powder, sifted into the flour

225g (8oz) natural yogurt

pinch of salt

50g (1¾oz) pistachios, roughly chopped

2 basil sprigs

Use two good sprigs of basil for this cake – or more if you're using an especially measly supermarket variety – dropping them into the hot lemon syrup for a sweet, redolent smell. When you pour the result onto this cake, fresh out of the oven, it gives a heart-stopping fragrance. These are flavours to fling spring firmly into action.

Preheat the oven to 170°C/150°C fan/325°F/Gas Mark 3. Line a 23cm (9in) cake tin with baking paper.

Using an electric mixer, beat together 200g (7oz) of the sugar with the lemon zest and the eggs for about 4–5 minutes, until the mixture is a thick and pale.

In a separate bowl, mix together the ground almonds or amaretti and the flour and baking powder.

Fold the yogurt and pinch of salt into the egg mixture, and then gently fold in the flour mixture to form a smooth batter.

Pour the batter into the prepared tin, scatter over the pistachios and place in the centre of the oven to bake for 40–45 minutes, until the cake is firm and a skewer inserted into the centre comes out clean. If it is browning too much, cover with a loose square of foil.

While the cake is baking, in a small saucepan over a moderate–high heat, boil the lemon juice with the remaining sugar for about 2–3 minutes, until the sugar has dissolved and the mixture turns syrupy. Remove from the heat and add the basil to infuse while the cake finishes baking.

When the cake is ready, remove it from the oven, use a skewer to poke the top with a few holes. Remove the basil sprigs from the syrup and pour the basil syrup over, leaving it to soak in before serving.

Rhubarb & Custard Cake

200g (7oz) caster (superfine) sugar, plus 1 tbsp more to sprinkle

2 eggs

100g (3½oz) self-raising flour, sifted

1 tsp baking powder, sifted into the flour

150g (5½oz) ground almonds

pinch of salt

250g (9oz) fresh custard

150g (5½oz) rhubarb (about 1 stalk), thinly sliced

Rhubarb and custard makes an all-time classic match. Fruity, vivid rhubarb goes beautifully with sweet, creamy custard. This recipe uses custard in lieu of yogurt. I have made many different yogurt cakes over the years, and, as cake preparations go, they have been some of the easiest – simply wet ingredients into dry. Shop-bought custard (I won't hear a word against it... the best illicit spoonful, fridge-cold, there ever was) gives this cake a crumb that is both moist and wonderfully custardy. Try to cut the rhubarb super thin while still keeping the form and arrange these in a casual lattice pattern. Feel free to serve the cake with another spoonful of custard on the side.

Preheat the oven to 170°C/150°C fan/325°F/Gas Mark 3. Line a 23cm (9in) cake tin with baking paper.

Using an electric mixer, whisk together the sugar and eggs for 4–5 minutes, until thick and pale. In a separate bowl, mix together the flour and baking powder, with the ground almonds and the salt.

Using a spoon, fold 175g (6oz) of the custard into the egg and sugar mixture. Then, fold in the combined dry ingredients and gently mix until fully incorporated.

Pour the cake batter into the prepared tin, then drizzle over the remaining custard and arrange the rhubarb and a dusting of sugar over the top. Bake for 40–45 minutes, until the cake is firm and a skewer inserted into the centre comes out clean. If the cake is browning too much, cover with a loose square of foil for the final 15 minutes. Cool the cake on a wire rack before removing from the tin.

Pasteis de Nata

250g (9oz) block of all-butter puff pastry, at room temperature

125g (4½oz) caster (superfine) sugar, plus 1 tsp to sprinkle

300ml (10½fl oz) whole milk

½ cinnamon stick

2 peeled strips of unwaxed lemon, pith removed

6 egg yolks

unsalted butter, for greasing

ground cinnamon, for sprinkling

MAKES 12

Pasteis de nata **are beautifully crisp on the outside and outrageously wobbly within. Unlike the English custard tart – very prim and proper, baked within an inch of its life – the Portuguese version is blasted in a fiercely hot oven, scorching the top, then dusted with cinnamon.**

Roll out the pastry to a rectangle about 20cm (8in) wide. Sprinkle with the teaspoon of sugar, then take one of the long sides and roll the pastry into a long log. Wrap the log in baking paper and refrigerate for at least 30 minutes.

In a saucepan, warm the milk over a moderate heat with the cinnamon stick and lemon peel for about 5 minutes. Remove from the heat and leave to infuse.

Put the 125g (4½oz) sugar in a small saucepan with 75ml (2¼fl oz) of water over a high–moderate heat and cook for 5 minutes, until syrupy. Set aside.

Whisk the egg yolks in a large bowl, then add 1 ladleful of the hot, infused milk (discard the cinnamon and lemon), whisking well to combine. Then, add all of the remaining milk and mix well again. Finally, beat in the sugar syrup.

Return the mixture to a pan and cook very gently over a low heat for 8–10 minutes, until the mixture thickens to the consistency of double cream. Remove from the heat, stirring occasionally to prevent a skin forming.

Preheat the oven to 220°C/190°C fan/425°F/Gas Mark 7. Place a flat baking sheet in the oven to preheat, too.

Generously grease the holes of a shallow 12-hole tart tin with softened butter. Slice the pastry log into 12 evenly sized disks. Lay one disk in each hole and, with floured fingers, squeeze each disk outward to line the hole, until the pastry just lips the top. Make sure the bottom half isn't much more than 1mm (⅟₃₂in) thick.

Pour the custard into each tart case, leaving about 5mm (¼in) of the pastry rim showing. Bake on the top shelf for 12–18 minutes, until the pastry is golden brown and the custard is nicely caramelized in patches. Leave the tarts to cool in the tins before removing to a plate to cool completely. Sprinkle with cinnamon to serve.

Elderflower & Crème Fraîche Ice Cream with Lemon Biscotti

FOR THE ICE CREAM

300ml (10½fl oz) whole milk

1 strip of unwaxed lemon zest

6 egg yolks

100g (3½oz) caster (superfine) sugar

300g (10½oz) crème fraîche

200ml (7fl oz) elderflower cordial

FOR THE BISCOTTI

200g (7oz) whole, skinned hazelnuts

2 eggs

175g (6oz) caster (superfine) sugar

300g (10½oz) plain (all-purpose) flour, plus 1 tbsp for dusting

1 tsp baking powder

zest of 1 unwaxed lemon

MAKES ABOUT 1 LITRE (35FL OZ) OF ICE CREAM AND ABOUT 16 BISCOTTI

Using crème fraîche in lieu of cream to make ice cream is a marvellous thing. What you get with crème fraîche is a clean, just-the-right-side-of-sharp flavour to the main body of the ice cream. One that makes you ever-so slightly pucker your mouth, like you've been told some shocking news and you need a second or two to adjust. With your mouth recalibrated and now clean as a whistle, in comes the elderflower, thundering along to the finish line. The biscotti will keep well enough stored in an airtight container for a month or more. I use a small domestic ice-cream machine to do the churning.

Bring the milk to a boil in a heavy-based saucepan, then remove from the heat and add the lemon zest.

Meanwhile, whisk the egg yolks and sugar together in a mixing bowl, and pour in the infused milk, whisking all the while.

Return the milk and egg mixture to the pan and cook over a low heat for about 5 minutes, stirring continuously with a whisk, without boiling, until thickened. Remove from the heat and whisk in the crème fraîche and elderflower cordial. Leave to cool, then churn in an ice–cream machine until thickened (how long this takes will depend on your machine). Decant into a clean container and place in the freezer.

Make the biscotti. Preheat the oven to 170°C/150°C fan/ 325°F/Gas Mark 3. Line a baking sheet with baking paper and toast the nuts in the oven for about 8–10 minutes, until nicely golden. Remove from the oven, put the nuts in a bowl and leave to cool. Turn the oven down to 150°C/130°C fan/300°F/Gas Mark 2. Keep the baking sheet ready to cook the biscotti dough.

Using an electric mixer, whisk the eggs and sugar together until pale and thick. Fold in the flour, baking powder and lemon zest, and, finally, the hazelnuts. Using your hands, work the mixture into a dough.

cont.

Lightly dust the worktop with flour and shape the dough into a long, smooth rectangle (or slightly oval-shaped is nice). It should measure about 5cm (2in) wide and 2cm (¾in) high. Shove any nuts that pop out back into the dough as these will catch during the bake time if they stay exposed.

Place the dough on the lined baking sheet (the one you used to cook the hazelnuts) and bake for 20–25 minutes, until firm to the touch (cracked a little on the surface is fine) and slightly risen.

Remove from the oven and place on a wire rack to cool for at least 30 minutes. When cool, place on a chopping board and, using a serrated knife, cut into slices 2cm (¾in) thick. Place the slices in an even layer back on the baking tray and bake for a further 10–15 minutes, until completely crisp. Remove from the oven and cool, then serve alongside the ice cream.

INDIAN SPRING LAMB FEAST

Slow-Cooked Lamb Shoulder with Pomegranate

Dried Cherry & Almond Peshwari Naan

Aloo Matar

Saffron Pilau

Cucumber, Pomegranate & Radish Kachumber

Mint Raita

Mango Kulfi

Cold beers

SERVES 6–8

This menu will take some planning. Don't let that daunt you – all the recipes are relatively easy to make, it's just your time management that will need to be well honed on the day to get everything ready at the same time. The time it takes for the lamb to cook in the oven should be ample to prepare the remaining recipes. Buy ghee to cook this menu, the flavour will be much better suited than melted butter or oil. Ghee is butter clarified until nearly all the milk solids and moisture have been removed. It is rich golden in colour, and it has a complex nutty, sweet taste. If your ghee has solidified, simply melt it and use as cooking fat in the recipes; brushed on the warm naans, you'll not only thank me for the recipe, but will no doubt cultivate a lifelong, dangerously addictive peshawari naan habit. Serve this menu with small glasses of icy cold beer (small, so the beer stays cold and is quickly replenished). One last thing, in this menu, and in this style of cooking, my handfuls, bunches and pinches of ingredients are altogether more personal – if you want more pomegranate seeds on your lamb, go for it; if you love ground cardamom or chilli powder more than my pinch or teaspoon, why not? What this menu offers is an uncompromising approach to flavour – ultimately, it's you who is in charge.

Slow-cooked Lamb Shoulder with Pomegranate

1 tbsp grated (shredded) fresh ginger

2 cloves of garlic, crushed

100g (3½oz) natural yogurt

1 tbsp Kashmiri chilli powder (or use 1 tsp hot chilli powder and 1 tsp unsmoked sweet paprika)

1 tsp ground turmeric

½ tsp freshly ground black pepper

juice of 1 lemon

50g (1¾oz) ground almonds

1 tsp salt

1 lamb shoulder or use 4 shanks (about 1.4kg/3lb 2oz total weight)

10 peppercorns

2 black cardamom pods (optional)

5 green cardamom pods

2 cinnamon sticks

4 cloves

2 bay leaves, scrunched a little

300ml (10½fl oz) pomegranate juice

300ml (10½fl oz) double (heavy) cream

50ml (1¾fl oz) pomegranate molasses

1½ tbsp garam masala

1 small bunch of mint, leaves picked and roughly chopped, to serve

seeds of ½ pomegranate, to serve

25g (1oz) whole almonds, roughly chopped, to serve

Blend the ginger, garlic, yogurt, Kashmiri chilli, turmeric, black pepper, lemon juice, ground almonds and salt to form a smooth paste. Rub this into the lamb and leave it for at least 2 hours, but as long as overnight, to marinate in the fridge.

Preheat the oven to 200°C/180°C fan/400°F/Gas Mark 6.

Transfer the meat to a pan or baking dish. Add the whole spices, the bay leaves and the pomegranate juice. Cover the pan and place in the oven for 30 minutes. Then, lower the heat to 170°C/150°C fan/325°F/Gas Mark 3 and cook for a further 2½–3½ hours, until the meat is completely tender. Uncover the lamb for the last 20 minutes of the cooking time so that it can take on a bit of colour. Remove to a plate, cover and keep warm.

Add the cream, pomegranate molasses and garam masala to the cooking liquid and reduce over a moderate heat for about 10 minutes, until rich and thick, then strain through a sieve and return the lamb to the pan to coat and warm through in the sauce.

Serve strewn with the chopped mint, pomegranate seeds and chopped almonds.

Dried Cherry & Almond Peshwari Naan

130ml (4fl oz) whole milk

5g (⅛oz) dried yeast

20g (¾oz) caster (superfine) sugar

25g (1oz) desiccated (shredded) coconut

25g (1oz) dried cherries, finely chopped

25g (1oz) ground almonds

small pinch each of ground cinnamon, ground cardamom and ground cloves

bigger pinch each of ground coriander and ground cumin

½ tsp salt, plus a pinch

60ml (2fl oz) boiling water from a kettle

300g (10½oz) strong white bread flour or plain (all-purpose) flour, plus more for rolling

100g (3½oz) yogurt

2 tbsp sunflower oil

melted ghee to brush the cooked naan, or use melted unsalted butter

MAKES 4 LARGE NAANS TO FEED 8

Warm the milk in a saucepan over a gentle heat. When tepid, stir in the yeast and half the sugar and remove from the heat.

Put the desiccated (shredded) coconut, cherries, ground almonds, spices, remaining sugar and the pinch of salt in a bowl and pour over the boiling water.

Put the flour in a bowl and stir in the milk mixture along with the yogurt, the oil and the ½ teaspoon of salt. Knead to a smooth, soft and elastic dough (about 5 minutes should do), then place the dough in a bowl and cover with a damp cloth. Leave somewhere warm to rise for 30–45 minutes, until risen by about half.

Divide the dough into 8 equal pieces. Roll out or use your hands to flatten one piece into a circle about 15cm (6in) in diameter. Place one quarter of the soaked coconut mixture in the centre of the circle. Roll out another piece of dough in the same way and use this to sandwich the coconut mixture. Re-roll the two dough circles together to approximately 20cm (8in) in diameter.

In a large, cast-iron frying pan (skillet) over a moderate heat, dry fry the naan for a few minutes until the top starts to bubble and puff up, then turn the naan over and cook until it's beginning to char slightly on the other side (about 1½–2 minutes each side should do it). Remove from the pan, brush well with ghee or butter and wrap in foil while you cook the remaining breads.

Aloo Matar

20g (¾oz) ghee or unsalted butter

1 onion, finely chopped

2 cloves of garlic, finely chopped

2 tomatoes, finely chopped

1 tsp Kashmiri chilli powder
(or use 1 tsp hot chilli powder
and 1 tsp smoked paprika)

1 tsp ground turmeric

1 tsp cumin seeds, toasted
and ground

1 tsp coriander seeds, toasted
and ground

600g (1lb 5oz) floury potatoes,
peeled and chopped into
bite-size pieces

250ml (9fl oz) boiling water from
a kettle

½ tsp salt

300g (10½oz) peas (fresh or frozen)

1 tsp garam masala

1 tsp fenugreek seeds, ground,
or use fenugreek leaf

freshly ground black pepper

Melt the ghee or butter in a saucepan over a moderate heat. Add the finely chopped onion and fry for about 10 minutes, or until the onion is soft and translucent.

Stir in the garlic, tomatoes, Kashmiri chilli, turmeric, cumin and coriander and cook for 1 minute, then add the potatoes, boiling water and salt. Bring to a boil, then cover, reduce the heat and simmer for 15 minutes, or until the potatoes are cooked through.

Add the peas to the potatoes and cook, uncovered, for a further 5 minutes, until the peas are cooked and all the liquid has evaporated. Finally, stir in the garam masala and the fenugreek and check the seasoning, adding more salt and some black pepper to taste, if necessary.

Saffron Pilau

1 onion, finely chopped

25g (1oz) ghee or unsalted butter

big pinch of saffron

2 tbsp hot water

400g (14oz) basmati rice

600ml (21fl oz) boiling water from
a kettle

½ tsp salt

20g (¾oz) raisins

20g (¾oz) whole almonds, roughly
chopped, or use flaked almonds

1 large handful (about 30g/1oz)
crispy fried onions

In a medium saucepan over a moderate heat, fry the finely chopped onion in the ghee or butter for about 10 minutes, or until the onion is soft and translucent.

Meanwhile soak the saffron in the 2 tablespoons of hot water.

Stir the rice, boiling water and salt into the cooked onions in the pan. Pour over the saffron-infused water, and then cover the pan with a tight-fitting lid. Cook the rice for 15 minutes, or until all the water has been absorbed and the rice is tender.

Remove from the heat, fluff up the rice with a fork and top with the raisins, almonds and crispy fried onions.

Cucumber, Pomegranate & Radish Kachumber

1 cucumber, peeled and thinly sliced

seeds of ½ pomegranate

1 bunch of radishes, thinly sliced

juice of ½ lemon

pinch of caster (superfine) sugar

salt, to taste

Mix all of the ingredients together in a bowl and check the seasoning. Set aside until ready to serve.

Mint Raita

250g (9oz) natural yogurt

1 small bunch of mint, leaves picked and finely chopped

juice of ½ lemon

½ clove of garlic, crushed

pinch of ground cardamom (optional, but worth it)

salt, to taste

Mix all of the ingredients together in a bowl and check the seasoning. Set aside until ready to serve.

Mango Kulfi

2 ripe mangoes (about 400g/14oz), peeled, stoned and chopped into bite-size pieces

600g (1lb 5oz) condensed milk

400g (14oz) natural yogurt

juice of 1 lemon

30g (1oz) pistachio nuts, roughly chopped (optional)

Blend the mango flesh to a smooth purée together with the condensed milk, yogurt and lemon juice.

Divide the mixture between 8 ramekins or ice-lolly moulds and freeze for 3 hours, or until set firm (alternatively, freeze in a tub and serve as scoops). Remove from the freezer for 10 minutes before serving, and sprinkle the kulfi with pistachios if using.

ASPARAGUS FEAST

Asparagus with Hard-boiled Eggs, Watercress, Tarragon & Mayonnaise

Asparagus & Hollandaise Tart

Asparagus with Anchovy, Black Olive & Parmesan

Lemon Trifle

Sauvignon and Elderflower Spritzer

SERVES 8

I adore asparagus but am measured enough to exercise a bit of patience when these extraordinary spears first arrive in the shops. Much better, I think, to wait for the price per bunch to fall (midway through the short season), and sufficiently so, so that you can then set about it, buying up an avalanche of the stuff, leaving the shop, triumphant with great big armfuls. Get the asparagus home and use them with an extravagance that all truly devout asparagus lovers will recognize and delight in. Asparagus is notorious in reputation for clashing wildly with wine, especially wines with oak or tannin. Sauvignon blanc is the exception. A grassy sauvignon blanc with good acidity will play beautifully with the asparagus, and because this menu has all the makers for a first-lunch-outside-vibe (a warm, sunny lunchtime perhaps), pouring a great slug of elderflower cordial into your sauvignon blanc and topping it with sparkling water will make saints of you all as you kneel at the altar of asparagus.

Asparagus with Hard-boiled Eggs, Watercress, Tarragon & Mayonnaise

4 eggs

600g (1lb 5oz) new potatoes

2 egg yolks

pinch of salt

1 tbsp Dijon mustard

300ml (10½fl oz) sunflower oil

1 tsp white wine vinegar

3 bunches of asparagus, trimmed

a few radishes, thinly sliced

1 bunch of watercress

4 tarragon stalks, leaves picked and roughly chopped

freshly ground black pepper

flaky salt, to sprinkle

Put the eggs in a saucepan and cover with cold water. Bring to a boil, simmer for 6 minutes, then remove from the heat. Run cold water over the eggs until they are cool enough to peel. Peel, then set aside until you're ready to assemble the salad.

Boil the potatoes in plenty of well-salted boiling water for about 20 minutes, until tender, then remove from the heat and drain. Set aside until you're ready to assemble the salad.

In a mixing bowl, add the egg yolks, pinch of salt and mustard and season with a little pepper. Slowly add the oil, drop by drop to begin with, to the eggs, whisking all the time. Very slowly increase the quantity of oil added each time, whisking in each addition so it is properly amalgamated before adding any more. Once the mayonnaise has started to hold its shape, you can start to add the oil in a thin and steady stream. When you have added all the oil, you should have a thick and wobbly mayonnaise. Taste and check the seasoning, then add the vinegar to thin the mayonnaise and add acidity. You may also need to add a splash – a tablespoon or two – of cold water to thin the mayonnaise to use it as a dressing.

Boil the asparagus in plenty of well-salted boiling water for 2–3 minutes, depending on the thickness of the spears. Take them out and drain well. (You could plunge the spears into some salted ice-cold water, then drain and dry, but I rarely bother. Just don't overcook the spears in the first place.)

Halve the eggs and halve or quarter the potatoes.

Arrange the asparagus, potatoes, eggs, radishes and watercress on a large platter. Scatter over the tarragon and spoon over the mayonnaise dressing. Another sprinkling of black pepper and some flaky salt (especially) are also good.

Asparagus & Hollandaise Tart

plain (all-purpose) flour, for dusting

400g (14oz) shortcrust pastry (make your own or use shop-bought)

4 egg yolks

3 eggs

1 tsp white wine vinegar

500ml (17fl oz) double (heavy) cream

squeeze of lemon juice, to taste

2 bunches of asparagus, trimmed

salt and freshly ground black pepper

1 small bunch of chives, finely chopped, to serve

chive or wild garlic flowers, to decorate (optional)

Preheat the oven to 180°C/160°C fan/350°F/Gas Mark 4. Put a large pan of salted water on to boil.

Lightly flour the work surface, then roll out the pastry to fit a 23cm (9in) tart tin. The pastry should be about 3–5mm (⅛–¼in) thick. Leave the edges slightly bigger than the tin, as the pastry will shrink during cooking.

Using a fork, prick the pastry base all over and line with some baking paper. Fill it with baking beans and blind bake for 10–15 minutes, until golden.

While the pastry case is baking, whisk the egg yolks, 2 of the whole eggs and the white wine vinegar in a bowl set over a pan of barely simmering water. Whisk until doubled in volume, then remove from the heat. Keep whisking continuously and add the cream, little by little, until incorporated. Season to taste with salt, pepper and the squeeze of lemon juice and put to one side somewhere warm.

Remove the baking paper and baking beans from the pastry case, then return it to the oven for 10 minutes, until the pastry is golden brown and crisp throughout.

Meanwhile cook the asparagus in the salted boiling water for 2–3 minutes, depending on the thickness of the spears, until just tender (but don't overcook them). Drain them and set aside. (You could plunge the spears into some salted, ice-cold water, then drain and dry them, but I rarely bother. Just don't overcook the spears in the first place.)

Beat the remaining egg in a bowl and use it to brush the pastry case. Carefully trim the edges of the pastry with a very sharp knife, then reduce the oven to 170°C/150°C fan/325°F/Gas Mark 3.

Pour the egg and cream filling into the pastry case and position the blanched asparagus nicely across the tart. Bake for 20–25 minutes, until the filling is firm but still with a slight wobble in the middle.

Leave the tart to cool a little before removing from the tin. Scatter with the chopped chives and with the flowers (if using) before serving.

Asparagus with Anchovy, Black Olive & Parmesan

2 bunches of asparagus, trimmed

3 tbsp good olive oil, plus more to dress the salad

1 tsp salt

juice of 1 lemon

good pinch of chilli flakes, to taste

1 small bunch of rocket (arugula), roughly chopped

1 small bunch of flat-leaf parsley, leaves picked and roughly chopped

50g (1¾oz) black olives, pitted

8 anchovies, halved lengthways

50g (1¾oz) parmesan, shaved with a peeler

flaky salt, to taste

Preheat your oven or grill (broiler) to maximum.

In a big bowl, mix the asparagus with the oil and salt. Make sure the asparagus are well coated. Lay the spears in a single layer on a baking sheet. Cook in the fiercely hot oven or under the grill for about 5 minutes, until wizened and charred in places.

Immediately remove the asparagus from the heat and sprinkle the lemon juice all over. Add the chilli flakes to taste (a good pinch is a must). Leave to cool slightly.

Arrange the cooked asparagus, together with any of the cooking juices on a serving plate and add the rocket (arugula), parsley, olives, anchovies and parmesan. Add a touch more olive oil to dress the salad, then check the seasoning. Again, flaky salt is always nice.

Lemon Trifle

about 325g (11½oz) lemon curd
(1 jar)

100g (3½oz) sponge fingers,
cut into 2cm (¾in) cubes

200ml (7fl oz) Moscatel dessert
wine, or use diluted elderflower
cordial (for alcohol-free)

100g (3½oz) amaretti biscuits, plus
50g (1¾oz) crushed to decorate

600ml (21fl oz) double (heavy)
cream

120g (4¼oz) caster (superfine)
sugar

zest and juice of 2–3 unwaxed
lemons

30ml (1fl oz) elderflower cordial

500g (1lb 2oz) fresh or canned
custard

Spread the lemon curd over the base of a trifle bowl
and scatter over the sponge cubes. Pour 50ml (1¾fl oz)
of the dessert wine over the cake, scatter the amaretti
biscuits over the top, then pour over another 100ml
(3½fl oz) of the dessert wine. Refrigerate while you
prepare the cream.

Pour 300ml (10fl oz) of the double (heavy) cream into
a saucepan and add 70g (2½oz) of the sugar. Bring to a
boil over a moderate heat, then turn down the heat and
leave the sweetened cream to simmer for 2 minutes. Stir
in 60ml (2fl oz) of lemon juice (about 1½ lemons – but
could be more depending on your lemons), then pour
this mixture over the sponge fingers.

Refrigerate for a couple of hours or overnight, until set.

Stir the elderflower cordial into the custard and pour it
over the lemon cream layer to cover.

Whip the remaining cream with the remaining sugar,
two thirds of the lemon zest and the remaining 50ml
(1¾fl oz) of the dessert wine until it forms soft peaks.
Place spoonfuls of the flavoured cream over the
trifle and decorate with the crushed amaretti and the
remaining lemon zest. Chill until ready to serve.

Sauvignon & Elderflower Spritzer

100ml (3½fl oz) elderflower cordial

1 bottle of sauvignon blanc

500ml (17fl oz) sparkling water,
or more to taste

2 slices of lemon

2 elderflower sprigs, well checked
over for bugs

about 30 frozen green grapes
(as ice cubes)

Fill a large glass jug with the cordial, wine and sparkling
water. Add the lemon slices, elderflower sprigs and
frozen grapes. Top up with extra fizzy water, if you like,
for a more diluted drink.

SUMMER

Buttermilk, Sweetcorn & Jalapeño Polenta Fritters

30g (1oz) unsalted butter

1 bunch of spring onions (scallions), thinly sliced, green and white parts separated

1–2 jalapeño chillies, deseeded and finely chopped, plus more to serve

stripped kernels of 3 corn-on-the-cobs (about 400g/14oz unstripped weight)

150g (5½oz) fine polenta

150g (5½oz) plain (all-purpose) flour

1 tsp salt, plus more to season

2 tsp baking powder

2 eggs

300ml (10½fl oz) buttermilk, or use sour cream thinned with a little milk

200g (7oz) feta cheese, crumbled

2 tbsp sunflower oil, plus more for oiling the pan

freshly ground black pepper

small bunch of coriander (cilantro), roughly chopped, to serve

sour cream, to serve

lime wedges, to serve

Using a double whammy of corn in this recipe – sweetcorn and fine polenta – and adding some jalapeño to the mixture, makes terrific fritters that offer a speedily assembled midweek supper. You could use canned corn, but fresh sweetcorn is in season. I like to serve these fritters with sour cream and some hot sauce, or more sliced fresh jalapeño chilli.

Melt the butter in a saucepan over a moderate heat. Add the spring onions (scallions), jalapeños and corn, then cook for about 4 minutes, or until the corn is tender and cooked through. Remove from the heat and transfer to a plate to cool slightly, then season with salt and pepper.

Combine the polenta, flour, 1 teaspoon of salt and the baking powder in a mixing bowl. Mix in the eggs, buttermilk, feta, oil, and half the cooked corn mixture to form a batter.

Heat a large non-stick or cast-iron frying pan (skillet) over a medium heat and add a spot of oil for frying. Use a tablespoon to spoon the batter out into the hot pan. You'll need to work in batches. Cook each fritter undisturbed until the edges begin to set and bubbles start to break through the top of the surface (about 1½–2 minutes should do it). Carefully flip the fritters with a thin, flexible spatula and cook on the other side, until golden brown and set (about 2 minutes). Transfer the cooked fritters to a warmed plate while you fry the remainder.

Serve topped with the remaining corn mixture and the coriander (cilantro), with sour cream and lime wedges on the side.

Stir Fried Flank Steak with Bird's Eye Chillies, Lime Leaves & Basil

450g (1lb) flank steak, skirt steak, hanger steak or leftover roast beef, cut into 1cm (½in) strips

1 tbsp light soy sauce

2 tbsp fish sauce, plus more to taste if necessary

20g (¾oz) palm or light brown soft sugar, plus more to taste if necessary

2 shallots, thinly sliced

5 cloves of garlic, ½ whole and ½ thinly sliced

2–6 red or green Thai bird's eye chillies, thinly sliced, to taste

4 kaffir lime leaves, central stem removed, then very thinly sliced

3 tbsp sunflower oil

200g (7oz) green beans, cooked for 2 minutes in well-salted boiling water, then drained under cold running water

1 small bunch of basil (Thai, purple or normal), leaves picked and roughly chopped

1 small bunch of mint, leaves picked and roughly chopped if large

20g (¾oz) crispy fried onions or roughly chopped cashews or peanuts

lime wedges, to serve

cooked rice or rice noodles, to serve

This dish would be excellent alongside some glass noodles or steamed sticky rice. I've suggested two to six bird's eye chillies... I am allowing a little ambiguity in the recipe here, reliant as it is on your tolerance for chilli. These chillies, though diminutive in size, are extremely hot. If it were me, I'd be slicing the full quota, making this stir-fry super-scorching and wonderfully fragrant.

Mix the beef, soy sauce, 1 tablespoon of the fish sauce and 1 teaspoon of the sugar in a bowl and leave in the fridge for at least 20 minutes or up to 12 hours, to marinate.

Blend or chop half the shallots, the whole garlic cloves and half the chillies with the remaining fish sauce to a very coarse paste.

In a bowl, mix the remaining shallot, sliced garlic and chilli with the lime leaves and leave to one side.

When ready to cook, heat half the oil in a wok or large, cast-iron frying pan (skillet) over a very high heat. Working in batches, stir-fry the beef for 2–3 minutes, until just cooked through (or still a bit pink, if you like), if raw (just heat through if you're using leftover roast). Transfer each cooked batch to a plate, wiping out the wok each time before you add the next. Put to one side.

Heat the remaining oil in the very hot wok or frying pan and add the paste. Fry over a high heat for 1 minute, until fragrant. Return all of the beef to the pan, along with the cooked green beans and the lime-leaf paste. Stir-fry the lot briskly over a very high heat for about 1 minute, or until the shallots have softened and there is little or no liquid left in the wok or frying pan.

Immediately stir in the herbs and season with a little more sugar, fish sauce and chilli, to taste.

Transfer the stir-fry to a serving dish and top with the crispy fried onions or nuts, and serve immediately with the lime wedges and noodles.

Cold Soba Noodles with Aubergine, Pickled Vegetables, Miso & Sesame

150ml (5fl oz) rice vinegar

50g (1¾oz) caster (superfine) sugar

1 tsp salt

2 cloves of garlic, crushed

chilli flakes or powder, to taste

1 heaped tbsp miso paste

1 tsp sesame oil

300ml (10½fl oz) sunflower oil

2 aubergines (eggplants), cut into 2cm (¾in) dice

600g (1lb 5oz) soba noodles

½ bunch of spring onions (scallions), thinly sliced

1 big handful of roasted peanuts (about 30g/1oz), lightly crushed or chopped

100g (3½oz) pickled vegetables (canned, jarred, packet or homemade)

2 tbsp sesame seeds, to serve

I stock up on packets of preserved, fermented vegetables (*pào cài*) from the Chinese supermarket here in Bristol. Served simply with some steamed broccoli or cabbage, along with some rice, this is one of my laziest possible, quick-fix meals. Mixed through in this noodle dish with soft, fried aubergines (eggplants), the pickled vegetables bring crunch and intensity that melds perfectly with the other ingredients. Soba are a favourite noodle for me to use at home. Made with buckwheat flour, on occasions mixed with wheat flour, these dark, freckled noodles have brilliant flavour and texture.

Put the vinegar, sugar and ½ teaspoon of the salt in a small saucepan and place over a moderate heat. Warm through until the sugar dissolves. Remove from the heat and stir in the garlic, chilli to taste, miso and sesame oil to make a dressing. Set aside to cool.

Heat the sunflower oil in a wok or large pan over a moderate–high heat. Add the aubergines (eggplants) and shallow-fry in batches until golden brown and soft through (about 3 minutes per batch), then transfer to a colander, sprinkle over the remaining ½ teaspoon of salt and leave to drain.

Cook the noodles in plenty of boiling, salted water, stirring occasionally, for 5–8 minutes, until just tender, then drain, rinse under cold water and drain again well.

In a large mixing bowl, toss together the noodles with the dressing and cooked aubergine, and add the spring onions (scallions), peanuts and pickled vegetables. Top with the sesame seeds to serve.

Kimchi French Toast

3 eggs

50ml (1¾fl oz) whole milk

½ bunch of spring onions (scallions), trimmed and thinly sliced

1 tbsp sesame seeds

8 slices of thick, day-old or stale bread

80g (2¾oz) unsalted butter or 80ml (2¾fl oz) sunflower oil

150g (5½oz) kimchi (see page 375, or use shop-bought), thinly sliced

salt and freshly ground black pepper

It's the tub or pouch in the fridge that, once opened, however tightly you try to reseal it, will permeate your fridge with an unruly, pungent, sour, garlic smell. Kimchi is a go-to addition for rice and steamed vegetables. Here, sandwiched between French toast as a snack, kimchi rocks, well and truly.

In a shallow bowl, beat together the eggs, milk, spring onions (scallions) and sesame seeds. Season well with salt and pepper. Dip the slices of bread into the egg mixture allowing the bread to soak through.

Melt half the butter or heat half the oil in a large non-stick or cast-iron frying pan (skillet) over a medium–high heat. Add 2 soaked slices of bread to the pan and fry for 1 minute, until the undersides are bronzed and firmed up a little. Top each with a quarter of the kimchi, then top with another slice of soaked bread to sandwich. Carefully flip over and cook for 2 minutes on each side, or until both sides of the sandwiches are deeply golden brown and crisp. Repeat with the remaining butter or oil for the remaining 4 slices of bread and the remaining kimchi. Eat immediately.

Green Panzanella

3 small, firm courgettes (zucchini), cut into 5mm (¼in) slices

½ bunch of spring onions (scallions), finely sliced

6 tbsp good olive oil

big pinch of salt, plus more to season

about 200g (7oz) ciabatta or sourdough, slightly stale and torn into bite-size pieces

lemon juice, to taste

2 cloves of garlic, finely chopped

2 tbsp red wine vinegar

1 small bunch of basil, leaves picked and roughly chopped

1 small bunch of mint, leaves picked and roughly chopped

50g (1¾oz) green olives, pitted

4 anchovy fillets, drained and halved

1 tbsp capers, (desalinated, if necessary), rinsed and drained

freshly ground black pepper

Conventional panzanella, made with grilled, skinned red (bell) peppers, tomatoes and red onions, is a favourite summer dish for me. Green panzanella… because, why not? Courgettes (zucchini), when cooked fiercely like this, turn soft, luscious even. Hot out of the oven and doused with lemon juice, they are especially delicious. I like to see a good blistering on both the courgettes and the spring onions (scallions) for this recipe. Lots of herbs – I say a small bunch, but you know the score, add as many herbs as you want to make this intensely flavoured, succulent salad look and taste fabulous.

Preheat the oven to 220°C/200°C fan/425°F/Gas Mark 7.

In a bowl, toss together the courgettes (zucchini) and spring onions (scallions) with half the olive oil and the big pinch of salt, then spread out the mixture in an even layer on a large baking sheet. Roast for 5 minutes, while you arrange the torn bread on a second baking sheet.

Place this in the oven alongside the courgette mixture. Continue to roast both for a further 10 minutes, until the vegetables are completely soft and the bread golden. Remove from the oven and immediately add the lemon juice to the courgette mixture. Put both baking sheets to one side.

Make a dressing. Mix the garlic with the vinegar and the remaining olive oil and season with salt and pepper to taste.

In a large bowl, toss together the courgette mixture and all the cooking juices with the bread, and the basil, mint, olives, anchovies and capers, add the dressing, check the seasoning and serve.

Spaghetti with Raw Tomato Sauce

1kg (2lb 4oz) ripe cherry tomatoes, halved (or quartered if chubby)

2 tbsp red wine vinegar

1 small bunch of basil, leaves picked and roughly chopped

2–3 tbsp good olive oil, plus more to serve

2 cloves of garlic, crushed

30g (1oz) black olives, pitted and roughly chopped

350g (12oz) dried pasta (I like spaghetti)

salt and freshly ground black pepper

chilli flakes, to serve (optional)

Disarmingly simple, this recipe will tax you only in the halving of a kilo of cherry tomatoes. Speaking of which, you will need the ripest, sweetest and just-about-ready-to-burst tomatoes that you can possibly find. Being summer, this shouldn't be all that difficult. Have the tomatoes ready and waiting in a large mixing bowl; in goes the cooked, drained spaghetti, mix well, adding more olive oil for gloss, sheen and, of course, taste for this dazzling, uncompromising pasta dish. I've used basil, but it could just as well be fresh marjoram or oregano.

Combine the tomatoes with all the remaining ingredients except the pasta in a large mixing bowl and season well to taste. Put to one side for at least 30 minutes for the flavours to meld.

Boil the pasta in plenty of well-salted water until cooked to your liking. Drain and immediately stir through with the chopped tomato mixture, checking the seasoning and adding salt and pepper to taste, if necessary.

Add a touch more olive oil to each portion to serve, sprinkling over chilli flakes to taste, if you like.

Jollof Rice

4 tbsp vegetable or coconut oil

1 red onion, thinly sliced

1 carrot, peeled and coarsely grated (shredded)

300g (10½oz) long grain or basmati rice

1 small red (bell) pepper, halved and deseeded

2 tbsp grated (shredded) fresh ginger

2 cloves of garlic, roughly chopped

1 x 400g (14oz) can of plum tomatoes

¼–1 Scotch Bonnet or 1–2 habanero chillies, to taste

1 tbsp curry powder (mild or hot, as you like)

1 tbsp paprika (unsmoked is best)

1 tsp cracked black pepper, plus more to season

2 bay leaves, scrunched a little

3 tbsp tomato purée

½ tsp salt, plus more to season

300ml (10½fl oz) very hot chicken stock

This is an essential west African rice dish – and there are a good many versions of it – that is often served with braised meat stews, sometimes fried plantain, and always with extra chopped fresh chillies or hot sauce of choice. Here, I'm giving it as a standalone midweek supper, because this rice dish is a magnificently fiery-hot and delicious one-pot recipe, which will stand you in good stead of a weeknight, and on many more occasions too. Blending the ginger, chillies, (bell) peppers, and some of the onions and tomatoes to then fry them with the tomato purée and the rest of the onions and spices gives you a rice dish with tremendous depth and complexity. If you would rather cook the rice in the oven, bring the rice with all the ingredients to a boil, cover and place in a preheated oven at 180°C/160°C fan/350°F/Gas Mark 4 for 30–35 minutes, until the rice is tender and all the liquid has been absorbed.

Heat the vegetable or coconut oil in a heavy-based saucepan with a tight-fitting lid over a moderate heat. Add half the onions and all the carrot and cook for about 10 minutes, until the onions are just beginning to colour and brown.

Meanwhile, wash the rice in plenty of cold water and leave to drain well.

Put the remaining onion in a food processor or blender with the red (bell) pepper, ginger, garlic, canned tomatoes and chillies. Blend until smooth.

Add the spices, bay leaves and tomato purée to the cooked onions and carrot and add the ½ teaspoon of salt. Cook over a moderate heat, stirring briskly, for 1 minute, then add in the tomato mixture. Reduce the heat to moderate–low and simmer for about 10 minutes, until rich and thick. Season well with salt and pepper.

Add the drained rice and the stock. Cover the pan and cook, still over a moderate–low heat, for about 20–25 minutes, until the rice is cooked through and all the liquid has been absorbed. Remove from the heat, fluff the rice with a fork, season with salt to taste and serve.

Eggs Cooked with Ricotta, Sage & Spinach

20g (¾oz) unsalted butter

3 cloves of garlic, finely chopped

2 large shallots, finely chopped

about 12 sage leaves

100g (3½oz) baby spinach

400ml (14fl oz) double (heavy) cream

½ tsp salt, plus more to season

250g (9oz) ricotta cheese

50g (1¾oz) parmesan, grated (shredded)

zest of ½ unwaxed lemon

6 eggs

¼ tsp red chilli flakes, or to taste

freshly ground black pepper

toasted baguette or sourdough, to serve

You'll need good bread at the ready to serve with these eggs: baguettes or thick rounds of toasted sourdough to swoop through the pan. Do try to keep the yolks runny, so err on the leaner side of cooking times. Best is for the whites to be just set with the yolks still gloriously liquid. I especially love the sage here, fried as it is in the butter with the garlic and shallots. Cooked like this, sage has a gorgeous pine-like scent that plays beautifully with the creamy clouds of cooked ricotta.

Preheat the oven to 180°C/160°C fan/350°F/Gas Mark 4.

Heat a 24cm (9½in) ovensafe pan over a medium heat. Add the butter and allow to melt, then add the garlic, shallots and sage. Cook for about 5 minutes, until softened. Add the spinach and cook for 1 minute, until wilted.

Pour in the cream and season with the ½ teaspoon of salt and a generous amount of black pepper. Bring the cream to a simmer and let it bubble away for 5 minutes, until reduced and thickened. Stir in the ricotta, parmesan and lemon zest and reduce the heat.

Carefully crack in the eggs, add the chilli flakes and transfer the pan to the preheated oven for 8–10 minutes, until the whites of the eggs have set. Remove from the oven and serve immediately.

Pork Chops Fried with Peach, Balsamic Vinegar & Shallots

4 bone-in pork chops

2 tbsp sunflower oil

2 large shallots, thinly sliced

2 tbsp balsamic vinegar

1 tbsp runny honey

1 tbsp thyme leaves

2 peaches, stoned and sliced

salt and freshly ground black pepper

boiled potatoes or good bread, to serve

Peaches are a favourite summer fruit for me. However discerning you are when it comes to peach selection, you will always find the odd one, more if I'm honest, that makes its way into the kitchen and falls short of peachy perfection. Some peaches miss the mark in taste and some in texture – but add sweetness and tartness by means of honey and vinegar, and fry them alongside some hefty pork chops as in this recipe and you will transform even the most ordinary peach. Serve with some boiled potatoes and a green salad.

Heat a large, cast-iron frying pan (skillet) over a medium–high heat. Season the pork chops all over with salt and pepper and rub with the oil. Add the pork to the pan and sear for 3–4 minutes on each side. Reduce the heat to medium, add the shallots, and continue cooking for about 8–12 minutes, until the pork chops are cooked through and the shallots are soft and caramelized.

While the chops are cooking, mix together the balsamic vinegar, honey, thyme and peaches. During the last 2 minutes of cooking, add the peach mixture to the pan, then when the 2 minutes are up, remove from the heat.

Allow to rest for 5 minutes, then serve the pork drizzled with the peaches and balsamic sauce, with some potatoes or good bread on the side.

Tuna on Toast with Roasted Peppers & Chermoula

FOR THE CHERMOULA

1 small bunch of coriander (cilantro), leaves roughly chopped

1 small bunch of flat-leaf parsley, leaves roughly chopped

50ml (1¾fl oz) olive oil

juice of ½ lemon

2 tsp smoked paprika

1 tsp ground cumin

2 cloves of garlic, peeled

1 small red chilli, destemmed

salt and freshly ground black pepper

TO SERVE

4 slices of sourdough, lightly toasted

150g (5½oz) drained tuna, or use drained sardine fillets in oil

1 jar roasted (bell) peppers, drained and thinly sliced

Chermoula is a sauce common in north African cuisine. It is made with coriander (cilantro), parsley, chilli and cumin, among other ingredients. Used as a condiment, it is especially flattering for fish. It should take you no more than 10 minutes to make the chermoula, leaving you enough time to slice and toast the bread and open the jars of tuna and (bell) peppers. Not so much a recipe here, more a serving suggestion. Stored under a film of oil, the chermoula will last, refrigerated, for up to 5 days.

Place all the ingredients for the chermoula together in a blender, season with salt and pepper, and blitz until smooth.

Top each piece of toast with some tuna or sardines and some slices of (bell) pepper. Spoon on the chermoula and serve straight away.

Grilled Courgettes with Chickpeas, Tahini & Mint

6 courgettes (zucchini), halved lengthways

1 tsp cumin seeds, toasted and lightly crushed

1 tsp coriander seeds, toasted and lightly crushed

1 x 400g (14oz) can of chickpeas (garbanzos), drained, rinsed and patted dry

½ tsp salt, plus more to season

3 tbsp olive oil

juice of 1 lemon

1 tbsp sumac

50g (1¾oz) tahini

2 cloves of garlic, finely chopped

1 small bunch of mint, leaves picked and roughly chopped

½ tsp chilli flakes, or more to taste

freshly ground black pepper

This recipe makes an excellent side dish, or a light lunch or supper with some flat breads. You will see when making the tahini sauce that the sesame paste appears to split. Don't worry – the water will bring it back, and it makes for a smooth, creamy sauce that is a very useful dressing for a good many salads. It's also very good with grilled meats – lamb and chicken, for example. Roast the chickpeas (garbanzos) as hard as you can. You want a good majority to shrivel and toast, turning nutty and moreish. To help with this, make sure the chickpeas are as dry as can be before roasting in the hot oven with the oil, salt and spices.

Preheat the oven to 220°C/200°C fan/425°F/Gas Mark 7.

Heat a grill pan or grill (broiler) to very hot. Season the courgettes (zucchini) well with salt and pepper and grill (broil) them cut sides downward for 3 minutes, until nicely charred. Turn over and cook on the other sides for a couple more minutes. Remove from the grill.

While the courgettes are grilling, mix the cumin and coriander seeds into the chickpeas (garbanzos) with the ½ teaspoon of salt and 2 tablespoons of the oil. Roast on a baking tray for 15–20 minutes, giving the tray a good shake to rotate the chickpeas halfway through cooking, until some of the chickpeas have begun to brown and crisp. Remove from the oven and season with another good dusting of salt. Transfer to a dish and set side.

Put the grilled, partly cooked courgettes on the baking tray and cook in the oven for 5–8 minutes, until tender. Remove from the oven and sprinkle over half the lemon juice. Arrange the courgettes on a large serving platter or individual plates and sprinkle with the sumac.

While the courgettes are in the oven, put the tahini in a bowl or blender with the remaining lemon juice and the garlic, and 100ml (3½fl oz) of water. Whisk or blend to the consistency of double (heavy) cream.

Spoon the tahini sauce over the courgettes, top with the roasted chickpeas, mint and chilli flakes and drizzle over the remaining olive oil.

Apricots Baked with Brioche, Bay Leaves, Honey & Hazelnuts

4 ripe apricots (more if small), stoned and halved

2–4 bay leaves, scrunched a little

3 tbsp runny honey, plus more to serve

zest and juice of ½ unwaxed lemon

unsalted butter, for greasing

4 slices of brioche

50g (1¾oz) hazelnuts (or use almonds or pistachios), roughly chopped

crème fraîche or Greek yogurt, to serve

Heat and honey work wonders on the apricots in this recipe. Bay leaf is a favourite herb of mine to use in desserts, giving subtle, sweet notes of cloves and cinnamon with just a whisper of eucalyptus. You can use dried bay leaves if you don't have fresh, but freshly scrunched bay leaves are a stealth ingredient for me and feature in much of my cooking, both sweet and savoury. Brioche bronzes nicely in the oven for this recipe, its soft buttery flavours pair very well with the accompanying ingredients.

Preheat the oven to 200°C/180°C fan/400°F/Gas Mark 6.

In a bowl toss the apricots with the bay leaves, honey and lemon zest and juice.

Lightly grease a baking tray with a little butter and arrange the slices of brioche over the tray. Distribute the apricots on top and add the nuts. Bake for 10–15 minutes, until the apricots have softened and the edges of the brioche have begun to caramelize.

Remove from the oven and serve with some crème fraîche or Greek yogurt and an extra drizzle of honey.

5-minute Berry Ice Cream

400g (14oz) frozen berries (I like blackberries) or any frozen soft fruit (kiwi, mango, banana)

2 tbsp runny honey, or more to taste

200g (7oz) Greek yogurt or crème fraîche

MAKES ABOUT 600G (1LB 5OZ)

This is a thrillingly easy, cheaty ice cream. Buy those frozen packets of berries from the supermarket, or freeze your own homegrown or foraged. Once you have them, very simply, using a good blender or food processor, quickly blend the berries from frozen along with the yogurt and honey. It's best eaten there and then. I've also had brilliant results with sliced frozen banana, blended as is with a spoonful or two of honey – no dairy necessary, as I find ripe bananas to be creamy enough when blitzed.

Put everything in the blender and purée until smooth. Serve immediately.

127

Baked Aubergine Pilaf with Yogurt & Mint

2 aubergines (eggplants), cut into 5mm (¼in) slices

2 tbsp olive oil, plus more for brushing

1 large onion, finely chopped

4 cloves of garlic, finely chopped

1½ tsp ground allspice

½ tsp ground cinnamon

¼ tsp ground cardamom

2 bay leaves, scrunched a little

1 tbsp tomato purée

50g (1¾oz) raisins or sultanas, soaked in warm water for 10 minutes

1 tsp salt, plus more to season

300g (10½oz) basmati rice, soaked for 10 minutes in cold water, rinsed, then drained

450ml (16fl oz) hot chicken or vegetable stock or water

20g (¾oz) unsalted butter, diced

freshly ground black pepper

1 small bunch of mint, leaves picked and roughly chopped, to serve

FOR THE SEASONED YOGURT

250g (9oz) yogurt

1 clove of garlic, crushed

juice of ½ lemon, remaining ½ cut into wedges

big pinch of salt

FOR THE BROWN BUTTER

60g (2¼oz) unsalted butter

juice of ½ lemon

½ tsp chilli flakes, or more to taste

about 40g (1½oz) crispy fried onions, to serve (optional)

Pilaf is one of my favourite ways to cook rice. Lidded and cooked along with softened onions, spices and good stock (although water will be fine, trust me), the rice swells, absorbing flavour from the off.

Preheat the oven to 190°C/170°C fan/375°F/Gas Mark 5.

Sprinkle the aubergine (eggplant) with a little salt and drain in a colander for at least 10 minutes, then pat dry.

Brush the aubergines with oil and arrange on a baking tray in an even layer. Bake for 10 minutes, until soft and beginning to brown at the edges. Don't let them scorch.

In a bowl, mix the yogurt with the crushed garlic, lemon juice and a big pinch of salt and put to one side.

Once the aubergines are ready, heat the olive oil in a saucepan over a moderate heat. Add the onion and fry for about 10 minutes, until softened. Add the garlic, then the spices and cook for 1 minute more, until fragrant. Add half the cooked aubergine slices, the bay leaves and the tomato purée and cook for a further 10 minutes over a moderate heat, until soft and rich.

Drain the raisins and add these along with the teaspoon of salt and the drained rice and stir to combine. Add the hot stock or water and put a lid on the pan; cook for about 15 minutes more, until the rice is cooked.

While the rice is cooking, make the brown butter. Heat the butter in a small pan until it melts, then foams and the sediments begin to turn nut-brown. Immediately add the lemon juice and the chilli flakes, remove from the heat and put to one side.

Open the lid of the rice and spread the remaining aubergine slices on top. Dot with the 20g (¾oz) of diced butter, giving an extra good seasoning of salt and pepper over the top. Replace the lid and place the whole dish in the hot oven for 10 minutes, until the rice is cooked through and there is no liquid left in the pan.

To serve, spoon over the browned butter and the crispy fried onions (if using), add the mint and serve the yogurt and lemon wedges on the side.

Roast Tomato & Bulgur Soup with Spiced Butter

8 large tomatoes, halved

2 tbsp sunflower or olive oil

300g (10½oz) split red lentils, rinsed and drained

3 tbsp coarse bulgur wheat

1 onion, finely chopped

1 small carrot, peeled and coarsely grated (shredded)

1.5 litres (52fl oz) chicken or vegetable stock or water

1 tsp salt, plus more to season

60g (2¼oz) unsalted butter or 4 tbsp olive oil

1 tbsp dried mint

1 tsp red (bell) pepper flakes, plus more to serve

juice of ½ lemon, remaining ½ cut into wedges

freshly ground black pepper

natural yogurt, to serve

If you don't have the time or inclination to roast the tomatoes, you could always use a can of peeled plum tomatoes added along with the lentils and bulgur when making the soup. This being summertime, however, fresh tomatoes should be plentiful and relatively cheap to buy. Dried mint has a distinctive flavour and is commonly used in Turkish cooking. I especially like it when it's fried in a little butter, then used to dress or finish a dish. The ingredients in this soup are all pretty thrifty, which makes this lavish spiced butter a real treat. Use olive oil if you would rather.

Preheat the oven to 220°C/200°C fan/425°F/Gas Mark 7.

Arrange the tomatoes, cut sides upward, on a roasting tray. Drizzle with the oil and season with salt and pepper. Roast for 15–20 minutes, or until tender, then blend until smooth.

While the tomatoes are roasting, put the lentils, bulgur wheat, onion, carrot and stock or water in a saucepan and place over a high heat. Season with the 1 teaspoon of salt, then bring to a boil. Reduce the heat to low, and simmer, stirring occasionally, for about 30–40 minutes, until the lentils and bulgur are tender. Add a little extra water if required.

While the soup is cooking, put the butter or olive oil in a small pan over a moderate heat, add the dried mint and red (bell) pepper flakes and cook for 2 minutes, until melted together and just beginning to bubble. Add the juice of ½ a lemon, then leave to one side.

With the soup cooked, stir through the blended tomatoes and check the seasoning, adding more salt and pepper, as necessary.

To serve, pour the spiced butter over the soup and have the yogurt and lemon wedges on the side.

Courgette Lauki Kofta Curry

3 tbsp sunflower oil, plus more to deep fry

1 small onion, ½ roughly chopped, ½ thinly sliced

2 cloves of garlic, crushed

1 tbsp grated (shredded) fresh ginger

6 tomatoes, roughly chopped

1 tbsp tomato purée

juice of 1 lemon

2 tsp ground turmeric

2 tsp Kashmiri chilli powder

2 tsp coriander seeds, toasted and ground

2 tsp garam masala

1 tsp salt

1 tsp caster (superfine) sugar

2 green chillies

1 bay leaf, scrunched a little

1 cinnamon stick

2 small courgettes/zucchini (about 400g/14oz), coarsely grated (shredded) and squeezed dry

100g (3½oz) gram or plain (all-purpose) flour

1 small bunch of coriander (cilantro), roughly chopped

A Gujarati curry, traditionally made using bitter gourd, this lauki is made with courgettes (zucchini) to great effect. The courgettes are grated (shredded) and mixed through with gram flour, among other ingredients, to form a thick batter. You then drop spoonfuls of the batter into the hot oil, frying to form these jagged little, courgette-flecked koftas, which you then heat through in the curry sauce all fragrant with tomatoes, ginger, turmeric and chilli. Serve alongside some steamed rice or flat breads.

Heat the 3 tablespoons of oil in a cast-iron frying pan (skillet) over a moderate heat. Add the onion, garlic and ginger and fry for about 10 minutes, or until the onion is soft and just beginning to brown.

In a blender or food processor, blend the cooked onion mixture with the tomatoes, tomato purée, half the lemon juice, half the ground spices, half the salt, the sugar and 250ml (9fl oz) of water to form a smooth sauce.

Put the sauce back in the pan. Add the chillies, bay leaf and cinnamon stick and simmer, covered, over a moderate heat for 15 minutes, or until rich and thick. Remove from the heat, check the seasoning and keep warm.

In a bowl, mix together the courgettes (zucchini), gram or plain (all-purpose) flour, and the remaining lemon juice, ground spices and salt with 50ml (1¾fl oz) of water, to form a thick batter.

Pour oil into a wide, deep pan until 5cm (2in) deep. Heat carefully over a high heat, until very hot (180°C/350°F) – the oil is ready when you drop in a small piece of the batter and it immediately sizzles and floats to the surface.

In batches, drop tablespoons of the batter into the hot oil and fry for a few minutes, or until golden on all sides. Drain each batch on paper towels and leave to one side while you use up the remaining batter to make all the koftas.

To serve, add the fried koftas to the curry sauce in the pan, warming through for a couple of minutes over a moderate heat. Finally, remove from the heat and add the chopped coriander (cilantro) before serving.

Potato, Aubergine & Pepper Stir-fry

2 large aubergines (eggplants), cut into bite-size pieces

big pinch of salt, plus more to season

1 tbsp Shaoxing wine (or use sherry)

2 tbsp light soy sauce

½ tsp caster (superfine) sugar

¼ tsp ground black or Sichuan pepper

1 tsp sesame oil

sunflower oil, for frying

1 large potato, peeled and cut into matchsticks 5mm (¼in) thick

2 tbsp cornflour (cornstarch)

1 red or green (bell) pepper, cut into bite-size pieces

1 bunch of spring onions (scallions), cut into 2cm (¾in) pieces

3 cloves of garlic, thinly sliced

cooked rice, to serve

This is a northern Chinese stir-fry dish named *dì sān xiān*, which appropriately, given that the season is summer and the bounty of ingredients on offer, roughly translates into English as 'three treasures from the Earth'. Moreover, being that cooking on a budget is one of the maxims this cookery book champions, I don't think many can stray far from this principal if you stick to ingredients at their seasonal peak. Serve this stir-fry, packed full of flavour, alongside some steamed rice. In Chinese cuisine this recipe might more usually accompany other Chinese-style dishes, so by all means do that. That said, cooked on its own and served with some rice, this stir-fry is pretty cheap and delicious.

Sprinkle the aubergine (eggplant) with the big pinch of salt and leave in a colander for at least 10 minutes to release some liquid, then pat dry. Put to one side.

Mix the Shaoxing wine, soy sauce, sugar, pepper and sesame oil in a small bowl with 2 tablespoons of water.

Heat 3cm (1¼in) of sunflower oil in a wok or large, cast-iron frying pan (skillet) over a moderate heat. When sizzling hot, add the potato and cook, scraping often, for 5 minutes, until the matchsticks are tender and just beginning to brown. Remove to a plate.

Toss the aubergine pieces with the cornflour (cornstarch) until coated. Top up the oil to 1cm (½in) deep, if needed.

Working in batches, fry the aubergine in the oil over a moderate–high heat for 10 minutes, until nicely browned and cooked through. Set aside each batch to drain on paper towels, while you fry the remainder.

Return all of the cooked aubergine to the pan, then add the (bell) pepper and cook for 2 minutes, until softened, then add the spring onions (scallions) and garlic, and return the potato to the pan. Cook for 1 minute, stirring well. Finally, tip in the sauce and stir-fry briskly for 30 seconds, until everything is well coated and glossy. Serve with rice.

Fried Eggs with Spinach, Garam & Turmeric Yogurt on Toasted Pita

200g (7oz) natural yogurt

1 tsp ground turmeric

30ml (1fl oz) sunflower oil (or use melted unsalted butter or ghee), plus more for frying

1 tbsp grated (shredded) fresh ginger

3 cloves of garlic, thinly sliced

1–2 green chillies, thinly sliced

1 tbsp garam masala

400g (14oz) baby spinach

4 large eggs

4 pita breads (or use naans)

1 small bunch of coriander (cilantro), leaves finely chopped

salt and freshly ground black pepper

More than a sandwich, but still a sandwich, its components are a simple lot, but together they triumph. Keep the egg yolks runny, but fry the whites fiercely so the edges lace and crisp up nicely. Garam masala is an indispensable spice blend, most commonly including cumin, coriander, green and black cardamom, cinnamon, nutmeg, cloves, bay leaves, peppercorns, fennel, mace and also dried chillies. Used in cooking as a multifunctional blend and also as a fragrant seasoning, garam masala is one to buy little and often, so that you're always using it in tip-top, aromatic condition.

Mix together the yogurt and the turmeric and season well with salt and pepper. Leave to one side.

Heat the oil in a pan over a moderate heat. Add the ginger, garlic and half the chilli and cook for 1–2 minutes, until softened. Stir in half the garam masala and cook for 30 seconds, until fragrant. Add the spinach and cook for 2–3 minutes, until completely wilted. Check the seasoning, adding more salt and pepper as necessary, then remove from the heat and keep warm.

Heat a spot of oil in a non-stick or cast-iron frying pan (skillet) over a moderate–high heat. Add the eggs and fry until the undersides are crisp, but the yolks remain runny (about 3 minutes).

Meanwhile toast the pita breads (or naans).

Spread the turmeric yogurt inside the toasted breads and top each with the cooked spinach. Finally, add a fried egg.

Sprinkle each egg with a little of the remaining garam masala, as well as the chopped coriander and remaining green chilli. Serve immediately.

Baked Tomatoes, Courgettes & Potato with Dill & Sour Cream

600g (1lb 5oz) courgettes (zucchini), cut into 5mm (¼in) slices

600g (1lb 5oz) small, waxy new potatoes (such as Charlotte), peeled and cut 5mm (¼in) slices

500g (1lb 2oz) ripe tomatoes, cut into 5mm (¼in) slices (or use 2 x 400g/14oz cans of plum tomatoes, drained)

1 red onion, thinly sliced

4 cloves of garlic, thinly sliced

small bunch of dill, stalks and leaves separated, both roughly chopped

100ml (3½fl oz) good olive oil

1 tsp chilli flakes, or more to taste

salt and freshly ground black pepper

sour cream, to serve

You'll want to use the ripest, most delicious ingredients and season them well. Eat the results warm or at room temperature for the flavours to really meld and sing.

Preheat the oven to 190°C/170°C fan/375°F/Gas Mark 5.

Arrange all the vegetables in a large ovenproof dish, layering them evenly, distributing the garlic, dill stalks and a good amount of salt and pepper as you do. Add 150ml (5fl oz) of water and top with the olive oil.

Cover with foil and bake in the oven for 45 minutes, then remove the foil and increase the heat to 210°C/190°C fan/415°F/Gas Mark 6–7. Cook until all the vegetables are completely tender and the uppermost vegetables are beginning to colour and crisp in places. Remove from the oven and leave to settle for at least 15 minutes before adding the chopped dill leaves and the chilli flakes and serving with the sour cream.

White Beans with Tomatoes, Peppers & Olives

2 x 400g (14oz) cans of cooked white beans, drained and rinsed (or use chickpeas/garbanzos)

100g (3½oz) black olives, pitted and roughly chopped

1 red onion, very finely diced

500g (1lb 2oz) ripe tomatoes, finely diced

1 large red (bell) pepper, destemmed and finely diced

1 clove of garlic, very finely chopped

enough good olive oil

enough (at least 1 tbsp) red wine vinegar

1 large bunch of flat-leaf parsley, leaves finely chopped

salt and freshly black ground pepper

I can't give you the exact quantity of olive oil or red wine vinegar you'll need for the dressing. Suffice to say, it all must be a luscious assembly that is best left to sit and wait, wallowing in its own juices, before you serve it.

In a big bowl, mix all the ingredients together adding enough olive oil and red wine vinegar to dress and coat everything lusciously. Season with salt and pepper.

Leave for at least 30 minutes for the flavours to meld and for the beans to soak up some of the juices. Serve.

Flamiche with Leeks & New Potatoes

250g (9oz) strong white bread flour, plus more for dusting

5g (⅛oz) salt

175ml (5½fl oz) warm water

5g (⅛oz) quick yeast

olive oil, for greasing the worktop

10g (¼oz) unsalted butter

500g (1lb 2oz) leeks, white part only, thinly sliced

2 eggs

150g (5½oz) crème fraîche or sour cream

½ tbsp chopped thyme leaves

¼ nutmeg (or to taste), grated (shredded)

6 small new potatoes, very finely sliced with a mandoline or sharp knife

15g (½oz) parmesan, grated (shredded)

salt and freshly ground black pepper

MAKES 1 FLAMICHE
(40 X 30CM/16 X 12IN)

A classic dish from Picardy in northern France, flamiche is half quiche, half pizza. You could make it with a pastry crust, but I like a bread-dough base. It makes for a brilliant lunch or picnic.

Mix the flour and salt in a large bowl. In a large jug, mix the warm water and yeast together. Leave for at least 5 minutes for the yeast to froth a little.

Add the liquid to the flour and salt and mix together vigorously with a metal spoon (alternatively, use a food processor fitted with a dough hook). Mix well for at least 5 minutes to form a smooth, cohesive dough.

Turn out the dough onto a lightly oiled surface and knead rhythmically for 2 minutes, folding the dough in on itself repeatedly. It should be smooth and elastic-looking.

Wipe out the mixing bowl. Shape the dough into a round and place it back in the bowl. Cover with a clean, damp tea towel and set aside until doubled in size (about 2 hours in a warm kitchen).

While the dough is rising, melt the butter in a saucepan over a moderate heat and add the leeks. Sweat for about 8–10 minutes, until softened. Do not let them colour. Remove from the heat and leave to cool.

Preheat the oven to 220°C/200°C fan/425°F/ Gas Mark 7. Line a 40 x 30cm (16 x 12in) flat baking tray with baking paper.

Beat the eggs in a bowl with the crème fraîche or sour cream, thyme and nutmeg, and season with salt and pepper to taste. Add the cooked leeks.

Lightly flour a work surface and roll out the dough to fit the lined tray. It should be about 5mm (¼in) thick. Make a small lip around the edge of the dough, or, push the dough up to the very edges of the baking tray. Add the leek mixture, distributing it evenly. Add the potato slices and finally sprinkle over the parmesan. Cook for 20–25 minutes, until the top is nicely coloured and the base is crisp. Remove from the oven, cut into squares, and serve.

Spelt Cooked in Cider with Ricotta, Grapes & Lamb's Lettuce

180g (6¼oz) spelt or farro

150ml (5fl oz) apple cider

2 bay leaves, scrunched a little

100ml (3½fl oz) good olive oil

juice of ½ lemon

100g (3½oz) lamb's lettuce, rocket (arugula) or watercress

1 small bunch of mint, leaves roughly chopped

150g (5½oz) red grapes, halved

200g (7oz) ricotta cheese

50g (1¾oz) walnuts, chopped

salt and freshly ground black pepper

Essential, I find, when cooking grains to serve in a salad like this one is to cook them with a good amount of aromatics so, when dressed, the finished salad has layer upon layer of flavour. Making a good salad is a discreet art – it's quite a challenge to make an ambient dish that can sustain as much as provide interesting texture and taste throughout. As ever, olive oil is a crucial flavouring. Use a good one when dressing finished dishes, certain salads especially. Grapes, although in the shops year-round, come into season at the tail end of summer and on through to the autumn. Make the most of them being at a more affordable price.

Pour 400ml (14fl oz) of water into a medium saucepan. Add the spelt or farro, cider, and bay leaves, season with salt and bring to a simmer over a moderate heat. Cook until the grains are tender and all the liquid has evaporated – about 30 minutes should do. If all the liquid evaporates before the grains are tender, add a little more water. Remove from the heat, let cool and discard the bay leaves.

In a salad bowl, whisk together the olive oil, lemon juice and a good seasoning of salt. Add the spelt or farro and mix well.

To serve, add the lamb's lettuce (or other leaves), mint and grapes, seasoning the mixture well with salt and pepper. Finish with the ricotta and the nuts.

Green Bean, Yellow Bean, Peppers & Capers with Coriander

4 tbsp good olive oil

2 yellow (bell) peppers, deseeded and thinly sliced

2 tsp coriander seeds, toasted and coarsely ground

2 cloves of garlic, thinly sliced

600g (1lb 5oz) fresh green and yellow beans, stalks trimmed

1 small bunch of coriander (cilantro), leaves roughly chopped (or use dill)

30g (1oz) capers (desalinated, if necessary), rinsed and drained

zest and juice of 1 unwaxed lemon

salt and freshly ground black pepper

Do try to get hold of both yellow and green beans for this salad. I find I can pick up both fairly easily come summertime. Likewise, use yellow (bell) peppers. Yellow and green, green and yellow, this, like so many of my favourite salad assemblies, is a soft jumble of flattering ingredients. Serve warm, at room temperature or from the fridge. It's great for convivial lunch gatherings and hearty barbecue spreads.

Heat half the olive oil in a saucepan over a moderate heat. Add the (bell) peppers with the coriander seeds and half the garlic and cook for about 10 minutes, until soft (try not to colour). Season with salt and pepper to taste. Remove from the heat and put to one side.

Meanwhile boil the beans in well-salted water for 5–8 minutes, until tender, then drain and leave to one side to cool.

Mix together the coriander (cilantro) leaves and capers along with the remaining garlic and the lemon zest. Chop the mixture together on a board or blitz to form a coarse paste, then stir in the lemon juice and the remaining olive oil and check the seasoning for salt and pepper.

Toss the beans in the pan with the cooked peppers, then stir through the herb dressing and pile onto a serving plate.

Avocado with Pak Choi, Sesame Fried Tofu & Pickled Carrot

2 large carrots, coarsely grated (shredded)

big pinch of salt, plus more to season

juice of 2 limes

6 tbsp light soy sauce or tamari

3 cloves of garlic, very finely chopped

1 tbsp sesame oil

2 tbsp runny honey

70g (2½oz) sesame seeds (both black and white is nice)

1 tbsp chilli sauce, plus more to serve (optional)

100g (3½oz) cornflour (cornstarch)

450g (1lb) firm tofu, sliced 1–1.5cm (½–⅝in) thick

about 4 tbsp sunflower oil, for frying

2 pak (bok) choi, halved lengthways

2 avocados, stoned and cut into bite-size pieces

1 small bunch of spring onions (scallions), trimmed and finely sliced

freshly ground black pepper

Sesame-coated fried tofu together with some pak (bok) choi and quick, lime-pickled carrots ratchets this recipe up high in the dazzling salad stakes. Keep the tofu warm as you assemble the rest of the ingredients. Avocado – good-size, super-dense, ripe and creamy with it – is a fine match for this recipe.

In a bowl, mix the carrots well with the big pinch of salt and leave in a sieve to drain for 5 minutes, then squeeze dry and add half the lime juice.

In a bowl mix the soy sauce or tamari, remaining lime juice, garlic, sesame oil, honey, 2 tablespoons of the sesame seeds and the chilli sauce and leave to one side.

Mix the remaining sesame seeds and the cornflour (cornstarch) together in a bowl and add the tofu. Toss to coat.

Heat about 3 tablespoons of the sunflower oil in a non-stick or cast-iron frying pan (skillet) over a moderate–high heat and, working in batches, fry the coated tofu pieces for 5 minutes, until crisp and golden brown all over. Set each batch aside to drain on paper towels while you cook the remainder. Keep warm.

Wipe out the pan and heat about 1 tablespoon of oil in it. Fry the pak (bok) choi over a high heat until heated through and slightly wilted.

To serve, arrange the pak choi and avocado on a large plate, add the fried tofu and pickled carrot, spoon over the dressing, check the seasoning, adding more salt and pepper as necessary and top with the spring onions (scallions).

Tomatoes, Peaches & Toasted Pistachios

75ml (2¼fl oz) good olive oil

30ml (1fl oz) red or white wine vinegar or cider vinegar

½ red onion, very thinly sliced

3 ripe peaches, stoned and cut into bite-size pieces

400g (14oz) tomatoes, mixed colours and sizes is nice, all cut into bite-size pieces

1 cucumber, deseeded and cut into bite-size pieces

1 small bunch of basil, leaves picked

50g (1¾oz) pistachios, lightly toasted

salt and freshly ground black pepper

Two of summer's best ingredients, peaches and tomatoes – sweet, perfumed and perfectly ripe – are meant for one another. This is a gorgeous salad. Cut the tomatoes, peaches and cucumber all the same size. Pistachios and basil are another great combination – although you could equally use almonds here, if you prefer.

Mix the oil and vinegar together and stir in the red onion. Season with salt and pepper to taste, then put to one side to macerate.

Spread the peaches, tomatoes and cucumber over a wide serving plate or bowl, and season with salt and pepper. Add the basil and spoon over the dressing. Top with the toasted pistachios and serve immediately.

Melon & Serrano Ham with Mint & Black Olives

1 nicely ripe Charentais or cantaloupe melon, peeled, seeded and cut into wedges

70g (2½oz) sliced jamón Serrano or prosciutto

2 tbsp good olive oil

salt and freshly ground black pepper

80g (2¾oz) black or kalamata olives, pitted, to serve

small bunch of mint, leaves picked and roughly chopped, to serve

SERVES 2 AS A STARTER
OR 4 AS AN APPETIZER

An oldie, but a goldie. The melon must be ripe, on the right side of dripping, and must also have a fragrance to stop you in your tracks. You're looking for luscious melon, sweet Spanish ham, salty black olives and good olive oil, with chopped mint cavorting through and invigorating the lot. Match made in heaven... or at least, all good Spanish eateries.

Arrange the melon and ham on a serving platter. Add the olive oil and season well with salt and cracked black pepper. Finally, scatter over the mint and the olives to serve.

Crab Caesar Salad

2 cloves of garlic, 1 crushed,
1 unpeeled and slightly bashed

1 tsp Dijon mustard

100g (3½oz) brown crab meat

2 egg yolks

100ml (3½fl oz) sunflower oil,
plus 3 tbsp for the bread

juice of ½–1 lemon, to taste

30g (1oz) parmesan, grated
(shredded)

4 thick slices of sourdough (or any
robust bread), crusts removed and
torn into pieces

3 little gem hearts (or cos or
romaine lettuce), leaves separated

200g (7oz) white crab meat

salt and freshly ground black pepper

Sweet, crunchy gem lettuce all plastered here with a good Caesar dressing. I've added brown crab meat to the dressing and used the white crab meat to top the leaves, along with the croutons. With a glass of white wine – rounded, with a little weight to the grape – this dish would be a stellar offering for lunch or a light supper.

Preheat the oven to 180°C/160°C fan/350°F/Gas Mark 4.

Whisk together the crushed clove of garlic and the mustard, brown crab meat and egg yolks. Whisk in the oil, drop by drop to start with, then in a very thin stream, until the mixture has thickened and the dressing is glossy. Add the lemon juice to taste and season well with salt and pepper. (You can do this by hand in a bowl or use a food processor. Just be sure to add the oil very slowly to begin with, so the dressing doesn't split. Essentially you are making a mayonnaise.)

Add all but 1 heaped tablespoon of the parmesan to the dressing. Loosen with a splash of cold water, if necessary, until the dressing has the consistency of double (heavy) cream.

Toss the bread with the 3 tablespoons of oil and the bashed whole garlic clove. Place the bread slices on a baking tray and season with salt and pepper. Bake for about 10 minutes, until golden and crisp. Remove the croutons from the oven and set to one side.

In a large salad bowl, mix together the lettuce, croutons and dressing. Top with the white crab meat and the remaining parmesan.

Pasta Salad with Sicilian Flavours

50g (1¾oz) basil, leaves picked

2 cloves of garlic

150g (5½oz) cherry tomatoes, roughly chopped

1 tsp fennel seeds, toasted and lightly crushed

40g (1½oz) pine nuts, lightly toasted

120ml (4oz) good olive oil

40g (1½oz) pecorino or parmesan, grated (shredded)

400g (14oz) short pasta

40g (1½oz) raisins

30g (1oz) capers (desalinated, if necessary), rinsed and drained

60g (2¼oz) black or kalamata olives, pitted

4-6 anchovy fillets, roughly chopped

zest and juice of 1 unwaxed lemon (or use orange, if you prefer)

salt and freshly ground black pepper

1 tsp chilli flakes (or more to taste), to serve

Pasta salads have a terrible reputation for being tired, soggy pasta dressed with little or no enthusiasm. It needn't be so. Paramount for pasta-salad success is cooking the pasta al dente – tender, but still firm enough to hold its own when cooling down (and never refreshed in cold water – you'll lose the glossy, starchy film to the cooked pasta). Plus, the pasta needs to be dressed very, very well. Buy good pasta, bronze dyed – never the cheaper stuff that cooks all flabby and disingenuous. Catch-all 'Sicilian' sounds lazy for a recipe title, but this isn't the case. This salad has flavours that, when pooled together, bring sunshine and, above all, personality to so many different dishes. Remember what was said about pasta salads?

Bring a large saucepan of well-salted water to a boil.

Set aside a few whole basil leaves for the finished salad, then put the remaining basil, along with the garlic, tomatoes, fennel seeds and half the pine nuts in a blender or gather them together on a chopping board. If using a blender, add half the olive oil and pulse a few times to create a thick paste. If using a chopping board, use a sharp knife to finely chop the ingredients together, then transfer to a bowl and stir in half the olive oil.

Add the pecorino or parmesan to the mixture, stir, then season well with salt and pepper and leave to one side. (Essentially, you're making a pesto with tomatoes here.)

Cook the pasta in the boiling water until al dente. Drain, then place in a large serving bowl, add the remaining olive oil and all the raisins and toss together well. Leave to cool.

Stir the pesto into the cooled pasta, mixing well to coat. Check the seasoning, adding more salt and pepper if necessary, then add the capers, olives, anchovies, and the lemon (or orange) zest and enough juice to taste. Scatter with the remaining pine nuts and reserved basil leaves and sprinkle with chilli flakes to serve.

New Potatoes Cooked in Lemon, Olive Oil & Coriander Seeds with Tzatziki & Feta

800g (1lb 12oz) small, waxy new potatoes (such as Charlotte), halved

zest and juice of 2 unwaxed lemons

4 tbsp good olive oil

3 cloves of garlic, roughly chopped

2 tsp dried oregano

1 tbsp coriander seeds, roughly cracked

½ small bunch of dill, finely chopped

small bunch of flat-leaf parsley, leaves roughly chopped

½ bunch of spring onions (scallions), thinly sliced

salt and freshly ground black pepper

1 recipe quantity of tzatziki (see page 76), to serve

150g (5½oz) feta cheese, crumbled, to serve

Cooking the potatoes in lots of lemon juice and good olive oil makes for the kind of potatoes people dream about, really. Add lots of cracked coriander seeds, as well as herbs (of course) and spring onions (scallions), and you're on track for the finest potatoes ever cooked. Gilding the lily? Never. Spoon on some tzatziki and add a blizzard of snowy feta. Top 10 potato dishes of all time.

Preheat the oven to 200°C/180°C fan/400°F/Gas Mark 6.

Place the potatoes in a single layer in a baking dish. Pour over the lemon juice, olive oil and 80ml (2½fl oz) of cold water. Stir in the garlic, oregano and coriander seeds, then season to taste with salt and pepper and toss together well to coat.

Cover the dish with foil and bake for 25 minutes, then remove the foil carefully and gently turn the potatoes over in the dish. Return to the oven uncovered and cook for a further 10–15 minutes, until tender and cooked through. Remove from the oven and stir through the dill, parsley and spring onions (scallions) and check the seasoning.

To serve, pile the warm potatoes onto a serving plate, scraping up all the pan juices, herbs and coriander seeds, then spoon over the tzatziki and add the crumbled feta to serve.

Duck Sours

FOR THE POMMES ANNA

600g (1lb 5oz) small, waxy new potatoes (such as Charlotte), cut into 2mm (¹⁄₁₆in) slices and put into cold water

50g (1¾oz) melted unsalted butter or duck fat

½ tbsp thyme leaves

salt and freshly ground black pepper

FOR THE DUCK

2 duck breasts

2 tbsp finely chopped stem ginger

1 shallot, finely chopped

1 tbsp runny honey

80g (2¾oz) blackcurrant jam

1 tbsp red wine vinegar, plus more for the watercress

salt and freshly ground black pepper

TO SERVE

a few handfuls of watercress

walnut or hazelnut oil

flaky salt

SERVES 2

Tart, fruity flavours work beautifully alongside duck. I've used blackcurrant jam here, adding good red wine vinegar (merlot, cabernet sauvignon – varietal vinegars are great and commonplace) for balance. Cooked rare but rested a decent amount of time in the fruity, gingery juices makes this dish an especially succulent and worthwhile one to master. You'll need a bit of time to sort the pommes anna (sliced potatoes cooked in butter), but really, while this recipe sounds flash and restaurant-y, it's a pushover to make. The method given for the pommes anna is slightly cheaty – assembling them, then cooking them in the oven rather than all the way on the stovetop is easier, trust me. Be sure to get a good, even scoring on the duck fat. This way, the duck breast will cook evenly, and also look attractive. And lastly, this being the treat yourself chapter, why not get hold of some lovely walnut oil to dress the watercress, along with some of that good vinegar. And buy good duck, it goes without saying.

Preheat the oven to 190°C/170°C fan/375°F/Gas Mark 5. Line a baking tray with some baking paper.

Start with the pommes anna. Drain the potatoes from the water and pat very dry, then coat in the butter or duck fat, sprinkle with the thyme leaves and season with salt and pepper.

Using the potato slices, make a circle of potatoes on the tray, add another, slightly smaller circular layer on a different rotation. Build up a further 4 layers, each slightly smaller and each on a slightly different rotation, so that slices roughly look like the petals of a flower. Bake for 30–35 minutes, until the potatoes are golden brown at the edges and tender.

Using a sharp knife, score the fat side of the duck breasts in a crosshatch pattern all over. Season well with salt and pepper. Place the breasts, skin-sides downward, in a cold, ovensafe or cast-iron frying pan (skillet). Place the pan over a moderate heat and cook for about 8 minutes, or until much of the fat has rendered and the skin is crisp and brown all over.

cont.

Turn over the duck breasts and transfer the pan to the oven. Cook for 5–6 minutes, or until rare in the middle (a meat thermometer should read about 55–60°C/ 130–140°F). Transfer the duck breasts, keeping the fat in the pan for the time being, to a plate and rub all over with the chopped stem ginger. Rest somewhere warm, while you prepare the sauce.

From the pan, pour off all but 2 tablespoons of the duck fat. Place the pan over a moderate heat and add the shallot. Cook for about 2 minutes, stirring briskly, then add the honey, blackcurrant jam and, finally, the vinegar. Cook for about 3 minutes, stirring occasionally, until the mixture has reduced to a bubbling, syrupy consistency. Season well with salt and pepper.

Return the duck breasts to the pan, skin-sides downward, reducing the heat to medium–low. Spoon or brush the sauce over the breasts to coat evenly. Turn the duck breasts skin-sides upward, spooning the sauce over the top of the breasts for about 30 seconds, then remove from the heat. Let the duck breasts rest for a final 5 minutes in the pan before slicing.

While the duck is resting, dress the watercress leaves with walnut oil and some red wine vinegar, to taste. Sprinkle with flaky salt.

Serve the duck with the sauce from the pan, the pommes anna and the dressed watercress.

More Than Tonnato

150g (5½oz) best-quality canned tuna, drained

1 clove of garlic, thinly sliced

75g (2½oz) capers (desalinated, if necessary), rinsed and drained

1 tsp Dijon mustard

4 anchovy fillets

3 egg yolks

juice of ½–1 lemon, to taste

2 tbsp good olive oil

salt and freshly ground black pepper

Tonnato is a truly delicious sauce, one that has an affinity with and is commonly served alongside cold roast veal in Italian cooking. Now, veal, in my experience, just isn't something many people buy or cook with at home, which I think makes veal tonnato a bit redundant as recipes go in a family cookbook. Just as well, then, that I have truncated the recipe so that you can make, then serve the sauce with a number of other complementary ingredients – to include veal, should you wish. Buy the best-quality tuna you can get your hands on, stored in oil is often best. Likewise anchovies. You are essentially making a tuna-and-anchovy-flavoured mayonnaise, of a pouring consistency, with garlic and capers. It will be excellent spooned over any of the following (here I go...): cold roast pork, veal or chicken; hard-boiled eggs; sweet, crunchy lettuces; ripe-to-bursting tomatoes; and radishes, lots of radishes.

Blend the tuna, garlic, 50g (1¾oz) of the capers, the mustard, anchovies and egg yolks in a food processor for about 30 seconds, then add half the lemon juice and blend for another 10 seconds.

With the motor running, add the oil in a thin stream until you have a thin mayonnaise texture and all the oil is used up. Season with salt, pepper and more lemon juice to taste.

Sprinkle the remaining capers over the top when you serve the tonnato.

Tiger Prawn Curry

FOR THE SPICE BLEND

1 tbsp raw basmati rice

½ tsp chilli flakes

1 tbsp coriander seeds

1 tbsp cumin seeds

1 tbsp black peppercorns

1 tsp black mustard seeds

1½ tsp fennel seeds

2 cloves

½ tsp ground turmeric

FOR THE CURRY

3 tomatoes, roughly chopped

1 tbsp tomato purée

2 cloves of garlic, roughly chopped

1 tbsp grated (shredded) fresh ginger

juice of 1 lime, plus more wedges to serve

3 tbsp spice blend (above)

1 tsp salt, plus more to season

2 tbsp sunflower oil

10 curry leaves (optional, but worth it)

200ml (7fl oz) full-fat coconut milk

650g (1lb 7oz) whole, raw tiger prawns

1-2 green chillies, finely sliced

freshly ground black pepper

chapati, to serve

Certainly, an extravagance. Purchasing some good-size tiger prawns from a sustainable source (one that encourages good fishery practice) will set you back a fair bit. As it should be... this is not everyday eating, after all. Taking care and time to toast and grind the rice and spices to make the curry paste, which you then fry off before adding the coconut milk and finally the prawns, feels like a process of due care and attention, befitting of the money spent. Buy some good chapati to serve with the curry. You could of course make your own, but better I think is to focus on the curry preparation here. Warm the chapati in the oven at the last minute. No one will ever know.

First, make the spice blend. Dry fry the rice in a large, dry saucepan over a moderate heat for 3–4 minutes, until it toasts and begins to turn light brown. Add the spices, minus the turmeric, and toast for 2 minutes, until aromatic. Move the pan constantly to prevent any of the spices burning. Remove from the heat and add the turmeric, then transfer to a mortar and grind with a pestle (or use a spice grinder) until you have a powder.

Make the curry. Blend the tomatoes, tomato purée, garlic, ginger, lime juice, the 3 tablespoons of spice blend and the salt to a smooth paste (add a splash of water, if necessary).

Heat the oil in a saucepan large enough to eventually fit the prawns over a moderate heat. Add the curry leaves, if using, and fry for 1 minute, until they sizzle, then add the tomato and spice paste and cook for 5 minutes, stirring often, until the paste begins to stick to the pan and smells fragrant.

Add the coconut milk, reduce the heat and simmer, uncovered, for 20 minutes, until the sauce starts to thicken. Check the seasoning, adding more salt and pepper to taste, if necessary.

Add the prawns to the curry and simmer for 5 minutes, until cooked and fully heated thorough. Remove from the heat, add the chilli slices and serve immediately with the chapati and lime wedges on the side.

Scallops with Shallot & Caper Butter, Baguette & Peas

1 shallot, peeled and very, very finely chopped

1 tbsp capers (desalinated, if necessary), rinsed and roughly chopped

1 small bunch of flat-leaf parsley, finely chopped

½ small bunch of tarragon, chives or thyme (or a mixture), leaves picked as necessary and finely chopped

1 unwaxed lemon, zested then quartered

100g (3½oz) unsalted butter

4 large scallops in the shell (or 8 smaller ones), cleaned and shells reserved

200g (7oz) peas (fresh or frozen)

salt and freshly ground black pepper

baguette, to serve

SERVES 4 AS A STARTER

I wanted to include a recipe in this section that was served simply with a baguette – a good baguette, the sort you buy a from a good bakery and that forces you to tear off an end to eat on your way home. Eating extravagantly, treating yourself shouldn't, to my mind anyway, just be about expense and propriety. It must, above all, be about unbridled indulgence. I think it's about buying ingredients to suit your mood right at that moment and then cooking and eating them exactly how you wish to enjoy them. This meal is just that. Scallops are a treat, but do you really, really want to eat them with a knife and fork, prim and proper with a stiff napkin on your lap? Or, would you rather tear off great hunks of baguette and drag these through the bubbling, buttery juices, spearing scallops with just a fork, and cramming all in with an absolute glee. The peas are there for good measure (also cooked in some of the butter) and are very happy as an aside, spooned into some of the spent scallop shells, then swooped on with more baguette. Elbows on the table, napkins round the neck, both perfectly fine.

Heat the grill (broiler) or barbecue to a high heat.

First, make a herby butter. In a bowl, mix the shallot, capers, herbs, and the juice of 1 lemon quarter and all the lemon zest with the butter and season well to taste with salt and pepper. Put to one side.

Divide all but 1 tablespoon of the herby butter equally between the scallop shells, ensuring each scallop gets a good covering.

Place the scallops in their shells on a baking sheet and grill (broil) or barbecue for 2–5 minutes, depending on their size, until the scallop meat is opaque and the butter is bubbling and hot. Don't overcook them.

Meanwhile, cook the peas until tender, then drain and stir through the reserved tablespoon of the herby butter.

Remove the scallops from the grill (broiler) or barbecue and serve immediately with the baguette and also the peas, with the remaining lemon quarters on the side.

Crab Gnudi with Butter Baked Cherry Tomatoes & Tarragon

350g (12oz) coarse semolina flour (cream of wheat)

300g (10½oz) ricotta cheese, strained

2 tbsp brown crab meat

1 egg yolk

2 tbsp type '00' flour or plain (all-purpose) flour

30g (1oz) parmesan or pecorino, grated (shredded)

100g (3½oz) unsalted butter

150g (5½oz) ripe cherry tomatoes, halved

100g (3½oz) white crab meat

salt and freshly ground black pepper

½ small bunch of tarragon, leaves picked, to serve

½ tsp chilli flakes, to serve

SERVES 2 AS A RICH MAIN,
OR 4 AS AN APPETIZER

Dumplings by any other name, gnudi are sensational – featherlight and only just holding their form. When boiled, they float and puff with a sense of fragility that makes the making and eating of gnudi a bit like standing on a ice cap with warm winds circling. Start this the day before you want to serve. Two days is better: the gnudi sit, and wait, and wait some more, under a duvet of semolina, gently leaching out moisture, crystallizing, creating a very, very tender shell for the ricotta and more. I've added brown crab meat, keeping the white meat to warm through and serve. Butter, lots of it, to cook the tomatoes, makes for a sauce so sublime the gnudi will be well at home.

Spread half the semolina (cream of wheat) in a baking dish big enough to hold 16 walnut-size gnudi, but small enough to fit in your fridge.

In a bowl, mix the ricotta with the brown crab meat, egg yolk, flour and parmesan or pecorino. Season with salt and pepper to taste.

Use your hands to roll the mixture into 16 walnut-size balls and transfer these to the baking dish. Gently roll the gnudi in the semolina to completely coat each ball. Refrigerate, with the gnudi submerged and the dish uncovered, overnight.

To cook, bring a large saucepan of well-salted water to a boil.

Melt the butter in a wide pan over a moderate heat and add the cherry tomatoes. Cook for 3–5 minutes, until softened.

Add the gnudi to the boiling water. Wait until they rise to the surface (about 3 minutes), then continue to gently cook for 1 minute to heat through. As each gnudi is ready, scoop it straight into the pan with the butter and tomatoes. Very gently mix through the white crab meat to warm it through in the juices.

Season with salt and plenty of pepper and divide between 4 shallow bowls. Scatter with the tarragon and a pinch of chilli flakes to serve.

Burrata with Courgette Scapece

600–800g (1lb 5oz–1lb 12oz) small courgettes (zucchini), cut into 2mm (1/16in) slices

sunflower oil, for frying

1 tbsp good red wine vinegar

1 small bunch of mint, leaves picked and roughly chopped

1 good tsp flaky salt

½–1 tsp chilli flakes, or more to taste

½–1 burrata per person

good olive oil, for dressing the burrata

Burrata has a bit of a cult status. Good mozzarella will work for this dish, but it won't have the same vaunted cream-filled wobble that spills when split open that so many seem to lust after in a burrata. It's my bet that any bigger supermarkets (and Italian delicatessens) will stock burrata so do search it out. If it remains elusive, remember: good mozzarella will work, the earth will spin and the trees will stand... let's keep some perspective. On a lighter note, I love to make scapece when courgettes (zucchini) come thick and fast during their peak season in the summertime. Try to use the little, firm ones as they will fry better. Laying the courgettes out to dry a little on a cloth might seem a faff, but (again) they will fry better if dried a little. An hour will do. Doused with the vinegar, given some chilli and finished with a frenzy of chopped mint, this is, unquestionably, one of my favourite things to eat in the summer.

Arrange the courgettes (zucchini) in a single layer on a clean tea towel (or two) for at least 1 hour (or all day, if you like) to dry out a little. Turn them over halfway through drying if you can.

In a heavy-based saucepan suitable for frying, add a good amount of sunflower oil (at least 5cm/2in) and heat until very hot (180°/350°F on a digital thermometer).

Working in batches, fry the courgettes until lightly brown and wizened. Remove each batch with a slotted spoon and set aside on a tray lined with paper towels to drain while you fry the remainder.

Douse the fried courgettes all over with the vinegar and mint. Sprinkle over the salt and chilli flakes and serve a pile of the courgettes alongside the burrata, dressed, as it must be, with good olive oil.

Linguine with Saffron & Lemon with Fennel Seed Pangrattato

a good-size pinch of saffron

about 20ml (¾fl oz) hot water

4 tbsp good olive oil, plus more to serve

2 tsp fennel seeds, cracked a little

4 cloves of garlic: 2 whole, unpeeled and bashed a little; 2 peeled and finely sliced

60g (2¼oz) stale, good white bread, crusts removed and blitzed to a rough crumb

¼–½ tsp chilli flakes

300g (10½oz) linguine or spaghetti

zest and juice of 1 unwaxed lemon

1 small bunch of flat-leaf parsley, leaves picked and finely chopped

salt and freshly ground black pepper

Saffron is a luxury ingredient and the world's most expensive spice. Incredibly labour intensive to harvest, saffron is the stigma, stamen and styles picked from the crocus plant; with 1g of saffron requiring the threads from about 200 crocuses, harvesting is back-breaking work. Dried, these intensely rusty, ruby-red filaments have an unmistakable and beguiling flavour that is hard to pinpoint exactly – try, honey and hay with sweetly bitter notes. There are a good many recipes that showcase this extraordinary spice (the bouillabaisse on page 192 is a case in point). I'm also including this simple pasta dish, with so few ingredients alongside the saffron, as a fitting treat. Just a pinch and you can feel like the richest person on Earth.

Put the saffron in a small dish and cover with the hot water. Leave to soak for 5 or so minutes.

Heat half the oil in a cast-iron frying pan (skillet) over a moderate heat, and add the fennel seeds, whole garlic cloves and breadcrumbs and season well with salt. Toast the breadcrumbs, tossing the pan frequently, for about 5 minutes, until golden brown and crisp. Remove from the heat and add the chilli flakes, mixing well. Tip into a bowl and put to one side.

Cook the pasta in well-salted boiling water according to the packet instructions until al dente. Drain, reserving a little of the cooking water.

Heat the remaining olive oil in a pan over a moderate heat and fry the sliced garlic for 2 minutes, until fragrant. Add the cooked pasta and the saffron, including the soaking water, mixing well to coat the pasta. Add the lemon zest and juice, chopped parsley and a splash of the pasta cooking water, to loosen, if necessary. Taste the pasta, and season with salt and pepper as necessary. Remove from the heat.

To serve, divide the pasta equally between 4 bowls and serve topped with the pangrattato and an extra slick of olive oil.

Cherry, Marshmallow & Dark Chocolate Chip Cobbler

800g (1lb 12oz) cherries, pitted

50g (1¾oz) caster (superfine) sugar

230g (8¼oz) self-raising flour

pinch of salt

140g (5oz) cold unsalted butter, diced

2 eggs, beaten

60ml (2fl oz) whole milk

60g (2¼oz) dark (bittersweet) chocolate chips

150g (5½oz) marshmallows

A cobbler is a cross between a crumble and a scone, celebrated in the USA, where home cooks consider it an all-time favourite dessert. It would seem this is also becoming the case here in the UK, a nation of flippant crumble-lovers. Crucial to a good cobbler is a good cobbler topping. It must be a light and crumbly crust, artfully splodged on top of the fruit. You want there to be gaps in the crust so that the fruit can bubble and breathe, turning syrupy as it bakes. Cherries are an unbeatable seasonal treat. Wonderful eaten just as they are, they offer a whole other kind of incredible when baked in a pudding. Marshmallows and dark chocolate chips are in with the cherries here for a full-throttle pudding.

Preheat the oven to 180°C/160°C fan/350°F/Gas Mark 4.

Put the cherries in an ovenproof dish, scatter over the sugar and add a splash of water. Cover the dish with foil and bake for 10 minutes, or until the cherries are just soft. Remove from the oven and leave to cool for a couple of minutes while you prepare the topping. (Leave the oven on.)

Mix together the flour and salt and then, using your fingertips, rub in the cold diced butter until the butter is broken up and the mixture resembles breadcrumbs.

In a separate bowl, mix together the eggs and milk. Make a well in the flour mixture, add the milk and egg mixture and swiftly combine to make a batter, then add the chocolate chips.

Spoon the marshmallows around the cooked cherries, then use a spoon to drop large spoonfuls of cobbler batter all over the surface of the cooked cherries leaving a few gaps here and there (you don't need to entirely cover the surface).

Bake, uncovered, for 15–20 minutes, until the cobbler is crisp and golden and the edges are bubbling beneath.

Hot-smoked Salmon & Sour Cream Fishcakes

FOR THE FILLING

80g (2¾oz) unsalted butter

1 large shallot, finely diced

80g (2¾oz) plain (all-purpose) flour

300ml (10½fl oz) whole milk

200g (7oz) crème fraîche or
sour cream

¼ nutmeg, grated (shredded)

1 unwaxed lemon, zested then
halved

200g (7oz) hot-smoked or cooked
salmon, flaked into large pieces

1 small bunch of dill, finely chopped

salt and freshly ground black pepper

FOR FRYING

100g (3½oz) plain (all-purpose)
flour

1 egg, beaten

150g (5½oz) dried breadcrumbs
(panko are best)

sunflower oil, for frying

Hot-smoked salmon is a very different product from smoked salmon – use it as you would fresh salmon that has first been cooked. The texture of these fishcakes is incredible. The salmon and crème fraîche mixture is stirred through the shallot-infused, super-thick béchamel. With no potato in the mixture (sometimes stodgy in a fishcake), you'll get instead a yielding creaminess that complements the fish perfectly.

Melt the butter in a pan over a moderate heat. Add the shallot and fry for 2 minutes, then stir in the flour, until you have a thick paste. Gradually add the milk, stirring all the time. When all the milk is incorporated, reduce the heat and simmer, stirring often, until you have a thick, smooth sauce (about 8–10 minutes).

Add the crème fraîche or sour cream, and the nutmeg and lemon zest. Season to taste, then remove from the heat. Put 100g (3½oz) of the sauce to one side.

Stir the salmon, half the dill and the juice from half the lemon into the remaining sauce and mix well. Spread the mixture over a baking tray lined with baking paper, cover and refrigerate for at least 1 hour, but overnight is best, until firm, cool and set.

When ready to fry, put the flour, beaten egg and breadcrumbs in separate bowls. Divide the salmon mixture into 8 equal portions. Lightly oil your hands, then gently roll each portion into a ball; flatten slightly to form the fishcake. Coat each one first in flour, then egg and finally breadcrumbs. Set to one side.

In a non-stick frying pan (skillet), in batches, shallow fry the fishcakes in 1cm (½in) oil over a moderate heat for 5–6 minutes on each side, or until golden brown and crisp. Turn the heat down if they start to look too brown. When the fishcakes are piping hot throughout, remove from the pan and drain on paper towels. Keep warm while you cook the remaining fishcakes.

Warm the reserved sauce and spoon onto 4 plates. Serve the fishcakes on top, sprinkled with the remaining dill, and the remaining lemon half cut into wedges.

Oaxacan-style Fried Tortilla with Courgettes, Burnt Salsa, Black Beans & Lime

6 tomatoes

2 red onions, 1 roughly chopped, 1 thinly sliced

4 cloves of garlic, unpeeled

4 courgettes (zucchini), halved lengthways

salt

2 limes

1 tsp oregano (Mexican, if you can get it)

1 tsp chilli flakes

1 tsp cracked cumin seeds, toasted

1–3 tsp chipotle sauce or hot smoked paprika, to taste

2 tbsp sunflower oil, plus more for frying the tortillas

1 x 400g (14oz) can of black beans, drained

2 bay leaves, scrunched a little

1 cinnamon stick

1 small bunch of coriander (cilantro), leaves picked and roughly chopped

4 large corn tortillas

200g (7oz) feta cheese or queso fresco, crumbled

150g (5½oz) sour cream

freshly ground black pepper

I have seen this dish referred to as Oaxacan pizza. As comparisons go, I don't approve. From Oaxaca, a southern state in Mexico, the tortilla is fried to form a crisp disk on which you then pile all number of other ingredients. In this recipe, I especially love how the vegetables are grilled until blackened, with some then blended to form a sauce to cook the beans, and some chopped with lots of coriander (cilantro) and lime to make the salsa. Called a *tlayuda* in Oaxaca, this Mexican dish is all about building flavour. Place on a board when good to go and chop into quarters, and that's about it as far as pizza comparisons go.

Preheat the grill (broiler) to very hot.

Char the tomatoes under the grill, along with the roughly chopped onion and the whole garlic cloves for 10 minutes, or until the tomato skins are charred, blackened in places, and the flesh is very soft. Put to one side.

Sprinkle the courgettes (zucchini) with salt and char under the grill for 5 minutes, until they are beginning to brown and are tender. Put to one aside.

Bring a small saucepan of salted water to a boil. Add the sliced red onion and boil for 2 minutes, then drain. Mix the onions with the juice of half a lime and a pinch of salt. Put to one side.

Discard the skins of the charred garlic and tomatoes, leaving the soft, cooked flesh of both. Scrape half each of the grilled tomatoes, onion and garlic into a blender along with half the oregano, half the chilli flakes, half the cumin, half the chipotle sauce or hot smoked paprika and a ½ teaspoon of salt. Blend to a smooth sauce.

Heat the 2 tablespoons of oil in a saucepan over a moderate heat. Add the sauce and fry for 5 minutes, until thickened, then add the black beans, 100ml (3½fl oz) of water, and the bay leaves and cinnamon stick and simmer for 5 minutes, until rich and thick. Check the seasoning.

cont.

To make the salsa, finely chop or mash on a board the remaining grilled garlic, tomatoes and onions. Add the juice of the remaining half lime, along with half the chopped coriander (cilantro), and the remaining chilli flakes and chipotle or paprika, seasoning with a big pinch of salt. Leave to one side.

Heat a spot of oil in a large non-stick or cast-iron frying pan (skillet) over a moderate heat. Add 1 tortilla and fry for about 1 minute, or until the bottom begins to brown nicely in patches. Flip and brown the other side. Repeat with the remaining tortillas, adding another splash of oil each time. Set each tortilla aside on a plate lined with paper towels, while you cook the remainder.

Chop the courgette into bite-size pieces, then sprinkle with the remaining cumin and oregano and a final pinch of salt.

To serve, top each fried tortilla with courgette, black beans, salsa, pickled red onions, feta cheese or queso fresco and sour cream and strew with the remaining coriander. Serve with the remaining lime cut into wedges on the side.

Fresh Egg Tagliatelle with Basil & Butter

FOR THE PASTA

350g (12oz) type '00' pasta flour

1 tsp salt

2 whole eggs

5 egg yolks

1 tbsp olive oil, plus more for greasing the worktop

fine semolina flour (cream of wheat), for dusting

FOR THE SAUCE

1 egg yolk

zest of ½ unwaxed lemon, plus a squeeze of juice to taste

70g (2½oz) parmesan, grated (shredded)

1 small bunch of basil, leaves picked and chopped

40g (1½oz) unsalted butter, softened

salt and freshly ground black pepper

Making pasta epitomizes an unhurried and relaxed approach to cooking. I like using a food processor to make the dough; you could do this by hand on a worktop, making a well with the flour and gradually adding the eggs, but a food processor does a great job. A pasta machine is an essential piece of kit, though. The simple sauce, with the egg yolk for creaminess and the basil and lemon to brighten, ensures the fresh pasta is given star billing.

To make the pasta, put the pasta flour and salt in the bowl of a food processor. With the motor running, add the whole eggs, egg yolks and olive oil and process until the dough comes together in a rough ball.

Turn out the dough onto a lightly oiled surface and knead well for 3–5 minutes, until the dough is smooth and soft and doesn't tear when you rub the surface with your thumb. Wrap and refrigerate for at least 1 hour.

Meanwhile, make the sauce. In a small bowl, whisk together the egg yolk, lemon zest and half the parmesan, then add the basil and put to one side.

Cut the chilled pasta dough into 4 pieces. Flatten with your hand and roll each piece through your pasta machine on its thickest setting. Fold the dough over on itself a few times to form a wide, neatly shaped ribbon the width of the pasta attachment, then roll each piece through the next smallest setting, folding the rolled sheet over each time. Do this at least 5 times for each setting – it will make the pasta extra silky. Finally, process the sheets though the tagliatelle setting, keeping the tagliatelle loosely arranged on a tray lightly dusted with semolina (cream of wheat) until ready to cook.

Bring a large pan of well-salted water to a boil and cook the pasta for around 1½–2 minutes, until al dente. Drain, reserving a little of the cooking water.

Add the pasta back to the pan and stir through the sauce, then add the butter, a slosh of the cooking water to loosen, and a squeeze of lemon juice. Check the seasoning and serve, topped with the remaining parmesan.

Trinidadian-style Fried Bread, Fried Fish & Hot Green Sauce

1 small bunch of coriander (cilantro), leaves picked and roughly chopped

1 tsp thyme leaves

2 cloves of garlic

½ bunch of spring onions (scallions), chopped

1 green chilli, halved

4 x 150g (5½oz) fillets of firm, white fish

juice of 1 lime

250g (9oz) self-raising flour or plain (all-purpose) flour mixed with 2 teaspoons of baking powder, plus more for dusting and dredging

½ tsp salt, plus more to season

½ tsp caster (superfine) sugar

180ml (5¾fl oz) whole milk

sunflower oil, for deep frying

freshly ground black pepper

TO SERVE

sliced tomato

sliced cucumber

lettuce leaves

pepper sauce or hot sauce

Eaten like a sandwich, this classic Trinidadian dish (known as 'bake and shark') of fried bread and fish, specifically shark, is first marinated in a blend of herbs, chilli and garlic. As shark is a species under urgent threat, I'm suggesting you ask your fishmonger to recommend another firm, white fish species caught from sustainable stocks. Or, buy farmed fish – organically reared is always best.

Blend the coriander (cilantro), thyme, garlic, spring onions (scallions) and green chilli with a splash of water to a smooth sauce and season with salt and pepper to taste.

Place the fish in a bowl and pour over the lime juice. Season with salt and pepper and add half the blended green sauce. Mix well, cover and let marinate in the fridge for about 30 minutes–1 hour.

In a mixing bowl combine the flour, the ½ teaspoon of salt, and the sugar and milk to form a soft dough. Turn out the dough onto a floured surface and knead for 2 minutes, until smooth and cohesive. Divide the dough into 4 equally sized balls and roll each ball into a disk 5mm (¼in) thick.

Heat 3cm (1¼in) oil in a large saucepan and fry the first dough disk for 2 minutes on each side, until puffed up and golden brown. Remove from the heat and set aside on a plate lined with paper towels. Repeat for the remaining dough disks to give 4 tortillas.

Dredge the marinated fish in flour and, using the same oil leftover in the pan from frying the dough, fry for 2–4 minutes, depending on thickness, until golden brown and cooked through (the fish should be opaque throughout and very hot to touch in the centre).

Slice the fried breads in half, like you would a roll or bap, spread with the remaining blended green sauce, add the fried fish, salad ingredients and hot sauce to taste, and serve.

Braised Lamb with Tomatoes, Cinnamon & Oregano with Buttered Aubergines

FOR THE AUBERGINE

4 aubergines (eggplants)

30g (1oz) unsalted butter

2 tbsp plain (all-purpose) flour

400ml (14fl oz) whole milk

50g (1¾oz) hard goat cheese
(or use parmesan or pecorino),
grated (shredded)

juice of 1 lemon

salt and freshly ground black pepper

FOR THE STEW

2 tbsp olive oil

800g (1lb 12oz) diced lamb

20g (¾oz) unsalted butter

1 onion, finely diced

2 large cloves of garlic, finely
chopped

1 green (bell) pepper, deseeded and
finely diced

1 x 400g (14oz) can of whole plum
tomatoes, drained and chopped

1 tsp dried oregano

¼ tsp Turkish chilli flakes (Aleppo
or Urfa)

2 bay leaves, scrunched a little

1 tsp salt, plus more to season

1 cinnamon stick

1 small bunch of flat-leaf parsley,
leaves picked and roughly chopped,
to serve

This Ottoman dish, *hünkar begendi* ('the sultan enjoyed it'), is a sheer delight. Cooked whole, the aubergines take on a smoky aroma, turning soft and silken. Their magnificent bulk is then mixed through a béchamel to form a voluptuous sauce on which to serve the aromatic slow-cooked lamb.

Preheat the oven to 220°C/200°C fan/425°F/Gas Mark 7.

Bake the whole aubergines (eggplants) for 25 minutes, until completely soft (it doesn't matter if the skins burn). Remove from the oven and leave to cool.

Heat the oil for the stew in a large casserole over a moderate heat. Fry the lamb in batches for 5 minutes, until browned, then remove to a plate. Melt the butter in the same pan and cook the onion, garlic and green (bell) pepper over a moderate heat for about 10 minutes, until softened. Add the chopped tomatoes, oregano, chilli flakes, bay leaves, 1 teaspoon of salt and the cinnamon stick and cook for 5 minutes, until bubbling up and thickened.

Return the lamb to the pan along with 200ml (7fl oz) of water. Bring to a boil, reduce the heat and season to taste, then cover and cook slowly for 1–1½ hours, until the meat is tender and the sauce is rich and thick. Check the liquid level in the pan occasionally to make sure it doesn't reduce too much, and top up if necessary. Check the seasoning again. Remove from the heat when the meat is cooked and put to one side.

Remove the aubergine skins and roughly chop or mash the flesh with a knife or fork on a chopping board.

In a saucepan over a moderate heat, melt the butter until foaming. Stir in the flour and cook for 2 minutes, briskly mixing. Gradually whisk in the milk, bring the sauce to a boil, then reduce the heat to low and cook, stirring often, for 10 minutes to form a smooth sauce.

Mix the chopped aubergine, grated (shredded) cheese and lemon juice (to taste) into the sauce. Season well.

To serve, spoon the aubergine sauce over a serving plate and top with the lamb. Sprinkle with parsley to serve.

Courgette, Black Olive & Rice Gratin

250g (9oz) short grain, risotto or paella rice

1 tsp salt, plus more to season

4–5 tbsp olive oil

1kg (2lb 4oz) courgettes (zucchini)

2 onions, finely diced

3 cloves of garlic, finely diced

1 tsp dried oregano

1 unwaxed lemon, zested then cut into wedges

150ml (5fl oz) double (heavy) cream

100ml (3½fl oz) chicken or vegetable stock, or water

120g (4¼oz) black olives, pitted and roughly chopped

80g (2¾oz) parmesan, grated (shredded)

freshly ground black pepper

¼–½ tsp chilli flakes (optional), to serve

salad leaves, dressed, to serve

This is not a dish to serve piping hot, but warm with a green salad (rocket/arugula leaves are especially good for their lively bite). Work in batches to get some colour on the vegetables; other than that, this is a lazy, leisurely, bung-it-in-the-oven ensemble. Use the same method and switch around the summer vegetables if you like: baked cherry tomatoes, fried aubergines (eggplants) or squash, or blanched broad (fava) beans or green beans would all suit.

Put the rice in a saucepan and cover with plenty of cold water. Add the 1 teaspoon of salt and bring to a boil. Reduce the heat and simmer for 8–12 minutes, until cooked. Drain and spread the rice out to cool in a baking dish with 1 tablespoon of the olive oil mixed through.

Thinly slice the courgettes (zucchini) 2.5mm (¹⁄₁₆in) thick – a mandoline is good for this if you have one; if not, a sharp knife will do. Heat 2 tablespoons of the olive oil in a wide saucepan and, in batches, fry the sliced courgettes over a moderate heat, until soft and coloured in places (3–5 minutes per batch). Drain each batch in a colander while you fry the remaining batches.

Preheat the oven 180°C/160°C fan/350°F/Gas Mark 4.

With the courgettes draining, heat the remaining olive oil in the same pan over a moderate heat. Add the onions and fry for 10 minutes, until soft and translucent. Add the garlic and oregano and fry for 2 minutes more. Remove from the heat. Add the drained courgettes back into the pan with the onions, mix well, add the lemon zest and season well with salt and pepper.

Add the courgette mixture to the rice in the baking dish. Add the cream, chicken stock, olives and half the parmesan and mix well.

Put the baking dish in the oven and cook, uncovered, for 35–40 minutes, until the mixture is bubbling and nicely coloured at the edges. Remove from the oven and cool for 10 minutes before serving with the remaining parmesan and the chilli flakes (if using) sprinkled over the top. Serve the lemon wedges alongside with some dressed salad leaves.

Summer Vegetables Stuffed Full with Turmeric & Cinnamon

4 large tomatoes: 2 of them coarsely grated (shredded); 2 with tops cut off and kept as lids, flesh scooped out and reserved

1 large aubergine (eggplant), halved and flesh scooped out and reserved, keeping the stalk end separate as a lid

2 large courgettes (zucchini), halved and flesh scooped out and reserved, keeping the stalk ends separate as a lid

40g (1½oz) basmati rice

40g (1½oz) red lentils

1 tbsp olive oil

2 onions, coarsely grated (shredded)

1 tsp ground turmeric

½ tsp chilli powder, or more to taste

½ tsp ground cinnamon

1 tsp freshly ground black pepper, plus more to season

2 tbsp tomato purée

1 tsp salt, plus more to season

2 tsp dried mint

1 small bunch of flat-leaf parsley, leaves picked and finely chopped

50g (1¾oz) raisins

2 large red, orange or yellow (bell) peppers, stalks cut off and reserved as lids

150g (5½oz) Greek yogurt

This recipe exorcises any previous crimes against stuffed vegetables you may have come across. It is best enjoyed after 30 minutes – an hour even – out of the oven. Warm enough for all the ingredients still to be soft and fragrant, but cool enough for the flavours to be harmoniously melded, and so really sing.

Finely chop the flesh of the 2 tomatoes, aubergine (eggplant) and courgette (zucchini) and set aside.

Pour 500ml (17fl oz) of water into a large saucepan and bring to a boil. Add the rice and lentils and boil, uncovered, for 7 minutes, then drain.

Heat the oil in a pan over a moderate heat. Add the onion, the chopped vegetable flesh, turmeric, chilli powder, cinnamon and the teaspoon of black pepper and cook for 10 minutes, or until softened. Put half this mixture to one side.

Add the coarsely grated tomato together with the tomato purée to the remaining onion mixture in the pan, then add ½ teaspoon of the salt and cook for 5 minutes, until thickened. Add 300ml (10½fl oz) of water and bring to a boil, then pour the sauce into a baking dish and put to one side.

In a bowl, mix the rice and lentils with half the mint, half the parsley, half the raisins, the remaining ½ teaspoon of salt and the reserved onion mixture.

Preheat the oven to 180°C/160°C fan/350°F/Gas Mark 4.

Stuff the rice and lentil mixture into the hollowed-out vegetables, including the (bell) peppers, top each with its lid and arrange in the baking dish, on top of the sauce. Cover with foil and cook for 2 hours, until the vegetables are very soft. Check the seasoning of the sauce, adding more salt and pepper to taste, and remove from the oven to cool a little (at least 30 minutes) before serving sprinkled with the remaining parsley.

Meanwhile, mix the yogurt with the remaining dried mint and remaining raisins together with a big pinch of salt. Serve alongside the stuffed vegetables.

Fougasse with Apricots & Thyme served with Goat Cheese

200ml (7fl oz) warm water

5g (⅛oz) dried yeast

1 tsp runny honey or caster (superfine) sugar

1 tbsp good olive oil, plus more for greasing and serving

350g (12oz) strong white bread flour

3 good thyme sprigs, leaves picked if the stems are woody

1 tsp salt

2 apricots, stoned and each sliced into 8

½ tsp flaky salt, for sprinkling

soft goat cheese or full-fat cream cheese, to serve

MAKES 1 FOUGASSE
(ABOUT 30 X 20CM/12 X 8IN)

I recently told a chef who specializes in cooking food from southern France, 'I've got a fougasse recipe going in my next book. It's baked with apricots and I'm serving it with goat cheese.' 'Oh really?' said the chef with a fair bit of incredulity. I felt myself hesitate... was I about to besmirch a bread recipe celebrated throughout Provence and beyond? Here, in print now, I'm sorry Alex: fougasse dough slashed authentically, but with apricots, honey and thyme in the mixture, and slathered with goat cheese. It's great. But is it fougasse? I think I'll be forgiven.

Pour the warm water into a jug and add the yeast, honey or sugar and olive oil.

Put the flour and thyme in a large mixing bowl and add the yeast liquid. Mix vigorously, then add the salt, mixing well to form a cohesive mass. Tip out the dough onto a lightly floured or oiled surface and knead well for at least 5 minutes, until the dough is smooth and elastic with a good sheen on its surface. (Use an electric mixer with a dough hook, if you prefer.) Place the dough in an oiled bowl and cover with a clean cloth. Leave to rise somewhere warm for 1 hour or so, until doubled in size.

Tip out the risen dough onto a baking tray lined with baking paper and press with fingers into a roughly oblong shape (about 30 x 20cm/12 x 8in). Drizzle with a little olive oil, gently press the slices of apricot into the dough and sprinkle with the flaky salt. Use a pizza cutter or sharp knife to make 2 distinct cuts down the middle of the dough, then to make 4 or 5 diagonal cuts either side of the central cuts to form a leaf design. Stretch the dough out to emphasize the holes. (See page 172.)

Cover again and allow to prove for about 45 minutes, until nicely risen. Meanwhile, preheat the oven to 220°C/200°C fan/425°F/Gas Mark 7.

Bake for about 13–15 minutes, until golden brown and the base sounds hollow when tapped. Remove from the oven and, while still hot, brush or drizzle the fougasse all over with a little extra olive oil. Serve warm, torn into pieces and slathered with goat or cream cheese.

Aubergine Flat Breads
with Parsley, Tomato & Pine Nuts

FOR THE TOPPING

1 large aubergine (eggplant)

1 red (bell) pepper

2 tomatoes

1 small onion

2 tbsp good olive oil, plus more for roasting

1 tbsp tomato purée

1 tsp coriander seeds, toasted and ground

½ tsp ground cinnamon

1 tsp ground cumin

1 tsp Turkish chilli flakes (Aleppo or Urfa), plus optional extra to serve

1 tsp salt

freshly ground black pepper

FOR THE DOUGH

500g (1lb 2oz) strong white bread flour

1 tsp dried yeast

1 tsp salt

good olive oil, for kneading and serving

TO SERVE

tomatoes, sliced

3 tbsp pine nuts, lightly toasted, or use lightly toasted almond flakes

1 small bunch of flat-leaf parsley, leaves picked and roughly chopped

1 lemon, cut into wedges

MAKES 4 FLAT BREADS

I have included a recipe for *lahmacun* (Turkish flat breads) in a previous book. That recipe used spiced, minced (ground) lamb; this revised version uses baked aubergine (eggplant), chopped to a pulp with onions, (bell) peppers and tomatoes. This soft mixture of roasted vegetables behaves in much the same way that the lamb mince does on a meat-based lahmacun. Intensely flavoured, with a good hit of chilli flakes, these flat breads are typically rolled and stuffed full of sliced tomatoes with the parsley used more like a salad leaf, bright and robust in flavour. I like to add a good amount of chilli flakes and enough lemon juice and good olive oil to each bread before rolling to soak and soften in the cooking juices. Unbeatable, really.

Preheat the oven to 200°C/180°C fan/400°F/Gas Mark 6.

Begin the topping. Pierce the aubergine (eggplant) a few times with a fork, then put it on a baking tray along with the red (bell) pepper, tomatoes and onion and rub them all over with olive oil. Roast for 25 minutes, then remove the pepper and tomatoes and put these to one side. Cook the aubergine and onion for a further 10 minutes, until soft and well coloured. Remove from the oven and put to one side with the pepper and tomato.

Meanwhile, make the dough. Put the flour and yeast in a big mixing bowl. Using a spoon, mix in 300ml (10½fl oz) of water, stirring vigorously for a couple of minutes. Add the salt and mix again until you have a dough. Turn out the dough onto a lightly floured surface and knead well until smooth and cohesive. Put the dough back in the bowl (wiped out if necessary and oiled a little), cover with a clean tea towel and leave to rise for 1 hour or so, until almost doubled in size.

With the vegetables cool enough to handle, deseed and peel the pepper, slip the skin from the tomatoes, slip the peel from the onion and scoop out all of the aubergine flesh from the skin. Roughly chop all the vegetables together on a board and place in a bowl.

cont.

Add the tomato purée, spices and the 1 teaspoon of salt, along with the 2 tablespoons of olive oil and a grinding of black pepper. Mix everything together well and put to one side.

When the dough is ready, preheat the oven to maximum (220°/200°C fan/425°F/Gas Mark 7 is ideal). If you have a pizza stone, preheat it now; otherwise use a baking tray.

Turn out the dough onto a lightly floured surface and knead it gently with lightly oiled hands for 1 minute. Cut the dough into 4 equal pieces. On a lightly floured surface, roll out each dough ball into an oval, getting it as thin as possible without tearing it.

Carefully remove the pizza stone or baking tray from the oven and place it on a heatproof surface. If using a baking tray, one at a time, lay a flat bread on some baking paper and place it on top; if using a pizza stone, lay the flat bread directly on to it.

Spread one quarter of the topping all over the flat bread, keeping a 1cm (½in) border around the edge. Bake in the very hot oven for 6–8 minutes, until the dough is crisp and the topping has a good colour to it. Repeat with the remaining flat bread pieces and topping.

To serve, add some of the tomatoes, toasted pine nuts (or flaked almonds) and parsley to each flat bread. Squeeze with the lemon wedges and add another generous slick of olive oil. Some extra chilli flakes are also good. Roll or fold and eat immediately.

Beer-brined BBQ Chicken with Mustard & Miso Mayonnaise Sauce

100ml (3½fl oz) warm water

50g (1¾oz) coarse salt

50g (1¾oz) caster (superfine) sugar

about 660ml (21½fl oz) light beer such as larger

1 whole chicken (about 1.5kg/ 3lb 5oz)

FOR THE SPICE RUB

1 tbsp sweet or hot paprika, as you like

1 tbsp mustard powder

1–2 tsp chilli powder (chipotle, if you have it)

1 tsp ground cumin

2 tsp coarsely ground black pepper

2 tbsp olive oil

FOR THE SAUCE

200g (7oz) mayonnaise

100ml (3½fl oz) cider vinegar

1 tsp coarsely ground black pepper

1 clove of garlic, crushed

1 tsp caster (superfine) sugar

1 tbsp Dijon mustard

1 tbsp miso (optional)

salt

TO SERVE

½–1 hispi cabbage, cored, leaves thinly sliced

½ small bunch of flat-leaf parsley, leaves picked and chopped

good bread

SERVES 4–6

This is hands down a brilliant method to master when cooking whole chicken on a barbecue. Taking the time to brine the chicken in a mixture of beer, salt and sugar will make all the difference to the final texture. And that's not all: once brined, making a spice mixture to coat a spatchcocked chicken (flash, although really terribly easy to do) ramps flavour like nothing else. Until, that is, you begin basting the chicken with the sauce – mayonnaise made punchy with miso, mustard and cider vinegar. More salt, more sugar – this American-style barbecue chicken is outrageously good. It's my guess you'll never barbecue a chicken any other way again. Buy a meat thermometer – I've said it before, but they are inexpensive and will give you rock-solid assurance when the meat is ready to serve; no ifs, no buts.

Pour the warm water into a large bowl. Add the salt and sugar and allow to dissolve. Add the beer and top up with 900ml (30½fl oz) of cold water. Place the chicken in the brine, adding more cold water if necessary to completely immerse the chicken. Refrigerate for at least 2 hours and up to 12 hours.

Remove the chicken and discard the brine. Pat dry with paper towels.

To spatchcock the chicken, place it on a large baking sheet, breast-side downward (this helps to keep things orderly). Using sharp kitchen scissors, cut along both sides of the backbone. Remove the backbone and flip the chicken over so that the breast side is now upward. Press down firmly to flatten the chicken. If you have time, refrigerate, uncovered, for another hour to further dry out the chicken (this will help to get crisper skin).

Combine the paprika, mustard powder, chilli powder, cumin and black pepper in a bowl to make the spice rub. Rub this all over the chicken, then rub in the olive oil.

cont.

To cook the chicken, heat the grill (broiler) or barbecue for indirect heat. If you're using a gas grill this means turning off the centre burner and reducing the side burners to medium. If you're using charcoal, place the coals to heat up on one side of the grill.

Place the chicken, breast-side upward, on an indirect heat. Cook for about 45–50 minutes, turning every 10 minutes, until the juices run clear on the thickest part of the thigh and the chicken is cooked through (the internal temperature should read 70°C/150°F on a meat thermometer).

While the chicken is cooking, mix all of the ingredients for the sauce together and season with salt. Divide the sauce equally into 2 bowls. After 20 minutes of cooking time, begin to baste the chicken using one of the portions of sauce. Do so every 10 minutes.

Once the chicken is cooked through, move the chicken to cook over direct heat, breast-side downward, for about 5 minutes, until the skin is charred and crisped. Remove the chicken from the grill and let it rest on a serving plate for 10 minutes.

Carve the chicken and serve with the remaining sauce and with the cabbage and parsley and good bread on the side.

To cook in an oven

Heat the oven to 190°C/170°C fan/375°F/Gas Mark 5. Roast the chicken, skin-side upward, basting often with the sauce, for 1 hour–1 hour 15 minutes, or until the chicken juices run clear when skewered in the thickest part of the leg (the internal temperature should read 70°C/150°F on a meat thermometer). Rest the chicken for 10 minutes before carving.

Charred Corn Chaat with Tandoori Fish

FOR THE MARINATED FISH

3 tsp Kashmiri chilli powder,
or 1 tsp chilli powder plus
1 tsp unsmoked sweet paprika

1 tsp ground turmeric

2 tsp cumin seeds, toasted
and ground

½ tsp ground cinnamon

1 tsp fennel seeds, toasted
and ground

150g (5½oz) natural yogurt

1 tbsp grated (shredded) fresh
ginger

2 cloves of garlic, finely crushed

1 tsp salt

1kg (2lb 4oz) firm, white sustainable
fish fillets (such as ling or hake),
cut into 5cm (2in) pieces

TO SERVE

1 small bunch of mint, leaves picked
and finely chopped

1 small bunch of coriander
(cilantro), leaves picked and
finely chopped

2 green chillies, finely chopped

1 tsp caster (superfine) sugar

2 lemons

4 corn-on-the-cobs

1 red onion, very thinly sliced

1 tbsp chaat masala, or more
to taste

salt and freshly ground black pepper

warmed naan breads, to serve

This might just be my favourite of all the summer recipes in this book. Not only do I think this a beautiful dish, it's also a recipe that suggests you've taken some time to source the ingredients and you've cooked them with care and attention for the season. This is a recipe that will demonstrate to your guests your innate cookery skill, your ingredient know-how, if you like. Make your own tandoori marinade for the fish using the recipe below, or you could buy a ready-made tandoori spice blend to mix in with the yogurt, or even a ready-made tandoori sauce – there are lots of good options available. But, making from scratch is really easy. Chaat masala is one of my favourite spice blends – it brings a hot, sour, spicy clout to everything it touches. Buy it little and often. My kids love it mixed through popcorn.

To make the tandoori marinade, mix all the ingredients except the fish together in a large bowl. Add the fish and mix well to coat. Refrigerate for at least 1 hour and up to 4 hours.

In a bowl, mix together the mint, half the coriander (cilantro), and the green chillies, sugar, juice of 1 lemon and a big pinch of salt and put to one side. (Alternatively, for a smoother sauce, blend these ingredients together in a food processor.)

Preheat the oven to 180°C/160°C fan/350°F/Gas Mark 4, or heat a barbecue or chargrill pan to medium–high heat.

Boil the corn cobs in well-salted water for 5 minutes, until just tender, then remove from the pan and put to one side to drain. Pat dry when cool enough to handle.

Sprinkle some salt onto the sliced red onion, then rinse in cold water and drain well, then add the juice of half a lemon together with another big pinch of salt. Put to one side.

Grill the corn all over for about 5 minutes, until nicely charred, then place to one side to cool.

cont.

181

Thread the marinated fish onto skewers (if you're using wooden skewers, soak them in water beforehand).

To cook these on the barbecue or in the grill pan: turn often, for 5–8 minutes, until lightly charred all over and piping hot throughout (the internal temperature should read 65°C/149°F on a digital thermometer).

To cook in the oven, place the skewers on a baking tray and bake for about 8 minutes, until cooked through. Remove from the heat and put to one side to keep warm.

Meanwhile, firmly hold each of the grilled corn upright on a chopping board and shuck the kernels using a sharp knife. Season the kernels well with salt and black pepper, then stir through the red onion and the remaining coriander.

To serve, pile the corn onto a serving plate, add some of the green sauce, add the fish skewers and a generous amount of chaat masala to each portion. Serve with the remaining lemon cut into wedges and warm naan breads.

Peach & Dulce de Leche Cake

180g (6½oz) dulce de leche from a jar or can

2 ripe peaches, stoned and thinly sliced

120g (4¼oz) unsalted butter, softened

100g (3½oz) caster (superfine) sugar

2 eggs, beaten

240g (8¾oz) plain (all-purpose) flour

1 tsp baking powder

pinch of salt

120ml (3¾fl oz) whole milk

SERVES 6-8

Dulce de leche is a wonder stuff. Sometimes called Mexican caramel, unlike caramel, which is made by cooking sugar, dulce de leche is made by cooking milk. There are many tales of boiling cans of condensed milk to make the stuff, hours (and hours) they will rattle away in a pan filled with water on the stovetop. Some explode, some don't. Far better, and far more sensible, is to just buy a jar or can of the stuff from the supermarket or, better still, any specialist Mexican shops. Dulce de leche has a deeply, smooth caramel, butterscotch flavour. It's dangerous stuff, indescribably sweet and very, very delicious. This recipe will show you why it goes together so well with peach.

Preheat the oven to 180°C/160°C fan/350°F/Gas Mark 4. Grease a 25cm (10in) cake tin and line it with baking paper.

Spoon 120g (4¼oz) of the dulce de leche over the bottom of the lined tin and arrange the peach slices in a single layer on top.

Using an electric stand mixer fitted with the whisk attachment, beat the butter and sugar together until light and fluffy. Add the eggs, little by little, followed by the remaining dulce de leche. Beat until combined.

In a mixing bowl, combine the flour, baking powder and salt. One large spoonful at a time, mix this into the creamed butter and sugar mixture, alternating with spoonfuls of the milk, and beating well after each addition.

Spoon the batter over the peaches and dulce de leche and bake for 45–50 minutes, or until a skewer inserted into the centre comes out clean. Cool for 10 minutes in the tin before inverting onto a serving plate.

Best served warm or at room temperature.

Raspberry Ripple Frangipane Tart

FOR THE PASTRY

250g (9oz) plain (all-purpose) flour, or use 70:30 plain to wholewheat, plus more for dusting

50g (1¾oz) icing (confectioner's) sugar, plus optional more to serve

pinch of salt

125g (4½oz) very cold unsalted butter, chopped

1 egg, beaten

zest of 1 unwaxed lemon, plus a squeeze of the juice for the raspberries

FOR THE FRANGIPANE

300g (10½oz) raspberries

160g (5½oz) caster (superfine) sugar

130g (4½oz) unsalted butter, softened

200g (7oz) ground almonds

2 eggs, beaten

SERVES 6-8

A good tart is one of my favourite things to make when I have proper time to spare and people to feed – for a special occasion or family gathering perhaps. This recipe with the frangipane swirled through with raspberry sauce is a knockout. It involves so few ingredients and yet together they produce something so elegant, so lovely, so very memorable.

First, make the pastry. Use a food processor or your fingertips and a mixing bowl to pulse or rub the flour, icing (confectioner's) sugar and pinch of salt together with the cold butter until it resembles breadcrumbs. Add the egg and lemon zest and pulse or mix until the mixture just comes together. Press the dough firmly together and flatten into a disk. Wrap it and refrigerate for about 1 hour while you prepare the filling.

Blend half the raspberries with 40g (1½oz) of the caster (superfine) sugar and a squeeze of lemon juice to form a smooth sauce.

In a bowl, beat together the softened butter and remaining caster sugar until just combined, then add the ground almonds and eggs, mixing well to combine.

Grease a 25–30cm (10–12in) tart tin and line it with baking paper. Preheat the oven to 180°C/160°C fan/ 350°F/Gas Mark 4. Take the pastry out of the fridge for 10 minutes before you need to use it.

Roll out the pastry on a lightly floured worktop to about 3mm (¹/₈in) thick and use it to line the tin, pressing it firmly inside. Trim the edges neatly, using the trimmings to patch any holes. Refrigerate for at least 30 minutes.

Spoon the frangipane mixture into the lined tart tin and spread it out evenly, then spoon in a few tablespoons of the raspberry sauce, carefully marbling it into the frangipane mixture. Scatter with the remaining raspberries and bake for 35–40 minutes, until the pastry is crisp and golden and the frangipane filling is set.

Cool for 30 minutes or so before removing from the tin and dusting with a little extra icing sugar, if you like. Serve with the remaining raspberry sauce on the side.

Flourless Dark Chocolate Cake
made with Turkish Delight, Halva & Dates

6 egg whites

200g (7oz) caster (superfine) sugar

125g (4½oz) ground almonds

¼ tsp ground green cardamom seeds

pinch of salt

300g (10½oz) halva, crumbled or chopped into small pieces

200g (7oz) Turkish delight, ½ finely chopped, ½ chopped slightly bigger to decorate

150g (5½oz) pitted dates, finely chopped

200g (7oz) 70% dark (bittersweet) chocolate, finely chopped

TO DECORATE

100ml (3½fl oz) double (heavy) cream

150g (5½oz) 70% dark (bittersweet) chocolate, finely chopped

30g (1oz) pistachios, roughly chopped

rose petals, optional

SERVES 8-10

Truly a great cake, fudgy and moist. The egg whites are whipped as for a meringue, then folded through with chunks of Turkish delight, pieces of halva, chopped dates and dark chocolate. Cardamom works its characteristic and ethereal magic with all of these ingredients.

Preheat the oven to 170°C/150°C fan/325°F/Gas Mark 3. Grease and line a 24cm (9½in) springform cake tin with baking paper.

Using an electric stand mixer fitted with the whisk, beat the egg whites to stiff peaks. Gradually add the sugar, beating continuously, then continue to beat for 5 minutes, until you have a thick and glossy meringue.

Fold in the ground almonds, cardamom, and pinch of salt, then add the halva and the finely chopped Turkish delight. Next, add the dates and finally the chocolate. Stir briefly until just combined. Spoon into the prepared cake tin and bake for 1 hour–1 hour 10 minutes, until the cake is set and firm to the touch (it will still be moist in the centre, so a skewer will not come out clean). Cover with a loose square of foil if the cake catches too much before it's ready.

To decorate, first make a ganache. Pour the cream into a saucepan and place over a high heat. Bring to a boil, then remove from the heat. Little by little (but still fairly rapidly), whisk in the chocolate, so that the cream doesn't cool too much and will melt all the chocolate. Once all the chocolate has melted, allow the ganache to cool for 10 or so minutes in the pan, by which time it will stiffen a little to a thick pouring consistency.

Transfer the cooled cake to a large serving plate and pour over the chocolate ganache, allowing it to drip down the sides. Decorate with the chopped pistachios and the remaining Turkish delight. Some fresh rose petals will add extra va-va-voom, if you have them.

Vietnamese or Laotian Coffee Ice Cream

250ml (9fl oz) hot strong black coffee

150g (5½oz) sweetened condensed milk, or more to taste

MAKES ABOUT 400G (14OZ)

Rather a long time ago now, before children, Matt and I travelled overland from Beijing to Bangkok. The trip took us ages and the many photos I have from that time are brilliant. Quite apart from looking a good deal younger, we had backpacker physiques. What I find particularly amusing is not only that we are both super-tanned, but our changing waistlines – photos taken in some places show us much trimmer than we are in others. I put it down to our unbridled enjoyment in finding the most delicious things to eat and drink in any place we visited. In particular, the bao buns we often ate for breakfast in Chengdu; and also, without a doubt, the pints of iced condensed-milk coffee, served clunking with ice in a bag, which you slurped through a straw in Vietnam and Laos. I could not get enough of the stuff. Intensely sweet and creamy with an invigorating wallop of freshly brewed coffee, just two ingredients here, churned in my very ordinary domestic ice-cream machine, takes me back. Take me back.

Mix together the coffee and the condensed milk, stirring well to combine. Refrigerate to cool, then churn the mixture in an ice-cream maker until frozen.

The ice cream is best eaten straight away, but if you're freezing it, take it out of the freezer at least 30 minutes before serving.

A FRENCH SEASIDE ONE

Lillet Blanc with Sliced Peach & Soda

Fig Tapenade Toasts

Bouillabaisse

Peaches Roasted in Lillet Blanc with Crème Fraîche

SERVES 6-8

I do so love a recipe that comes with such mighty and historical baggage. First up, I am duty-bound to note that on no account can the main dish be called a bouillabaisse if the place in which it is made is all that far from the town of Marseille, where the fish are caught and the catch is cooked. The inclusion of rascasse is said to be a must, an absolute must. The inclusion of molluscs is up for debate – the thought of adding langoustines or lobster is a heresy that might cause some to froth at the mouth... One thing is for sure, there are a good many food writers well versed in bouillabaisse and none better than the late, straightforward and brilliant Alan Davidson in his book *Mediterranean Seafood*: 'Bouillabaisse is a simple dish and quite a good one. But it does not deserve or benefit from the mystique which has been built up around it or the costly ingredients which are sometimes put into it.'

Davidson's voice is one of gentle reason and knowing persuasion, so let's take his lead. Bouillabaisse is an excellent dish and you can and must make it with whatever sustainable fish you'd like to use. I'm giving a fairly orthodox recipe here – one that encourages a variety of fish, with the fish soup served separately to the fish in which it is cooked. The recipe includes saffron, fennel and leek – which is authentic – and the rouille is served alongside the croutons, which you can spread with the rouille and serve on the side or drench in the soup to soak in the stew. Up to you.

As for the tapenade, this preparation made with fresh figs is entirely inauthentic, but lovely. Sweet, salty, intense, these toasts whet the appetite and get the taste buds working overdrive in anticipation. The accompanying Lillet blanc with peach and soda is a great start for what will be an extraordinary dinner. After that, I'd recommend drinking a dry white wine with good acidity, preferably of seaside origin; something French, naturally. Finally, and full circle – which I find to be thoughtful practice in most menu planning – any remaining Lillet blanc is to be sploshed over the peaches to bake with some orange blossom honey... transformed, incandescent, like a sunset, and served simply with crème fraîche.

Lillet Blanc with Sliced Peach & Soda

1 bottle of Lillet blanc (keep 100ml/3½fl oz back to roast the peaches for pudding)

1 bottle of soda water

1 ripe peach, stoned and sliced

ice, to serve

In a large jug mix together the wine and soda water, using a ratio of two thirds Lillet blanc to one third soda and use lots of ice. Put a slice of peach in each glass. Top with the drink and serve immediately.

Fig Tapenade Toasts

100g (3½oz) good-quality black olives, drained and pitted

2 ripe black figs

2 anchovy fillets in olive oil, drained

1 tbsp capers (desalinated, if necessary), rinsed and drained

1 small clove of garlic, crushed

1 tsp finely chopped thyme leaves

a few sprigs of flat-leaf parsley, leaves picked and finely chopped

50ml (1¾fl oz) good olive oil

juice of ¼ lemon

sourdough or ciabatta bread, sliced

salt and freshly ground black pepper

Put all the ingredients, except the olive oil, lemon juice and bread, into a mortar and pound to a paste, or use a food processor, or simply chop together on a board (then transfer to a bowl). Add the olive oil and lemon juice and mix to a paste. Put to one side.

Toast the bread slices, spread with the tapenade and serve with the drink (see above).

Bouillabaisse

FOR THE FISH SOUP

100ml (3½fl oz) good olive oil

1 large onion, finely chopped

2 small leeks, finely chopped

1 large fennel bulb, tough stalks removed, remainder finely chopped

1 tsp fennel seeds, lightly toasted and crushed

4 cloves of garlic, finely chopped

large pinch of saffron threads, soaked in a little warm water

3 peeled strips of unwaxed orange zest, pith removed

¼ tsp chilli powder, chilli flakes or cayenne pepper

2 tbsp tomato purée

1 tbsp thyme leaves

2 bay leaves, scrunched a little

1 big flat-leaf parsley sprig

1 x 400g (14oz) can of plum tomatoes, drained

1kg (2lb 4 oz) whole small fish or fish bones and heads, gills removed and blood rinsed off

200ml (7fl oz) dry white wine

50ml (1¾fl oz) Pernod or pastis (optional)

salt and freshly ground black pepper

FOR THE ROUILLE

3 cloves of garlic, roughly chopped

25g (1oz) stale white bread or use good-quality breadcrumbs

large pinch of chilli flakes, chilli powder or cayenne pepper

pinch of saffron threads, soaked in a little warm water

pinch of salt

2 egg yolks

120ml (4fl oz) good olive oil

A food processor or blender is very useful for this recipe, to blend the broth and to make the rouille.

Make the soup. Heat the olive oil in a good-size saucepan over a moderate heat. Add the onion, leek, fennel and fennel seeds and fry for 10 minutes, until soft and translucent. Add the garlic and cook for 5 minutes more, to soften. Do not allow the mixture to brown.

Add the saffron and its soaking water, along with the orange zest, chilli or cayenne pepper, tomato purée and herbs and cook for 2 minutes, until fragrant, then add the tomatoes and cook for 2 minutes, until thick and rich.

Add the quantity of whole fish or fish bones and stir well to combine. Cook for 5 minutes, stirring, until the fish and aromatics are beginning to stick to the bottom of the pan without browning.

Add the wine and Pernod or pastis (if using), stirring to scrape up any bits from the bottom of the pan, then boil for about 2–3 minutes, until any raw alcohol fumes have cooked away.

Add 2 litres (70fl oz) of water, making sure all of the ingredients are covered. Bring to a vigorous boil and allow to boil rapidly for 5 minutes, then lower the heat to a low simmer and cook for 45 minutes, seasoning well with salt and pepper.

While the fish soup is simmering, make the rouille. Use a pestle and mortar or a blender to pound or blend the garlic, bread, chilli or cayenne, soaked saffron (reserve the soaking liquid), a pinch of salt and the egg yolks to a thick paste. Thin the rouille using 3 tablespoons of liquid, made up using the saffron soaking liquid topped up with the broth from the fish-soup pan.

With the blender motor running, or by mixing continuously in the mortar, add the olive oil in a thin, steady stream to create a thick mayonnaise. Check the seasoning and put to one side in a bowl.

1.5–2.5kg (3lb 5oz–5lb 8oz) mixed whole and fish fillets (some with firm meaty flesh and some with delicate white flesh; weight will depend on how many whole, bone-in fish you use), gills removed

450g (1lb) mussels, cleaned and beards removed (optional, but I rate highly)

1 good rustic-style baguette, cut into 1cm (½in) slices and toasted

When the soup is ready, give it a good stir and remove any large fish bones you can see – this will help when blending (unless you have an especially powerful blender). Working in batches, transfer the broth and all the ingredients, including smaller fish bones, to the blender. Be careful not to overfill. Remove the stopper and cover with folded clean paper towels to stop the dangerously hot stock coming out. Begin blending with the motor on low speed, then gradually increase the speed to high, blending until you have as smooth a mixture as possible.

In batches, transfer the blended soup to a large sieve or conical set over a clean, wide, large saucepan and use a wooden spoon or ladle to scrape and pass, or press, the broth through the mesh. Discard any of the dry, mushy remnants in the sieve or conical. Season to taste and return to a low heat.

To get ready to serve: season the fish fillets and the whole fish and add to the broth, beginning first with the whole fish and any thicker fillets. Gently simmer until each piece of fish is just cooked, hot and opaque throughout, then transfer the cooked fish to a serving platter and keep warm.

If you're using mussels, discard any raw ones that fail to close when tapped securely. Add those that do to the gently simmering broth and cook until all the mussels have opened. Discard any that remain shut.

To serve, arrange the cooked fish on the warm platter and put the fish-soup broth (with the mussels) in a large soup tureen or serving bowl. Serve each guest a portion of the fish and they can then choose to ladle the soup over the fish or eat the two separately. Serve the toasted baguette on the side along with the rouille.

Peaches Roasted in Lillet Blanc with Crème Fraîche

8 large ripe peaches, halved and stoned

4 tbsp orange blossom honey (or regular runny honey will be fine)

100ml (3½fl oz) Lillet blanc

crème fraîche, to serve

Preheat the oven to 220°C/200°C fan/425°F/Gas Mark 7.

Place the peaches snugly, cut-sides upward, in a roasting tray. Add the honey, Lillet blanc and a splash of water. Mix gently to coat.

Roast for 20–25 minutes, or until the peaches are light golden in colour and tender throughout. Remove from the oven and baste the peaches with the juices.

Allow to cool slightly or serve at room temperature along with the crème fraîche and any of the syrupy cooking juices.

SUMMER BBQ MEZZE

Kofte

Baharat Chicken

Grilled Whole Halloumi

Grilled Flat Bread

Aubergines with Honey & Mint

Whole Herb Tabbouleh

Broad Bean Hummus & Fresh
Podded Broad Beans

Chilli Tomato Sauce

Figs & Dates with Honey
& Rose Water

SERVES 6–8

We were lucky enough to have a barbecue built for us to photograph the mezze feast for this book. On the day, a hot summer's day in a back garden here in Bristol, we lit this hulking great thing. As it raged with flames and we waited for the fire to die back and for the wood to glow bright, I think I gave my face something of a suntan (a grill tan)... at the very least, very rosy cheeks. An extraordinary piece of kit, with a solid plate of raised cast iron to lay the logs and light the fire, and a sturdy grill that sits above the heat and splits in two. I don't imagine many own a barbecue like this one but, should you wish to, I do think it's pretty terrific to cook on.

If, however, you have a smaller barbecue, or (shoot!) no barbecue at all, don't let that stop you. While this is an elaborate and, yes, a rather long menu, all the food on offer could just as well be cooked in a pan over a hob in the kitchen.

Get ahead: make the sauces, cook the grains for the salad, and mix the mascarpone for the figs in the morning, well before any guests arrive, leaving you to grill the kebabs and chicken, aubergines (eggplants), flat breads and halloumi when they get there. Have plenty of herbs at the ready and I think it absolutely worth your while getting hold of some Turkish chilli flakes, both Aleppo and Urfa if you can, to use in your cooking and to have at the table for your guests to help themselves. Sweet, hot, smoky... I find these chilli flakes an indispensable ingredient. Sumac (another favourite for this style of cooking) is a sour, pungent berry used in lieu of or in addition to lemons. It is an attractive colour and it's vital you track it down for this menu.

The figs and dates for pudding are a doddle to assemble and my thoughts on this as a dessert are pure and simple. Flavoured with rose water and honey and studded with pistachios, this is a wonderfully evocative and easy end to the meal. Find a rose and throw the petals over the plate for good measure.

Kofte

600g (1lb 5oz) minced (ground) lamb or beef

1 tsp cumin seeds, toasted and ground

½ tsp ground cinnamon

1 tsp Turkish chilli flakes (Urfa, in this case), or another chilli flake if necessary

½ tsp salt

1 small onion, coarsely grated (shredded)

½ small bunch of flat-leaf parsley, leaves picked and finely chopped

1 tsp dried mint

freshly ground black pepper

Mix the minced (ground) lamb or beef with the spices, the ½ teaspoon of salt, and the onion, parsley and mint, then knead for 1 minute, until completely combined.

Form the mixture into 8 sausage shapes, then refrigerate until ready to cook. (You can cook them like sausages, just as they are, or thread them onto skewers – I prefer skewers because it makes them easier to move about on the grill.)

Get the grill hot. Place the kofte on the heat and grill, turning often for 10 minutes, or until cooked through and beginning to char nicely.

Baharat Chicken

1 tsp ground black pepper

½ tsp ground cinnamon

¼ tsp ground green cardamom seeds

1 tsp cumin seeds, toasted and ground

1 tsp coriander seeds, toasted and ground

small pinch of ground cloves

2 tsp sweet paprika

2 tbsp olive oil

2 lemons

½ tsp salt

8 chicken thighs

In a big bowl, mix all the spices with the olive oil, the juice of ½ lemon and the ½ teaspoon of salt. Add the chicken and coat well. Allow to marinate for at least 1 hour, or for up to 8 hours refrigerated.

Get the grill hot.

Grill the chicken, turning often, on the barbecue for 15–20 minutes, or until cooked through and nicely charred (the internal temperature should read 74°C/ 163°F on a meat thermometer). Slice the rest of the lemons into wedges to serve with the chicken or kofte.

Grilled Whole Halloumi

1 or 2 x 250g (9oz) halloumi packets (depending how much you want)

good olive oil, to coat

Slice the halloumi into wide slices about 2cm (¾in) thick and lightly brush each side with olive oil. Grill whole until soft and yielding with good colour.

Grilled Flat Bread

10g (¼oz) dried yeast

350ml (12fl oz) hand-hot water

2 tbsp good olive oil, plus more to serve

500g (1lb 2oz) strong white bread flour, plus more for dusting

2 tbsp sesame seeds

½ tsp salt

Mix the yeast with the warm water and the olive oil until the yeast is dissolved.

In a big bowl, mix the yeast mixture into the flour along with the sesame seeds and the ½ teaspoon of salt to form a dough. Tip out the dough onto a floured surface and knead for 2 minutes until soft and smooth, then cover with a clean cloth and leave somewhere warm for 1–2 hours to rise, until nearly doubled in size.

Divide the dough into 8 equal pieces. On a lightly floured surface, roll out into ovals each about 15cm (6in) long and 5mm (¼in) thick.

Get the grill hot.

In batches, grill the dough ovals on the barbecue for 1–2 minutes, or until puffed up slightly and browning on the bottom. Flip over and grill on the other side, until cooked, nicely browned and puffed up in places.

Pop the cooked flat breads into a bowl and cover with a clean cloth while you cook the remainder. Drizzle or brush with olive oil just before serving.

Aubergines with Honey & Mint

2 aubergines (eggplants), cut into 1cm (½in) slices and sprinkled with salt

good olive oil

big pinch of salt, plus more to season

2 tbsp runny honey

freshly ground black pepper, or chilli flakes

½ small bunch of mint, leaves picked and roughly chopped, to serve

Allow the salted aubergines (eggplants) to sit in a colander for 5 minutes to release some liquid, then pat dry with a clean kitchen cloth. Drizzle the aubergines with olive oil and sprinkle with a big pinch of salt and grill for 3–5 minutes, until soft and nicely browned at the edges.

Lay the aubergines on a platter in a single layer and spoon over the honey. Season well with salt and pepper, or use chilli flakes, and add the chopped mint to serve.

Whole Herb Tabbouleh

60g (2¼oz) coarse bulgur wheat

200ml (7fl oz) boiling water from a kettle

2 little gem lettuces, leaves shredded

1 cucumber, peeled, deseeded and thinly sliced

1 large bunch of flat-leaf parsley, leaves picked

1 large bunch of mint, leaves picked

1 small bunch of dill, chopped large

juice of ½ lemon

2 tsp sumac

4 tbsp good olive oil

¼ tsp ground cinnamon (optional)

salt and freshly ground black pepper

Soak the bulgur wheat in the boiling water for 30 minutes, or until the grains are tender and the water has been absorbed. Drain any excess water away.

In a large bowl, mix the lettuce, cucumber and herbs together. Add the bulgur and stir through.

Make a dressing by mixing the lemon juice, sumac, olive oil, cinnamon (if using) and a good amount of seasoning in a small bowl. Toss the dressing through the salad and set aside ready to serve.

Broad Bean Hummus & Fresh Podded Broad Beans

400g (14oz) broad (fava) beans, podded

1 clove of garlic, finely chopped

juice of ½ lemon, plus more to taste

30g (1oz) tahini sauce

½ bunch of dill, roughly chopped

chilli flakes (Turkish Aleppo or Urfa), optional

salt and freshly ground black pepper

2 tbsp good olive oil, to serve

Cook the broad (fava) beans in well-salted water for 5 minutes, until tender, then drain and refresh in cold water and drain again. Shell the broad beans, leaving any tiny ones unpeeled (any smaller than a fingernail are good as they are). Reserve about 2 tablespoons of the tiniest beans to garnish.

Blend the beans with the garlic and lemon juice to a smooth paste. Season with salt and pepper and add a little splash of cold water to get the right consistency (think hummus). Check the seasoning again, adding more salt, pepper and lemon juice to taste, if necessary.

Spoon the paste onto a plate and serve topped with the reserved tiny broad beans and chopped dill. Sprinkle with the chilli flakes, if using, and serve drizzled with the olive oil.

Chilli Tomato Sauce

2 tbsp olive oil

2 cloves of garlic, finely chopped

3 tsp Aleppo chilli flakes (or use another, if necessary)

1 tsp unsmoked paprika

½ tsp salt, plus more to season

250g (9oz) cherry tomatoes, halved

juice of ½ lemon

freshly ground black pepper

Heat the olive oil in a pan over a moderate heat. Add the garlic, chilli flakes, paprika and salt and cook for 2 minutes. Add the tomatoes, lemon juice and a splash of water and cook for 10–15 minutes, or until the tomatoes have broken down to form a thick sauce. Season to taste, then leave to one side to cool.

Figs & Dates with Honey & Rosewater

4 tbsp runny honey

200g (7oz) mascarpone

½–1 tbsp rose water (not rose essence)

pinch of salt

8 ripe figs, cut with a deep cross

8 large pitted dates (such as medjool), split in half

50g (1¾oz) shelled pistachios, roughly chopped

petals of 1 rose, to decorate (optional)

Beat half the honey into the mascarpone. Add the rose water to taste and a pinch of salt and mix to combine.

Squeeze open the figs and dates and fill with the mascarpone mixture. Sprinkle over the pistachios and drizzle over the remaining honey to serve. Decorate with rose petals, if you have them.

AUTUMN

Green Apple, Thai Basil & Smoked Tofu with Shallots & Bird's Eye Chilli

2 cloves of garlic, finely chopped

1–3 Thai bird's eye chillies, thinly sliced, plus more to taste if needed

1 tbsp palm sugar (or use light brown soft sugar)

30g (1oz) roasted peanuts, lightly crushed

8 cherry tomatoes, halved

4 tsp fish sauce, plus more to taste if needed

juice of 1 lime, plus more to taste if needed

3 small shallots (or 1 large), very finely sliced

3 tart, firm green eating apples (such as Granny Smith)

2 little gem or 1 soft round lettuce, leaves separated

200g (7oz) smoked tofu, cut into bite-size pieces

1 small bunch of Thai basil (or use green or purple basil), leaves picked, and roughly chopped if large

salt and freshly ground black pepper

The apples and the smoked tofu are an excellent canvas for the dressing in this recipe, a dazzling combination of cherry tomatoes and peanuts, which are pestle-bashed in a mortar (or use a food processor, those little ones are often very handy, to bruise and break everything down just enough), then mixed through with the lime, fish sauce and shallots. Try to get hold of some Thai basil – it has a pungent, slightly spicy flavour redolent of liquorice and anise, quite different to standard sweet basil, which has more minty, grassy notes. Most larger supermarkets stock it these days, and (most likely of all) Asian grocery stores. This is a light lunch or supper dish that truly packs a punch.

In a food processor on pulse or in a mortar with a pestle, pound the garlic, chillies and sugar to a paste. Add 1 tablespoon of the peanuts and all the cherry tomatoes and pound or blitz a few times, just to bruise the tomatoes and release some juices. Stir in the fish sauce, lime juice and shallots and put to one side. Taste and adjust the seasoning with salt and pepper as necessary.

Fill a bowl with some salted water. Slice or shred the apples with a peeler or cut them into matchsticks (peel them, if you prefer), putting them straight into the bowl of salted water to prevent discolouration.

Drain the apples and transfer them to a large mixing bowl along with the lettuce leaves, tofu and basil. Add the dressing, adjusting with more lime, chilli or fish sauce, if necessary, and serve immediately with the remaining peanuts strewn over the top.

Spaghetti with Fried Breadcrumbs, Anchovies & Chilli

6 tbsp good olive oil

3 cloves of garlic, 1 slightly squashed, 2 finely chopped

40g (1½oz) fresh breadcrumbs

¼–½ tsp chilli flakes, or more to taste

about 1 x 100g (3½oz) can of anchovies, drained and roughly chopped

400g (14oz) spaghetti or linguine

½ small bunch of flat-leaf parsley, leaves picked and roughly chopped

zest of 1 unwaxed lemon

3 tbsp currants or raisins, soaked in warm water and drained

salt and freshly ground black pepper

Anchovies are one of my top five ingredients, without a doubt. They are a stealth ingredient that will boost many different dishes. What I especially love about them is their ability to bring unparalleled flavour to the simplest meals. There are few other ingredients in their league in this respect. With pasta; on vegetables, meat or fish; in sauces; or for breakfast even, on bread with thick slices of butter, deeply salty with a wonderfully powerful, savoury flavour – anchovies have a permanent place in my storecupboard. This is a southern-Italian inspired pasta dish – no parmesan necessary, because the fried, garlic-infused breadcrumbs do the job of finishing and flavouring the pasta.

Bring a large saucepan of salted water to a boil, ready for the pasta.

Heat 2 tablespoons of the olive oil in a small saucepan over a moderate heat. Add the squashed garlic clove and cook for 2 minutes to infuse the oil with flavour. Add the breadcrumbs and fry, stirring often, until crisp and golden brown. Transfer to a bowl lined with paper towels, discard the garlic, and set to one side.

Heat a further 2 tablespoons of the oil in a saucepan over a moderate heat. Add the chopped garlic and chilli flakes and gently heat for 1 minute until fragrant. Remove from the heat, add the anchovies and keep warm in the pan.

Boil the pasta according to the packet instructions, until al dente. When cooked, drain and mix the cooked pasta into the anchovies and garlic in the pan. Add half the breadcrumbs and mix well, seasoning with the chopped parsley, lemon zest, currants or raisins, remaining oil and any extra chilli, if you like. Season with salt and pepper to taste. Serve immediately topped with the remaining breadcrumbs.

Smoked Haddock with Curry Butter & Poached Egg

50g (1¾oz) unsalted butter

1 clove of garlic, finely chopped

1 tsp grated (shredded) fresh ginger

1 tbsp curry powder, mild or hot, as you like

zest of ½ unwaxed lemon, and a squeeze of juice to taste

pinch of salt, plus more to season

300g (10½oz) undyed smoked haddock fillets, skin removed and cut into 4 portions

150ml (5fl oz) whole milk

20ml (¾fl oz) white wine vinegar or cider vinegar

4 eggs

½ small bunch of flat-leaf parsley, leaves picked and finely chopped

freshly ground black pepper

warmed flat breads or hot buttered toast, to serve

Buy unsmoked haddock from a sustainable source – the yellow stuff is pointlessly and artificially dyed. With similar command, buy curry powder little and often from a stockist with a high turnover of spices and spice blends. Choose spices with a long sell-by date on them, a sign of most recent packaging. A good curry powder blend includes many different spices, so find one that suits your palate and tolerance for chilli. This simple dinner is as swift to assemble as it is delicious to eat. Serve with warm pita bread, good and puffy, to scoop and slather the spiced, buttery fish. A green salad wouldn't go amiss, or some steamed spinach or green beans.

Melt the butter in a saucepan over a medium heat. Mix in the garlic, ginger, curry powder, lemon zest and a pinch of salt. Simmer for 1 minute until fragrant. Remove from the heat and leave to one side.

Place the fish pieces in a frying pan and season with a little black pepper but no salt. Pour in the milk (it won't quite cover the fish), place it over a moderate heat and bring it up to a simmer. Poach the fish very gently, uncovered, for 7–10 minutes, until just about cooked through (it will keep cooking a bit in the residual heat), remove from the heat and cover to keep warm.

Bring a large saucepan of unsalted water to a boil over a high heat. Reduce the heat to medium and add the vinegar. Crack in the eggs and poach to your liking (a firm white, yolk still runny, is ideal and will take about 3 minutes). Using a slotted spoon, transfer the eggs to paper towels to drain. Keep warm.

Lift the fish pieces from the milk and place them in the pan with the melted butter. Gently fork into large flakes, season to taste and add a squeeze of lemon juice.

Place 1 poached egg in each of 4 bowls. Spoon over the melted, spiced butter and flaked fish, add the chopped parsley. Cut any remaining lemon into wedges and serve the fish with lemon wedges and warmed flat breads to scoop or hot buttered toast on the side.

Goan Green Chicken

1 small bunch of coriander (cilantro), leaves picked and roughly chopped

2 cloves of garlic, finely chopped

2–3 green chillies, finely sliced

1 tbsp grated (shredded) fresh ginger

2 tsp cumin seeds, toasted and ground

1 tsp ground turmeric

½ tsp ground green cardamom seeds

½ tsp ground cinnamon

good pinch each of ground cloves and ground star anise (or use ground fennel)

2 tbsp white wine vinegar or cider vinegar, plus 1 tsp to dress the cucumber

1 tbsp sunflower oil

½ tsp freshly ground black pepper

1 tsp salt, plus more to season

8 boneless chicken thighs, skins removed if you prefer

1 red onion, thinly sliced

2 tbsp poppy seeds

1 cucumber, peeled, deseeded and sliced

warmed chapati or flat breads, or steamed rice, to serve

This is a Goan dish, also known as cafreal chicken. It is a southern Indian curry preparation made with cardamom, cinnamon, ginger, chilli, coriander and vinegar, among other ingredients. Originally thought to be introduced to the Goan state by Portuguese and African soldiers during the Portuguese conquest in 1510, it has a fascinating and cosmopolitan lineage, indicative of the tumult at the time. Cooking, and the way recipes move across continents, different populations adapting them along the way, in times of both peace and war, offers a prophetic insight into our shared social history. I like to serve this curry with some chapati or paratha alongside a tangle of cucumbers, sharp with vinegar. If you wanted to make a vegetarian version, use some paneer cheese, cut into bite-size pieces, then marinated in the sauce before cooking in the oven until soft and charred in places – 25 minutes or so.

Blend half the coriander (cilantro) with the garlic, green chillies, ginger, ground spices, vinegar, oil, black pepper and salt to form a smooth sauce.

Put the chicken in a bowl and mix with the sauce to fully coat, then leave to marinate for at least 30 minutes or for up to 8 hours in the fridge.

Preheat the oven to 200°C/180°C fan/400°F/Gas Mark 6.

Line a baking tray with baking paper (to help ease the washing up) and spread out the marinated chicken over it. Scatter the onion and poppy seeds over the top. Roast the chicken for 25–35 minutes, until cooked through and beginning to char around the edges.

Meanwhile, season the sliced cucumber with the teaspoon of vinegar and a good amount of salt and put it in a serving bowl.

Using a carving knife and fork, shred or slice the cooked chicken, mixing it through with the onion and cooking juices, and sprinkle with the remaining coriander. Serve with the cucumber, and chapati, flat breads or rice at the table.

Yogurt & Leek Soup with Dill & Sunflower Seeds

60g (2¼oz) unsalted butter

1 tsp dried mint

2 tsp chilli flakes, plus more to taste

4 large leeks, thinly sliced

1 tbsp cornflour (cornstarch)
(or use plain/all-purpose flour)

2 eggs

500ml (17fl oz) natural yogurt

2 cloves of garlic, finely chopped

2 tsp cumin seeds, toasted
and ground

1 tsp coriander seeds, toasted
and ground

300–500ml (10½–17fl oz) vegetable
or chicken stock

2 tbsp sunflower seeds, lightly
toasted in 1 tbsp of good olive oil
or unsalted butter

½ small bunch of dill (or flat-leaf
parsley or mint), leaves picked and
finely chopped

salt and freshly ground black pepper

Yogurt soups are among some of my favourite to make, and I make a lot of soups. The key to making this style of soup is to not let the soup boil once you add the egg and yogurt mixture, heating it gently to cook out the egg and for the soup to thicken. Alchemy of the best sort. As is my wont and my way with soups, I think it is imperative that they are served with extra ingredients to add at the table per bowlful, alleviating any repetitive mouthfuls, bringing interest and texture right up to the very last spoonful. Here with brown butter laced with chilli and dried mint, toasted sunflower seeds and plenty of chopped dill, this soup and all its accompaniments are extraordinary.

Cook half the butter in a small saucepan over a moderate heat, until it foams and the sediments just start to turn golden brown, then pour into a bowl. Add half the dried mint and all the chilli flakes and keep warm.

Melt the remaining butter in a small saucepan over a moderate heat and add the leeks. Cook for 10–15 minutes, until very soft and sweet.

Meanwhile in another small bowl, mix the cornflour (cornstarch), eggs and yogurt together and leave to one side.

Add the chopped garlic and ground spices to the leeks and cook for a further 2 minutes, then add 200ml (7fl oz) of the stock and bring to a boil. Stir in the yogurt mixture, reduce the heat to moderate–low and very gently cook without boiling for 5 minutes, until rich and thick. Add more stock as necessary to thin the soup as much as you prefer. Check the seasoning, adding salt and pepper to taste.

Pour the soup into bowls and spoon the reserved brown butter over. At the table, sprinkle with sunflower seeds and the chopped dill and remaining dried mint, adding more chilli flakes to taste, if you wish.

Fig Leaf Pilaf with Aromatic Tomato Sauce & Toasted Almonds

200g (7oz) green lentils, puy or French

3 tbsp olive oil

2 onions, finely diced

1 tsp cumin seeds, toasted and ground

1 tsp coriander seeds, toasted and ground

4 cloves of garlic, finely sliced

1 tsp salt, plus more to season

400g (14oz) basmati rice, rinsed and drained

700ml (24fl oz) hot chicken or vegetable stock

3-5 fig leaves

20g (¾oz) unsalted butter or 20ml (½fl oz) olive oil

1 cinnamon stick or ½ tsp ground cinnamon

¼–½ tsp Turkish chilli flakes (preferably Aleppo or Urfa), to taste

1 x 400g (14oz) can of plum tomatoes

TO SERVE

crispy fried onions

40g (1½oz) flaked almonds, lightly toasted

1 lemon, cut into wedges

natural yogurt, seasoned with salt and finely crushed garlic

In northern Cyprus a few years back I spotted a woman gathering armfuls of fig leaves from the tree to the side of the restaurant kitchen where we'd ordered lunch. A short while later, plates began to arrive at the table; most intriguing of all was a whole baked halloumi cheese wrapped tightly in fig leaves, all blistered and charred from the wood-burning oven. It was a revelation to me: leaves peeled back, the cheese was soft and molten with a heavenly sweet, figgy, almond-like aroma. Used here as a seal, or cartouche, to the rice as it cooks, the fig leaves impart flavour that permeates the entire dish.

First, cook the lentils in well-salted, boiling water for 12–15 minutes, until tender. Drain and put to one side.

Heat the oil in a heavy-based saucepan with a tight-fitting lid and fry half the onions over a moderate heat for 10 minutes, until soft and translucent. Add the cumin and coriander, half the garlic and the 1 teaspoon of salt and cook for a further 2 minutes, until fragrant. Add the rice and cooked lentils and mix well to coat.

Add the hot stock, bring to a boil and stir well. Reduce the heat to a simmer and cover the rice as much as possible with the fig leaves, creating a seal. Cook the pilaf over a moderate–low heat for 15–20 minutes, until the stock is absorbed, and the rice cooked. Remove from the heat.

While the pilaf is cooking, make a tomato sauce. Heat the butter or olive oil in a saucepan over a moderate heat. Add the remaining onions and the cinnamon and cook for 10 minutes, until the onions are soft and translucent. Add the remaining garlic and the chilli flakes and cook for a further 2 minutes, until fragrant. Add the tomatoes, season and cook for 20–30 minutes, until the sauce is rich and thick. Keep warm.

To serve, at the table peel back the fig leaves and spoon the warm, aromatic tomato sauce over the rice. Add the crispy fried onions and toasted almonds and serve with the lemon wedges and seasoned yogurt on the side.

Tahini Baked Chicken on Hummus with Crispbread, Spring Onions & Whole Cloves of Garlic

12 cloves of garlic, 4 peeled and crushed, 8 peeled then left whole

2 tsp cumin seeds, toasted and ground

2 lemons

2 tsp paprika (sweet or hot, as you like)

120g (4¼oz) tahini

2 tbsp olive oil, plus more for the spring onions

8 boneless, skin-on chicken thighs

2 bunches of spring onions (scallions), cut into 3cm (1¼in) lengths

salt and freshly ground black pepper

200g (7oz) hummus (shop-bought or homemade), to serve

4 good-size crispbreads or crackers, broken into bite-size pieces

1 small bunch of flat-leaf parsley, leaves picked and roughly chopped

This recipe is based on *fatteh*, a dish from the southern Levant comprising toasted or stale flat breads layered with all number of flattering ingredients. I've used scrunched-up crispbreads, but you could just as well use good crackers or assertively toasted and torn pita breads. The tahini marinade does something ludicrously good to chicken skin when you bake it, super-crisp and golden. The hummus here (homemade or shop-bought, as you wish) is a non-negotiable bed on which to sink the accompanying fatteh ingredients. This is a recipe to take your time to plate, building flavour and texture to rousing delight.

In a large mixing bowl, whisk together the crushed garlic, cumin, juice of ½ lemon, paprika, half the tahini and all the olive oil. Season the chicken pieces with salt and plenty of black pepper, then add them to the marinade. Cover and refrigerate for at least 2 hours (up to 4 hours).

To make the tahini sauce, mix 100ml (3½fl oz) of water and the juice of another ½ lemon into the remaining tahini and whisk until smooth. Season to taste with salt and pepper. Set aside at room temperature.

Preheat the oven to 200°C/180°C fan/400°F/Gas Mark 6. Line 2 baking trays with baking paper. Put the marinated chicken on one of the lined baking trays and bake for 25–30 minutes, until the chicken is cooked through. Remove from the oven and rest it for at least 10 minutes before tearing or slicing into bite-size pieces.

Meanwhile, on the second lined baking tray, add the spring onions (scallions) and whole cloves of garlic. Add a good seasoning of salt and enough olive oil to coat. Cook for 15–20 minutes, until soft and charred.

To serve, choose a large, flat serving platter and begin building the dish, or make 4 individual servings. Smooth the hummus out all over the plate, then alternate with the chicken, crispbread, spring onion, whole roasted cloves of garlic and parsley. Spoon over the tahini sauce and serve immediately with the remaining lemon cut into wedges.

Cauliflower Korma with Cashew Nuts & Rose Water

30g (1oz) unsalted butter or ghee (or use sunflower oil)

2 tbsp sunflower oil

2 large onions, thinly sliced

100g (3½oz) unroasted cashews or almonds, plus a few more to serve

60g (2¼oz) raisins or sultanas

250ml (9fl oz) boiling water from a kettle

2 large cauliflowers, florets cut into bite-size pieces

1 tsp salt

4 cloves of garlic, finely chopped

1 tbsp grated (shredded) fresh ginger

2 tsp garam masala

½ tsp chilli powder or flakes

10 green cardamom pods, bashed a little

2 black cardamom pods (optional), bashed a little

1 cinnamon stick

2 bay leaves, scrunched a little

2 tsp rose water (optional, but worth it)

100g (3½oz) natural yogurt

This recipe is a series of simple steps to make what is essentially a complex curry. Soaking the nuts and raisins in the water, then blitzing with the onions and ground spices before adding the roasted cauliflower, whole spices and, finally, the yogurt, will give you a korma with the vaunted creamy, sweetly spiced and layered flavours that is so recognizable. With a slightly smoky, menthol flavour, black cardamom gives an earthy base note to the more aromatic spices. Rose water brings a delicate beauty to the dish. I buy mine in my local Turkish store, but it's widely available in supermarkets.

Preheat the oven to 180°C/160°C fan/350°F/Gas Mark 4.

Melt the butter and heat 1 tablespoon of the oil in a pan over a moderate heat. Add the onions and cook for 10–15 minutes, until very soft and starting to brown.

Meanwhile, soak half the nuts with half the raisins or sultanas in the boiled water for 10 minutes. Toss the cauliflower in the remaining oil and a ½ teaspoon of the salt, transfer to a baking tray and roast for 30 minutes, until tender. Add the remaining nuts 5 minutes before the end of the roasting time.

Add the garlic and ginger to the onions and cook for a further 2 minutes, until fragrant, then stir in half the garam masala and all the chilli and cook for 1 minute.

Place the onion mixture in a blender with the soaked nuts and raisins (including the liquid) and the remaining ½ teaspoon of salt. Blitz to form a thick sauce, then return the sauce to the pan and add the whole spices and the bay. Bring to a simmer over a high heat, then reduce the heat to let the sauce simmer gently while the cauliflower is roasting. Do not allow the sauce to boil.

When the cauliflower is roasted, stir it into the sauce, keeping a few uncoated bits to serve on top, then stir in the rose water and yogurt and gently warm through.

Serve the korma topped with the reserved cauliflower and sprinkled with the remaining garam masala, a few extra nuts and the remaining raisins.

Tuna, Egg & Grilled Green Peppers with Capers & Olives Stuffed in a Roll

4 eggs

2 green (bell) peppers, halved and deseeded

2 large tomatoes

150g (5½oz) tuna in oil, drained weight

30g (1oz) capers (desalinated, if necessary), rinsed, drained and roughly chopped

30g (1oz) green olives, pitted and roughly chopped

3 tbsp olive oil

juice of ½ lemon

salt and freshly ground black pepper

4 crusty rolls, or 1 large baguette cut into 4, to serve

½ bunch of flat-leaf parsley, leaves picked and roughly chopped, to serve

I'm a firm believer that if you put enough effort into the contents of a sandwich, such as this one, a sandwich then absolutely counts as a meal. Portable, of course, and with enough substance to sate even the biggest of appetites, sandwiches are often also mercifully speedy to assemble. If in doubt, as recipes go, sandwiches and variations of, are among some of the easiest recipes to upscale. Grilling (broiling) the (bell) peppers – and I like to use green ones for this recipe, enjoying their grassy, slightly bitter flavour – is worth the effort, along with the tomato, giving you luscious fat fingers of grilled pepper, a superglue for the hard-boiled eggs and tuna.

Put the eggs in a saucepan in one layer and cover with cold water. Bring to a boil and simmer for 6 minutes. Remove from the heat, drain and run the eggs under cold water until cool enough to peel. Peel and set aside.

Preheat the grill (broiler) to very hot.

Place the (bell) peppers, cut sides downward, and the tomatoes on a baking tray and grill (broil) for 8–10 minutes, until the skins begin to split and blacken. Turn everything over and grill for a further 5 minutes or so, until soft and luscious. Remove from the grill and allow to cool before peeling and discarding the skins from both the tomatoes and the peppers. Roughly cut the flesh into wide slices and put to one side in a bowl, seasoning with a bit of salt and black pepper.

Halve the eggs and add them to the bowl, then add the tuna, capers and olives to the peppers and tomatoes. Gently mix the lot together with the oil and lemon juice. Season well with salt and pepper.

Split the rolls or baguette pieces in half and fill with the tuna and egg mixture and grilled vegetables. Sprinkle with parsley to serve.

Nasi Goreng

FOR THE NASI GORENG

400g (14oz) jasmine rice or other long grain rice

3 tbsp sunflower oil

2 cloves of garlic, finely chopped

4 tbsp kecap manis (or use a mixture of dark soy sauce and brown sugar)

1 tbsp light soy sauce

1 bunch of spring onions (scallions), thinly sliced

2 eggs, beaten

FOR THE SAMBAL

100ml (3½fl oz) sunflower oil

100g (3½oz) red Thai bird's eye chillies, destemmed

4 cloves of garlic, roughly chopped

100g (3½oz) shallots, roughly diced

1 tsp shrimp paste (terasi) or Thai fish sauce, plus more to taste

juice of 1 lime

FOR THE TOPPINGS (OPTIONAL)

½ cucumber, sliced

1 handful of crispy fried shallots

1 handful of roughly chopped salted roasted peanuts

Nasi goreng is an Indonesian dish of fried rice. Crucial to the mixture is the use of kecap manis and shrimp paste. Widely available in supermarkets, kecap manis is ubiquitous in much Indonesian cooking, bringing a rounded, sweet and salty flavour. Shrimp paste, called *terasi* in Indonesian (although there are many other regional names throughout southeast Asia for fermented fish or shrimp pastes and sauces), might be trickier to come by unless you have a specialist shop, but it is readily available online. You could use fish sauce, *nam pla*, which is easily available, in lieu of the terasi, but it will lack in texture and deeply pungent profile. Making the sambal to mix through the fried rice and to serve as a condiment on the side elevates achievable mid-week cookery to something really quite special. To serve with the nasi goreng, I think thinly sliced cucumber and a handful each of crispy fried shallots (shop-bought, they offer an entirely addictive crunch to many different dishes) and salted peanuts gives a flawless finish.

For the nasi goreng, first boil the rice in 800ml (28fl oz) of water in a covered pan for 15–20 minutes, until tender. Rest for 5 minutes, then fluff with a fork and spread on a tray to cool for at least 30 minutes.

While the rice is cooling, make the sambal. Heat the oil in a wok or deep, cast-iron frying pan over a high heat and fry the chillies for 2 minutes, until darkened in colour, then remove with a slotted spoon and put to one side. Add the garlic and shallots to the hot oil in the pan and fry for 3–5 minutes, until beginning to brown and softened, then remove and add to the chillies. Take the pan off the heat, but leave the oil in it to use later.

Transfer the fried chillies, garlic and shallots to a blender or food processor, add the shrimp paste and blitz to a coarse purée.

Return the purée to the wok and cook in the oil over a low heat for 2 minutes, until bubbling and thick, then add the lime juice, seasoning to taste with more shrimp paste or fish sauce if you like, then put the whole lot into a bowl to serve (or a sealed jar if you're planning to keep it – it will keep for a couple of weeks in the fridge).

Finish the nasi goreng. Heat the 3 tablespoons of oil in a wok over a high heat, then add the garlic and fry for 2–3 minutes, until golden and crisp. Add the cooled rice, breaking up any clumps as you go, and fry until fully heated through (about 3–5 minutes), then stir in the kecap manis, soy sauce, spring onions (scallions) and 4 tablespoons of the sambal mixture.

Push the rice up the sides of the wok and pour in the beaten egg. Once the egg has just begun to set in the base of the wok, stir briskly to break it up and mix it into the rice. Stir-fry the lot for another 1 minute or so, then serve topped with the cucumber, crispy shallots and peanuts, if using. Serve the remaining sambal on the side.

Tray-baked Potatoes with Mushrooms & Chestnuts & a Slosh of Sherry

1kg (2lb 4oz) medium–small potatoes, diced or sliced bite-size if large

7 large cloves of garlic, 4 unpeeled and smashed, 3 peeled and finely sliced

4 tbsp good olive oil, plus more to serve

3 good thyme sprigs, leaves picked

500g (1lb 2oz) chestnut or button mushrooms, sliced

3 tbsp dry or medium sherry

75g (2½oz) chestnuts, roughly chopped

½ small bunch of flat-leaf parsley, finely chopped

100g (3½oz) manchego cheese or parmesan

salt and freshly ground black pepper

Waxy potatoes, mushrooms and chestnuts, these are three ingredients that sit very well together on a plate. Add a good slosh of sherry and you have a middle-of-the-week meal that is as impressive as it is easy. I like chestnut mushrooms, preferring them over bog-standard button. Although they are both cultivated and both something of a grocery staple, the freckled chestnuts with dark brown gills, I think, deliver more flavour. By all means use fat slices of portabella mushrooms, if you prefer – indeed use any mushrooms, and a mixture, yes, would be fabulous. I might serve this with some crusty bread or bruschetta on the side to mop up the juices, if I feel especially hungry.

Preheat the oven to 220°C/200°C fan/425°F/Gas Mark 7. Line a baking tray with baking paper.

Spread the potatoes out onto the lined tray along with the 4 smashed cloves of garlic, the olive oil and the thyme, and season with salt and pepper. Roast for 15–20 minutes, until the potatoes are softened but not yet fully cooked through.

Add the mushrooms, sliced garlic and sherry to the potatoes, mixing together to distribute evenly, and cook for a further 20–25 minutes, until the mushrooms and potatoes are cooked through and have taken on some colour. Remove from the oven and add the chestnuts and parsley, mixing well. Check the seasoning, adding more salt and pepper, if you like.

Using a potato peeler, shave the manchego or parmesan over the mushrooms and potatoes, sprinkle with more oil if you like, and serve.

Butter Beans with Spinach, Tarragon, Bacon & Cream

30g (1oz) unsalted butter

3 cloves of garlic, finely chopped (plus another whole clove for the toast)

200ml (7fl oz) double (heavy) cream

2 x 400g (14oz) cans of butter (lima) or cannellini beans, drained and rinsed

big pinch of ground nutmeg

100g (3½oz) baby spinach leaves

¼ small bunch of tarragon, leaves picked and roughly chopped

6 rashers of streaky bacon or pancetta, cut into lardon cubes

salt and freshly ground black pepper

4 slices of good bread, toasted and rubbed with garlic, to serve

juice of ½ lemon (optional), to serve

Use streaky bacon for this recipe. Thinly sliced it will exude its fat into the butter as it cooks and crisps in the pan. You could use pancetta, if you prefer. You must then absolutely make use of this bacon fat to marble and dress the creamy tarragon beans. It will boost the seasoning and give more pep to the finished dish. This is midweek cookery with little more than a can of beans, some bacon and spinach – and thick slices of toast, of course.

Melt half the butter in a medium saucepan over a moderate heat and add the chopped garlic. Fry for 2 minutes, until the garlic is just beginning to turn golden brown. Add the cream, beans and nutmeg, stirring to combine. Season well with salt and plenty of freshly ground black pepper. When the mixture begins to bubble up, reduce the heat to moderate–low and simmer, stirring occasionally, for at least 5 minutes, until the cream has thickened a little. Add the spinach and cook for 2–3 minutes, until just wilted, then add the tarragon and mix well.

If you would like the mixture to be more stew-like, mash some of the beans using a fork for a thicker consistency.

Melt the remaining butter in a cast-iron frying pan over a moderate heat. Add the bacon and fry for 3–5 minutes, until crisp and golden.

To serve, put a slice of toast on each plate, add the beans and top with the bacon, including any of the molten, buttery, bacon fat from the frying pan. Lots of black pepper is good, and you might like to add a little lemon juice to the beans, too.

Tahini with Pear, Walnuts, Honey & Greek Yogurt

500g (1lb 2oz) Greek yogurt

2 ripe pears, peeled, cored and sliced

2 tbsp light tahini

3 tbsp runny honey

30g (1oz) walnuts (or hazelnuts, almonds or pistachios), roughly chopped

1 tbsp sesame seeds (black or white)

Hands down, this is a very, very quick pudding. Tahini paste, made from sesame kernels ground to form an oily paste, is a staple in my kitchen and I often have at least a couple of different jars on the go. Smooth, nutty and rich, brands do vary considerably – more robust, wholegrain versions, for example, are most likely blended with the husks intact. Broadly speaking, I like tahini from Middle Eastern countries over Greek, Turkish or Cypriot brands, preferring the looser, oilier texture and more rounded, soft taste. Some varieties can be a bit too claggy in the mouth and taste a good deal more bitter than others. An easy way to remedy any thicker, more stodgy varieties is to mix the paste with a little cold water until you get your desired, creamy texture. For this recipe, choose ripe pears that glisten and drip as you slice into them. Juicy and sweet, they are the perfect foil for the other ingredients.

Divide the yogurt between 4 bowls, top with the sliced pear, drizzle with the tahini and honey and scatter with the nuts and sesame seeds. Job done.

Roasted Apples with Cider, Butter & Brown Sugar

4 large eating apples (such as russet)

30g (1oz) unsalted butter, softened, plus more for greasing

20g (¾oz) rolled oats

50g (1¾oz) light brown soft sugar

½ tsp ground cinnamon or big pinch of freshly grated (shredded) nutmeg

250ml (9fl oz) cider

crème fraîche, Greek yogurt, cream or ice cream, to serve

I'm not so keen on the baked apples of my childhood, all wrinkly skin and stuffed with a few forlorn raisins. This version, however, is quite another thing. Slicing the tops off the apples and also removing the core to plug, will ensure that the apples don't split and explode in the oven. If you're feeling especially dextrous, with a sharp knife you can cut a pretty pattern on the lid of the apple, as this should then furl and cook attractively in the oven. Cooked with cider, oats, brown sugar and butter, these apples blister and bake as usual, but also come with a buttery, cidery, caramel sauce to spoon over as the apples exit the oven. Midweek pudding cookery – same-same, but different.

Preheat the oven to 190°C/170°C fan/375°F/Gas Mark 5.

Slice a thin layer off the top of each apple and remove the core to create a cavity, but leaving about 2cm (¾in) in the base (in other words, don't go all the way through the apple). This will help to stop the apples from splitting when they cook. Put the apples snugly in a lightly greased baking dish.

In a small bowl, mix together the butter, oats, sugar and spice. Fill the cavity in each apple with the oat mixture and top each with a lid.

Pour the cider into the dish around the apples and cover the dish loosely with foil. Bake for 20 minutes, then remove the foil and bake for a further 10–15 minutes, until you can pierce a knife through each apple with no resistance. Remove from the oven and cool for at least 5–10 minutes before serving.

Koshari Rice with Butternut Squash & Sunflower Seed Dukkah

1 butternut squash (about 600g/
1lb 5oz), peeled, quartered
lengthways and deseeded

4 tbsp olive oil

1 tsp ground cumin

1 tsp ground coriander

1 large onion, finely diced

185g (6½oz) wheat vermicelli
or spaghetti, broken into about
5cm (2in) pieces

185g (6½oz) long grain rice, rinsed
and drained in cold water

2 bay leaves, scrunched a little

1 cinnamon stick

1 tsp salt, plus more to season

800ml (28fl oz) hot chicken or
vegetable stock or water

freshly ground black pepper

1 large bunch of flat-leaf parsley,
finely chopped, to serve

natural yogurt, seasoned with salt
and ½ clove of garlic, to serve

chilli flakes or chilli sauce, to serve

FOR THE DUKKAH

100g (3½oz) sunflower seeds

2 tbsp coriander seeds

2 tbsp cumin seeds

3 tbsp sesame seeds (black
or white)

Koshari rice is an Egyptian method of cooking rice along with lentils and small pasta. This thrifty and wholesome dish is one of my go-to recipes and is also one of my children's favourites; omitting lentils in this version and using wheat vermicelli to toast in the buttery onion before adding the stock, I love how the vermicelli cooks to a tangle in among the rice. Use butternut squash or any other squash or pumpkin you like – in autumn, the shops should all be toppling under the weight of these monstrous beauties.

Preheat the oven to 200°C/180°C fan/400°F/Gas Mark 6.

Put the butternut squash into a roasting tin, add half the olive oil, a good seasoning of salt, a good grinding of black pepper and the ground cumin and coriander and mix well to coat. Cover the tin tightly with foil and roast the squash for about 25–30 minutes, until tender, uncovering for the last 5 minutes so that it colours a bit.

Meanwhile, heat the remaining oil in a heavy-based casserole over a moderate heat. Add the onion and fry for 10–12 minutes, until soft, translucent and just beginning to turn a little brown.

Add the pasta and toast in the pan for about 3 minutes, until lightly coloured. Add the rice, bay leaves and cinnamon and stir to coat for another 1 minute. Add the teaspoon of salt and all of the hot stock or water, reduce the heat and simmer, covered, for 15–20 minutes, until the rice and pasta are cooked through and all the liquid has been absorbed.

While the rice is cooking, make the dukkah. Dry fry all the seeds in a cast-iron frying pan for 2–3 minutes, until just bronzed and becoming very fragrant. Use a pestle and mortar or food processor (or use a sturdy bowl and the end of a rolling pin) to grind the seeds very coarsely, then season to taste with salt and pepper.

To serve, tip the rice and pasta into a wide serving dish and top with the roasted squash. Scatter with the parsley and dukkah and serve with the seasoned yogurt and a sprinkling of chilli flakes or drizzle of chilli sauce.

Roast Squash with Chickpeas, Garam Masala & Pumpkin Seeds

800g (1lb 12oz) butternut squash or other squash, peeled if necessary, and cut into wedges

2 red onions, cut into wedges

5 tbsp sunflower oil

1 tbsp garam masala

50g (1¾oz) pumpkin seeds

2 x 400g (14oz) cans of chickpeas (garbanzos), drained and rinsed

½–1 tsp chilli flakes or powder, or to taste

salt and freshly ground black pepper

1 small bunch of coriander (cilantro), leaves picked and roughly chopped, to serve

FOR THE DRESSING

3 tbsp sunflower oil

2 cloves of garlic, finely chopped

1 tbsp grated (shredded) fresh ginger

1 tsp cumin seeds

1 tsp ground turmeric

1 tsp mustard seeds

1 tsp runny honey or light brown soft sugar, to taste

zest and juice of 1 unwaxed lemon

I serve this tray of baked squash and chickpeas (garbanzos) as a midweek meal with some toasted flat bread or pita to mop up all the juices. Some squash roast beautifully with their skins on – Crown Prince squashes a case in point. A good rule of thumb, though, is the smaller the squash, the thinner the skin and the more likely you might want to eat it. Whether you end up eating the roasted skin or you don't, I do think it's often better to roast squash and pumpkins as wedges with their skins on, imparting flavour, but also to help the structure of the fruit as it cooks. Garam masala is a crucial spice blend for me; it is good used at the beginning to add tone and depth, but also at the end for vibrancy.

Preheat the oven to 220°C/200°C fan/425°F/Gas Mark 7.

Place the squash on a baking tray along with the onion wedges. Sprinkle over 3 tablespoons of the oil and the garam masala and season with salt and plenty of freshly ground black pepper to taste. Bake for about 20–25 minutes, then add the pumpkin seeds and bake for a further 10 minutes, until the squash is tender. Remove from the oven and put to one side.

Place the chickpeas (garbanzos) on a separate baking tray with the remaining oil and the chilli flakes or powder. Season to taste with plenty of salt and pepper and mix well to coat the chickpeas. Bake for 8–10 minutes, until the chickpeas begin to sizzle and some turn brown and crisp. Remove from the oven and put to one side.

To make the dressing, heat the oil in a small saucepan over a moderate heat. Add the garlic, ginger, cumin, turmeric, mustard seeds and honey or sugar and cook for 1 minute, until fragrant. Add the lemon juice and season with salt to taste.

To serve, add the squash and chickpeas to a large serving dish or individual plates, scraping up all the cooking juices as you do so. Add the chopped coriander and spoon over the dressing.

Pav Bhaji

60g (2¼oz) ghee or unsalted butter or 60ml (2fl oz) sunflower oil, plus more to serve

1 red onion, finely diced

good pinch of salt

1 lemon, halved

1 tbsp grated (shredded) fresh ginger

2 cloves of garlic, finely chopped

1 tbsp garam masala

2 tsp hot curry powder

1 x 200g (7oz) can of chopped tomatoes or 200g (7oz) passata

200g (7oz) potatoes, peeled and coarsely grated (shredded)

2 carrots, peeled and coarsely grated (shredded)

½ cauliflower, very finely chopped

4 soft bread rolls, split in half

2 green chillies, finely sliced

1 small bunch of coriander (cilantro), leaves picked and roughly chopped

This is an Indian street-food dish – it is extremely popular and for very good reason. It is inexpensive to make, but my one stipulation would be to invest in a can of ghee. Frying the bread (the *pav*) in a bit of ghee until toasted and golden brown will give you an exceptional pav bhaji. Butter will do, but won't have the toasted, nutty flavour that makes ghee such an incredible and delicious fat to cook with. The rest of the ingredients cost next to nothing, so allow yourself this one little extravagance. Use the ghee as you would sunflower oil – it has a high smoking point and will not burn like butter can. This curry is a fairly simple one, loaded onto the fried bun all heaped with the onion, chilli and coriander with lots of lemon to squeeze.

Heat half the ghee, butter or oil in a saucepan over a moderate heat. Add half the onion and cook for about 10 minutes, until softened.

While the onions are cooking, in a small dish, add the remaining onion and mix in a good pinch of salt. Leave for 5 minutes before rinsing in cold water and draining well. Squeeze the juice of ½ lemon over the onion and leave to one side.

Add the ginger, garlic, garam masala and curry powder to the softened onions in the pan and cook for a further 1 minute, then add the tomatoes, potatoes, carrots and cauliflower along with 300ml (10½fl oz) of water. Bring to a boil, cover, reduce the heat to a simmer and cook for 20–25 minutes, until the vegetables are tender and the sauce is rich and thick. Remove from the heat and keep warm.

Add the remaining ghee, butter or oil to a large, cast-iron frying pan (skillet) over a moderate heat. Add the halved buns, cut sides downward, and toast until golden brown.

To serve, top the split, toasted rolls with the curry (an extra knob of ghee is great here) and serve with the macerated onion, sliced green chilli, chopped coriander (cilantro) and remaining lemon cut into wedges.

Speedy, Cheaty Soufflé

30g (1oz) parmesan, grated (shredded)

90g unsalted butter, plus more for greasing

50g (1¾oz) plain (all-purpose) flour

500ml (17fl oz) whole milk

½ tsp salt, plus more to season

about ⅛ nutmeg, grated (shredded)

6 eggs, well beaten

200g (7oz) gruyère or cheddar cheese, coarsely grated (shredded)

½ small bunch flat-leaf parsley or chives, finely chopped

freshly ground black pepper, to taste

I didn't know what to call this recipe. Cheat suggests not making a recipe correctly, cutting corners and the like, but this recipe is not that. This recipe is clever. By doing away with using one of those individual soufflé dishes and opting instead for a wide, low gratin dish, all dusted with cheese, you get a soufflé without the vaunted height, but still with a tender wobble and tempting – all the more to eat you with – crust. Serve the soufflé, straight out of the oven, with a big, green salad dressed in a good vinaigrette made with some Dijon mustard, red wine vinegar, olive oil and salt and pepper.

Preheat the oven to 200°C/180°C fan/400°F/Gas Mark 6. Grease a 1.5 litre (52fl oz) gratin dish with butter.

Sprinkle the greased gratin dish with half the parmesan and put to one side.

Melt the butter in a saucepan over a moderate heat, then whisk in the flour and cook for 20 seconds, until it bubbles a little. Vigorously whisk in the milk, then cook, whisking all the while (and making sure you get into the corners of the bottom of the pan), for 3–5 minutes, until the mixture comes to a boil.

Keep whisking over a low heat for a further 2 minutes, until the mixture thickens, then remove from the heat and stir in the ½ teaspoon of salt, the nutmeg and a generous amount of pepper. Allow to cool for about 10 minutes. Mix the beaten eggs into the white sauce along with the grated (shredded) gruyère or cheddar cheese and the herbs and mix well.

Pour the mixture into the buttered gratin dish and sprinkle with the remaining parmesan. Bake for 30–40 minutes, or until well puffed and nicely browned on top. Remove from the oven and serve immediately.

Cavolo Nero Polenta Soup

3 tbsp good olive oil, plus more to serve

1 onion, finely diced

1 carrot, peeled and finely diced

1 celery stick, finely diced

6 sage leaves, finely chopped, or 2 good rosemary sprigs, leaves picked and finely chopped

3 cloves of garlic, finely chopped

500g (1lb 2oz) cavolo nero, tough middle stalks discarded, leaves sliced into ribbons

1 litre (35fl oz) hot chicken or vegetable stock or water

80g (2¾oz) fine polenta

1 x 400g (14oz) can of borlotti or cannellini beans, drained and rinsed

juice of ½ lemon, or to taste

salt and freshly ground black pepper

parmesan, grated (shredded), to serve

You can rely on this sort of soup to feed you well and to make you feel rooted to the essentials of what it is to be a good cook. Take a slow, steady start with the crucial trio of onions, carrot and celery cooked down to a soft, sweet base (a *soffritto*), then hit it with the remaining ingredients, layer, after layer, after layer. You can't rush a good soup. You'll need good olive oil for this recipe, because you will want to dress the finished soup with a slick of it – the heat will send the oil's scent up and into your face as you inhale. Cavolo nero is wonderful cooked down like this. You're almost twice cooking these deep green and furrowed leaves – first in with the soffritto, then again in the liquid when you add the stock. The polenta thickens the soup. A large chunk of parmesan, grated (shredded) all over to finish, is essential.

Heat the oil in a heavy-based saucepan over a moderate heat. Add the onion, carrot and celery and cook for 10 minutes, until the onion is soft and translucent. Add the herbs and the garlic and cook for a further 2 minutes, until fragrant. Add the cavolo nero and cook for 8–10 minutes, until the leaves are well wilted and reduced in size.

Add the stock or water and season to taste with salt and plenty of freshly ground black pepper, then gently simmer for 15 minutes, until the cavolo nero is completely tender. Finally, add the polenta in a thin, steady stream, stirring all the time so it mixes in well among the cavolo nero and other vegetables.

Reduce the heat slightly to moderate–low and simmer until the polenta is fully cooked out (about another 15–20 minutes). Add a little more liquid if the soup gets too thick during this time. About 2 minutes towards the end of the cooking time, add the beans to warm through. Simmer until the flavours are melded and the soup tastes good. Check the seasoning, adding more salt and pepper, as necessary, and the lemon juice to taste.

Serve in warmed bowls with plenty of parmesan grated (shredded) on top and a good slug of olive oil.

Root Vegetables as Fritters & Slaw with Sausage & Mustard

150g (5½oz) parsnip, coarsely grated (shredded)

150g (5½oz) carrot or beetroot, peeled and coarsely grated (shredded)

1 large red onion, very thinly sliced

150g (5½oz) white or green cabbage, shredded

big pinch of salt, plus more to season

200g (7oz) potatoes, peeled and coarsely grated (shredded)

2 eggs, beaten

4 tbsp plain (all-purpose) flour

sunflower oil, for frying

100g (3½oz) crème fraîche, sour cream or Greek yogurt

1 tsp Dijon mustard, plus more to serve

salt and freshly ground black pepper

8 sausages, cooked, to serve

This recipe uses the same quantity of grated (shredded) and sliced vegetables in two very different ways. One portion is mixed through with eggs and a little flour and fried as a fritter, while the other portion is made into a slaw with crème fraîche and mustard. I suggest serving this with a couple of good sausages – pork or vegetarian, as you wish. I am never without a pot of Dijon mustard on the shelf at home, and I especially like those hefty earthenware jars with the waxy red seals – so big, so deep and opaque is the pot, you feel as if you'll never get to the end of it and, then, quite unexpectedly, you do.

Mix the parsnip, carrot (or beetroot), onion and cabbage together in a mixing bowl and add the big pinch of salt. Squeeze as much liquid out of the vegetables as you can, then divide into two equal portions.

Add the potatoes, eggs and flour to one portion, seasoning with salt and pepper. Mix well and press the grated (shredded) vegetables into 8 thin, equal-size patties (rostis).

Heat a couple of tablespoons of oil in a non-stick or cast-iron frying pan (skillet) over a moderate heat. Working in batches, fry the patties for about 3 minutes on each side, until crisp and golden all over. Put the fried patties on a plate lined with paper towels and keep somewhere warm while you cook the remaining batches.

Meanwhile, mix the remaining portions of vegetables with the crème fraîche and mustard. Season to taste with salt and pepper and put to one side.

To serve, put two rostis on each plate, pile on some of the slaw, then add sausages and some good mustard on the side.

Dan Dan Noodles

2 tbsp sunflower oil

200g (7oz) minced (ground) pork or beef

50g (1¾oz) pickled mustard greens, finely chopped or use another Chinese pickle or kimchi

½ bunch of spring onions (scallions), thinly sliced, white and green parts separated

1 tsp chilli flakes

2 tsp ground Sichuan peppercorns

1 tbsp Shaoxing rice wine or dry sherry

100ml (3½fl oz) light soy sauce

100ml (3½fl oz) chilli oil (shop-bought or homemade, see page 272), more to taste if you really like it hot

2 tbsp black rice vinegar

1 tsp caster (superfine) sugar, or to taste

350g (12oz) thin wheat noodles

You should serve these noodles hot as hell – so hot with the chilli oil and numbing with the Sichuan pepper as to make your top lip sweat a little... a lot. I have eaten these in Chengdu in China, in a small roadside restaurant famous for making the spiciest dan dan noodles in all of Sichuan. The chef brought the dish out to the table himself and, I won't lie, with a brazen and expectant grin on his face. He watched as we, the *laowai* (foreigner), readied ourselves to eat. If there had been a bath of yogurt or cream next to me that day, I would have jumped in headfirst. I couldn't hack it, the heat was too fierce and the chilli oil clung to the insides of my mouth with unnerving attack. Two mouthfuls in, I gave up. My husband Matt, however, ploughed on, sweating. All of us laughing – me with baby Grace on my hip, my stepmother Lily and my father – all of us clapping him on. We left heroes. Well, Matt did, but we all basked in his glory. As we left, the chef told my stepmother he had never before had a laowai able to complete the challenge.

Heat the sunflower oil in a wok or deep frying pan over a high heat and add the minced (ground) meat. In batches, stir-fry the mince for 5–8 minutes per batch, until it's beginning to brown and you have good caramelization.

Add the pickled vegetables, the white parts of the spring onions (scallions), the chilli flakes and the Sichuan pepper. Stir-fry for a further 5 minutes, until the mince begins to dry and crisp. Add the rice wine and 1 tablespoon of the soy sauce and cook for 5 minutes, until the mince begins to dry and crisp up again. Remove from the heat and put to one side.

Whisk together the remaining soy sauce with half the chilli oil, the vinegar and the sugar to taste.

Cook the noodles according to the packet instructions, then drain, reserving a ladleful of the cooking water.

Add the sauce to the noodles, loosening with a spoonful of the reserved cooking water, if necessary, and divide the noodles between the serving bowls. Top each bowl with the stir-fried mince, a sprinkling of the chopped green spring onion, and add more chilli oil to taste.

Green Lentils, Mint, Sherry Vinegar & Dates with Goat Cheese

400g (14oz) green or brown lentils

2 bay leaves, scrunched a little

8 cloves of garlic, 4 peeled then left whole, 4 finely chopped

½ tsp salt, plus more to season

80ml (2½fl oz) olive oil

60g (2¼oz) pitted dates, very finely chopped

2–3 tbsp sherry vinegar or red wine vinegar

freshly ground black pepper, to taste

1 small bunch of mint, leaves picked and roughly chopped, to serve

200g (7oz) soft goat cheese, sliced into rounds or bite-size pieces (or use good feta), to serve

Green lentils – French, specifically those grown in the Puy region of central France; or Italian, the Castelluccio variety from Umbria – are my favourite lentils to use in salads or dishes where you want the lentil to hold its form and not disintegrate in the cooking liquid. Also, key to using these lentils to their best potential is to dress them while still warm so they absorb the dressing, drinking up the flavours as they cool. Speaking of which, this is a perky dressing and suits the earthy, minerally lentils very well. Quite a bit of garlic here, both to cook the lentils and also in the dressing, moderated as it is with chopped dates and good sherry vinegar, then showered with invigorating mint. Serve this salad just warm or at room temperature, although cold will also be fine.

Rinse the lentils and put them in a saucepan with the bay leaves and the whole cloves of garlic and cover with 1 litre (35fl oz) of cold water. Bring to a boil, skim off any froth that surfaces, then simmer, covered, for 30–40 minutes, until the lentils are cooked through but still with slight resistance. Add the ½ teaspoon of salt 5 minutes before the end of the cooking time. Remove from the heat, drain and set to one side, discarding the bay leaves and whole cloves of garlic, which will have both done their work.

Immediately make a dressing. Heat the oil in a saucepan over a moderate heat. Add the chopped garlic and cook for 2–3 minutes, until the garlic is just beginning to turn golden brown. Remove from the heat and stir in the dates and the vinegar, adding salt and pepper to taste.

Stir the dressing through the still-warm lentils, then add the chopped mint and the goat cheese to serve.

Buckwheat Noodles with Avocado, Edamame & Walnut Pesto

1 large bunch of basil, leaves picked

2 cloves of garlic, finely chopped

50g (1¾oz) walnuts, roughly chopped

40g (1½oz) parmesan, grated (shredded)

50ml (1¾fl oz) good olive oil, plus more for the noodles and to serve

350g (12oz) buckwheat or soba noodles

200g (7oz) chard, stalks and leaves chopped

100g (3½oz) podded edamame beans (fresh or frozen)

zest and juice of 1 lemon

50g (1¾oz) rocket (arugula), roughly chopped

2 avocados, stoned, peeled and cut into small cubes

salt and freshly ground black pepper

I'm a big fan of buckwheat or soba noodles. From the buckwheat seed, and not a grain as the name suggests, buckwheat is gluten free and a reliably useful and versatile ingredient. Ground as a flour to make noodles or pasta, it has an intensely nutty flavour, which suits cold dishes such as this salad very well. While noodles might make you think more of Asia than Italy, as the pesto here might prompt, buckwheat pasta is also used in Italian cooking. Buckwheat, walnut pesto, avocado, chard and edamame – these are all flavours that work very well together, all earthy and nutty. You'll find buckwheat or soba noodles easily enough to make this recipe, or you could look for more elusive Italian buckwheat pasta varieties.

Blend or use a pestle and mortar to mix the basil, garlic, walnuts and parmesan to a coarse paste, then pulse or pound while slowly adding the olive oil to form a smooth sauce. Season well with salt and pepper.

Bring a large saucepan of unsalted water to a boil. Cook the noodles according to the packet instructions (about 4–5 minutes), then drain and rinse under cold water and toss them with 2 tablespoons of olive oil.

Fill the saucepan back up with well-salted water and bring to a boil. Add the chard stalks, then the leaves and finally the edamame. Cook for 3–4 minutes, until tender. Drain well and spread out on a plate to cool quickly.

To serve, in a large bowl or a wide platter, add the noodles, chard and edamame and stir through with the pesto (you can leave some to serve on the side, if you wish). Add the lemon zest and juice, then the rocket (arugula) and avocado and check the seasoning, adding more salt and pepper to taste.

Chipotle with Quinoa & Root Vegetables, Sour Cream & Lime

200g (7oz) quinoa

about 5 tbsp sunflower or olive oil

zest and juice of 1 unwaxed lime

500g (1lb 2oz) assorted root vegetables (carrots, beetroot, parsnips or sweet potatoes), peeled and cut into bite-size pieces

40g (1½oz) pumpkin seeds

1 red onion, roughly diced

2–4 tbsp chipotle paste, to taste

100g (3½oz) kale, stalks discarded, leaves roughly chopped

150g (5½oz) sour cream

salt and freshly ground black pepper

1 small bunch of coriander (cilantro), leaves picked and roughly chopped, to serve

I find those little jars or cans of chipotle in adobo sauce a very useful storecupboard ingredient. They can vary in heat, so find a brand you like best. As a marinade, used in a dressing, or stirred through cooked beans or a stew, these smoky, intensely flavoured chillies (some broken down as a sauce and some still in chilli form, and immersed in a thick and flavoursome sauce) will give a gorgeous, intense boost to many different dishes. I've added chipotle to the roasting vegetables and also in the sour cream, with lime juice, to make the dressing.

Rinse the quinoa and cook it in 800ml (28fl oz) of well-salted boiling water for 12–15 minutes, until tender. Drain and transfer to a serving bowl to cool. Once cool, mix it through with 3 tablespoons of the oil, the zest of the lime and half the juice and put to one side.

While the quinoa is cooking, preheat the oven to 220°C/200°C fan/425°F/Gas Mark 7.

Toss the chopped vegetables, pumpkin seeds and onion together on a baking tray with the remaining oil, a seasoning of salt and pepper and one quarter of the chipotle paste. Roast, uncovered, for about 20 minutes, until cooked through and nicely coloured in places. Remove from the oven.

In a mixing bowl, rub the kale with a good pinch of salt firmly with your fingertips for about 30 seconds (massaging the leaves, if you like) and put to one side. This will soften and break down the kale leaves.

In a small bowl, mix together the remaining chipotle with the sour cream and add the remaining lime juice and a good seasoning of salt to make the dressing.

Give the kale a good squeeze in a clean tea towel or cloth to remove any excess water.

To serve, add the roasted vegetables and softened kale to the quinoa and check the seasoning, adding more salt and pepper if necessary. Then top with the chipotle sour cream and the chopped coriander.

Lunchbox Salad with Beetroot, Carrot, Sesame Oil & Toasted Seeds

about 300g (10½oz) small, waxy potatoes

50g (1¾oz) mixed seeds (I prefer pumpkin, sunflower and especially sesame)

1 tbsp Dijon mustard

2 tbsp red wine vinegar

3 tbsp sunflower or olive oil

1 tsp sesame oil, or to taste

½ small clove of garlic, crushed with a little salt to a paste

2 carrots, peeled and coarsely grated (shredded)

1 raw beetroot, peeled and coarsely grated (shredded)

4 spring onions (scallions), finely sliced

60g (2¼oz) rocket (arugula) leaves

1 small bunch of flat-leaf parsley or coriander (cilantro), leaves picked and roughly chopped

salt and freshly ground black pepper

SERVES 2

These layered salads seemed to be very hip a while back. Layered in rainbow colours and squashed in a Kilner jar, well, Instagram was awash! If we can put trendy-looking salads to one side, there is, however, a good reason for making and presenting a salad like this, and it's a practical one I like. By dressing the bottom layer generously before adding all the other ingredients, this salad can sit very happily for a good, long while; the suitable ingredients soak in the abundant dressing to mix through, in turn, with the more delicate salad leaves and seeds, which might spoil if left to sit in the dressing for any length of time. This is a sensible salad to take in a lunchbox for work or to eat later on in the day. I'm all for it, although not perhaps in a Kilner jar, which is, frankly, just daft.

Boil the potatoes in plenty of well-salted water until tender. Drain and put to one side.

Put the seeds into a dry, non-stick frying pan over a moderate heat, until they toast and begin to crackle (about 2–3 minutes, depending on the seeds). Tip into a bowl and set aside.

In a mixing bowl, add the mustard, vinegar, oils, crushed garlic and salt and pepper to taste and give this all a good mix. Add the cooked potatoes while they are still warm and mix well to coat.

Place the potatoes and all of the dressing in the bottom of the lunchbox, then top with the grated (shredded) carrots and beetroot, then the spring onions (scallions) and rocket (arugula) and finally the chopped herbs and toasted seeds. Don't stir or toss the salad – do that when you are ready to eat it.

To serve, mix all the salad ingredients together, scooping up from the bottom layer, which holds much of the dressing.

Grapes & Fennel with Taleggio & Crispbread

2 plump fennel bulbs, trimmed of any tough stalks and sliced, green fronds reserved

200g (7oz) black grapes, halved

splash of red wine vinegar or lemon juice

3 tbsp olive oil

4 pieces of crispbread, or crackers or savoury olive-oil tortas, broken into bite-size pieces

1 small bunch of flat-leaf parsley, leaves picked and roughly chopped

salt and freshly ground black pepper

150g (5½oz) taleggio or soft goat cheese, to serve

The combination of textures here is crucial, an unbeatably crunchy trio of celery, fennel and shop-bought olive oil tortas (crispbreads), the grapes bring a juicy, sweet burst that flatters the salty, crystalline-skinned taleggio cheese. Speaking of which, don't remove the skin; it's delicious and a perfect foil for the creamy buttery interior of the cheese. Taleggio is a washed-rind cow's milk cheese from northern Italy. It is one Italy's oldest soft cheeses and is produced in the autumn and winter months. Matured for a minimum period of 25 days, the cheese's skin is rigorously washed with a brine to promote good bacteria, breaking down and softening the crust to make it edible, and delicious to say the least. Commonly available in most supermarkets with some cheeses more superior in quality to others, choose a soft, yielding cheese with an attractive peachy coloured skin all freckled with salt crystals.

In a bowl, mix together the fennel and grapes and season to taste with salt and freshly ground black pepper. Add the red wine vinegar or lemon juice and the olive oil. Add the pieces of crispbread (or alternative) and the parsley and, finally, distribute the cheese over to serve.

247

Squash Caponata

800g (1lb 12oz) butternut squash, peeled, deseeded and cut into bite-size pieces

2 red onions, cut into small wedges

80ml (2¾fl oz) good olive oil, plus more to serve

1 celery heart, thinly sliced, leaves reserved and finely chopped

4 cloves of garlic, finely chopped

½ tsp chilli flakes, or to taste

1 x 400g (14oz) can of plum tomatoes, chopped or ripped a little

2 tbsp red wine vinegar, plus more to taste if necessary

30g (1oz) capers (desalinated, if necessary), rinsed and drained

50g (1¾oz) raisins, soaked in hot water for 5 minutes, then drained

50g (1¾oz) black olives, pitted

salt and freshly ground black pepper

1 small bunch of flat-leaf parsley, leaves picked and roughly chopped, to serve

I have made many versions of caponata (also ratatouille) over the years. Most latterly, I have made it at a cookery school over in Sicily. And what I know most about this family of recipes is that the finished dish must be absolutely balanced, with each ingredient distinct. However, when we eat them, the ingredients must come together in perfect harmony with sweet, sour, salty and rich. Where ratatouille is French, caponata is a cornerstone of Sicilian cookery. Although caponata is most often made with aubergines (eggplants), I have also seen it made with artichokes, squash or pumpkin. Crucial is the addition of celery, which, for a caponata, must always be boiled, never fried. Make this and serve it just warm (although I think it is best at room temperature, and best of all, made the day before, refrigerated, then plated in advance to come back to room temperature). Use good olive oil, always.

Preheat the oven to 200°C/180°C fan/400°F/Gas Mark 6.

Toss the squash and onion with 50ml (1¾fl oz) of the olive oil and season with salt and pepper. Roast for 25–30 minutes, until soft and beginning to brown.

Meanwhile, boil the celery heart in plenty of well-salted water for 3–5 minutes, until tender but not too soft, then drain and put to one side.

Heat the remaining 30ml (1fl oz) of olive in a saucepan over a moderate heat. Add the garlic and cook for 1 minute, until fragrant, then add the chilli flakes, tomatoes and vinegar and cook for 10 minutes, until rich and thick, then season to taste with salt and pepper and stir in the capers, raisins and olives.

Stir the tomato sauce and the drained celery through the roasted squash and onion, then season to taste with salt, pepper and a splash more vinegar, if you like. Add the parsley and the celery leaves and a touch more olive oil to serve.

Apple & Blackberries with Chicory & a Walnut Vinaigrette

2 eating apples (such as russet), peeled, cored and finely sliced

1 white chicory, leaves separated and roughly chopped or torn (or use little gem lettuce)

1 celery heart, about 3 or 4 sticks complete with leaves, all finely sliced

2 tbsp cider vinegar or white wine vinegar, or to taste

1 bunch of watercress, picked into bite-size bunches, big, tough stalks removed

50g (1¾oz) crème fraîche or sour cream

2 tsp Dijon mustard

2 tbsp sunflower oil

2 tbsp walnut oil (or use more sunflower)

50g (1¾oz) walnuts, toasted, half finely chopped, half roughly chopped

salt and freshly ground black pepper

200g (7oz) blackberries, to serve

100g (3½oz) blue cheese (such as stilton, gorgonzola or roquefort), cut into smaller pieces, to serve

This salad is best made with chicory or endive. It will, of course, work with another leaf, but ideally you want a bitter salad leaf to complement the sweet apples and blackberries. Walnut oil is lovely stuff. It's not terribly expensive and most supermarkets stock one brand or another, richly flavoured with a sweet, nutty, almost milky quality. Like all nut oils, walnut oil is a terrific ingredient to use in salad dressings or to dress cooked vegetables. An autumnal salad, the best of sorts.

In a bowl mix the apples, chicory and celery and toss through with 2 teaspoons of the vinegar and a good pinch of salt. Spread out on a large serving platter or individual plates and top with the watercress.

In a separate small bowl mix the crème fraîche or sour cream, mustard and oils together with a little salt and pepper to taste, then add the remaining vinegar to taste and stir through the finely chopped walnuts. Spoon this dressing over the salad.

To serve, add the blackberries, blue cheese and the roughly chopped walnuts.

Salt-baked Beetroots with Ajo Blanco Dressing

350g (12oz) coarse sea salt

150g (5½oz) caster (superfine) sugar

½ small bunch of thyme, ½ roughly chopped with stalks, with the remaining leaves picked

2 egg whites

500g (1lb 2oz) raw beetroot

100g (3½oz) flaked almonds

1 small clove of garlic, roughly chopped

100ml (3½fl oz) good olive oil, plus more to serve

1–2 tsp sherry vinegar or red wine vinegar

salt and freshly ground black pepper

It's a misnomer to call this a salad – more a beautiful side dish or attractive starter. A frothy mixture of egg whites beaten with salt, sugar and thyme permeates the beetroots as they cook and in doing so seasons them to perfection. The mixture sets as it bakes, meaning that you will have to break through the golden crust to get to the beetroots inside. Some chefs like to wear gloves when prepping beetroots. I'm not one of them; I love the pink and purple stains left on my hands after peeling. More, though, I love beetroots when cooked, still warm and super-smooth, with the skins effortlessly slipping off. Ajo blanco is a Spanish soup, typical of Grenada or Málaga, served cold and made of almonds, garlic, water and good olive oil. It's looser here, made more as a dressing.

Preheat the oven to 180°C/160°C fan/350°F/ Gas Mark 4. Line a baking tray with foil (this will help contain the mess).

Beat the salt, sugar, roughly chopped thyme and egg whites together in a bowl to make the salt-crust mixture. Place the beetroots on the prepared tray, covering them well with the mixture. Bake for 1 hour.

While the beetroot is cooking, toast half the almonds on a separate baking tray in the oven, tossing once, for about 5 minutes until golden. Remove from the oven and put to one side.

Make an ajo blanco sauce. Blend the garlic, olive oil, 1 teaspoon of vinegar, the remaining almonds and 100ml (3½fl oz) ice-cold water in a blender until very, very smooth and creamy. Season generously with salt and add more vinegar to taste, if required. Put to one side.

Remove the beetroot from the oven and allow to cool. Crack open the salt crusts and peel the beetroots. When cool enough to handle, slice or cut them into wedges.

To serve, put the salt-baked beetroots on a large serving platter or individual plates, then spoon over the ajo blanco sauce and add the picked thyme leaves and toasted almonds. Some extra olive oil is important, too.

Venison with Wild Mushrooms & Pumpkin & Marsala Cream Sauce

600g (1lb 5oz) pumpkin or squash, peeled and cut into bite-size pieces

3 tbsp sunflower oil

20g (¾oz) unsalted butter

2 large shallots, finely diced

1 celery heart, 4 sticks finely chopped, any leaves roughly chopped and reserved

200g (7oz) wild mushrooms, roughly chopped if large (or use chestnut)

1 tbsp finely chopped thyme, rosemary or sage leaves

500g (1lb 2oz) venison loin or boneless haunch

100ml (3½fl oz) Marsala or Madeira (or use red wine)

50ml (1¾fl oz) double (heavy) cream

salt and freshly ground black pepper

½ small bunch of flat-leaf parsley, leaves picked and roughly chopped, to serve

SERVES 2-3

Venison is wildly underrated. Loin is especially easy to cook as it suits so well being fiercely seared, then shoved in a hot oven briefly, before being left to rest, when the meat becomes beautifully supple and tender, like cutting through butter. The pumpkin here is also roasted and then it is mixed through with the celery and shallots – softly, softly – with a good enough haul of wild mushrooms and a serious-though-simple sauce using marsala and cream.

Preheat the oven to 210°C/190°C fan/415°F/ Gas Mark 6–7.

Put the pumpkin in a baking tray and season with salt and plenty of freshly ground black pepper. Toss in 2 tablespoons of the oil, then roast for 15–20 minutes, until tender. Remove from the oven and keep warm.

Melt the butter in a large saucepan over a moderate heat. Add the shallots and chopped celery sticks and fry for about 15 minutes, until golden brown and very soft. Add the mushrooms for the last 5 minutes. Add the thyme (or rosemary or sage) and the celery leaves, and season to taste. Add this mixture to the cooked pumpkin and keep warm.

Heat the remaining oil in a heavy-based or cast-iron frying pan (skillet) until smoking hot. Season the venison all over, then add to the pan and cook for 2–3 minutes, until caramelized on the underside. Turn and cook for another 2 minutes, until well browned.

Place the meat on a baking sheet (put the cooking pan to one side, as it is) and place it in the oven for 5–6 minutes for rare or 8–10 minutes for medium. Allow to rest for at least 10 minutes before serving.

While the venison is resting, add the Marsala or Madeira to the venison pan over a high heat and boil until reduced by a half (about 3–5 minutes), then add the cream and bring back to the boil before removing from the heat and straining well.

Slice the venison and spoon over the pumpkin and mushrooms and sauce. Serve sprinkled with parsley.

Roast Pork Collar & Quince with Quince Aioli

1 x 1.8kg (4lb) pork collar (spare rib), skin scored

6 celery sticks, roughly chopped

1 onion, roughly diced

3-4 quinces, cored and cut into quarters

800g (1lb 12oz) waxy potatoes, peeled and halved

3 tbsp sunflower oil

salt and freshly ground black pepper

FOR THE AIOLI

1 clove of garlic

250g (9oz) membrillo (quince paste)

150ml (5fl oz) oil - use equal parts good olive oil and sunflower oil

juice of ¼ lemon, or to taste

SERVES 4-6 WITH LEFTOVERS

Quinces are the better fruit to apples and pears. The only glitch to their superiority is that they require a slow and steady cook, and cannot just be chomped on. Smudge the downy fur on a ripe quince and you should be able to smell notes of orange blossom, jasmine, candied peel and Turkish delight. Cooked, quince flesh takes on the colour of a sunset, radiant and ruby-red. In the aioli, membrillo emulsifies with the oil to make the sauce. You could use apples in lieu of the quince, but seeing as the quince are meant to be the real treat here, do what you can to find some.

Make the aioli. Crush the garlic with a little salt in a pestle and mortar or with a little salt on a chopping board using the back of a knife. Put the crushed garlic in a blender and blitz with the membrillo. Very slowly add the oil mixture in a thin and steady stream, until all the oil is emulsified into the garlic and membrillo paste. Add salt, pepper and lemon juice to taste. Set aside.

Preheat the oven to 210°C/190°C fan/415°F/ Gas Mark 6–7.

Season the pork all over with plenty of salt and pepper. Toss the celery and onion with a good amount of salt and place in a roasting tray with the pork on top. Surround the pork with quinces and potatoes and spoon the oil over both. Roast for about 15 minutes, or until the pork is nicely coloured, then reduce the temperature to 180°C/160°C fan/350°F/Gas Mark 4. Add a splash of water to the pan and cook uncovered for about 1–1½ hours, until the pork is cooked through (it should have an internal temperature of 72°C/161°F if you check it with a digital thermometer) and the quinces and potatoes are tender.

When the pork has cooked, remove it from the oven and rest it somewhere warm for at least 15 minutes.

To serve, carve the pork and serve with the quinces, potatoes, any juices from the pan and crackling and a large spoonful of the quince aioli.

Marsala Chicken with Roasted Garlic, Raisins & Almonds

8 skin-on, bone-in chicken thighs (or use breasts)

50g (1¾oz) flaked almonds

4 tbsp olive oil

1 whole garlic bulb, cloves separated and unpeeled

150ml (5fl oz) Marsala (or use medium sherry)

400ml (14fl oz) boiling chicken stock or water

2 bay leaves, scrunched a little

50g (1¾oz) raisins, soaked in warm water for at least 5 minutes, then drained

200g (7oz) couscous

½ tsp salt, plus more to season

freshly ground black pepper

1 small bunch of flat-leaf parsley, leaves picked and roughly chopped, to serve

Originating from northwest Africa, specifically the Maghreb region, couscous is here given the Sicilian touch with pan-fried chicken cooked with Marsala. And here's the trick: couscous likes a sauce. Never serve it plain as pebbledash, an afterthought. If you're going to serve couscous, do so impressively – make sure the sauce you serve it with is a delicious one. You could use chicken breasts for this recipe, but mostly I find bone-in thighs or legs to be the better cut to cook – more juicy, more flavoursome.

Season the chicken all over with salt and pepper.

Dry-roast the almonds in a large saucepan or casserole over a moderate heat for 2 minutes, until golden, remove from the heat and put to one side on a plate to cool.

Heat the oil in the same pan over a moderate heat. Add the chicken and fry for 5 minutes on one side, until deep golden brown. Add the whole garlic cloves and turn over the chicken to fry on the other side for a further 5 minutes, until a deep golden brown all over but not fully cooked through.

Pour the Marsala (or sherry) into the pan and cook for 2 minutes to evaporate some of the alcohol, then add 100ml (3½fl oz) of the stock or water along with the bay leaves. Cover with a lid and cook for 10–15 minutes, until the chicken is cooked through. Add the raisins for the last 1 minute of cooking to warm through. Check the seasoning, adding more salt and pepper to taste.

While the chicken is cooking, put the couscous in a mixing bowl and cover with the remaining 300ml (10½fl oz) of boiling stock or water and add the ½ teaspoon of salt. Cover and set aside for 10 minutes to soften.

To serve, fluff the couscous with a fork and divide it between the plates or bowls. Add the chicken and whole cloves of garlic before pouring over a good amount of sauce. Scatter with the toasted almonds, then the chopped parsley, to serve.

255

Vacherin Cheese Baked in a Box with Roasted Bread, Boiled Potatoes & Cornichons

1 x 250g (9oz) ripe vacherin in a wooden box (or use camembert)

30ml (1fl oz) white wine

1 good-size thyme sprig

TO SERVE

300g (10½oz) small potatoes

2 little gem lettuces, leaves separated

1 eating apple (such as russet or similar), cored and sliced

3 celery sticks, pale inner heart complete with any leaves, thinly sliced

30g (1oz) walnuts, toasted and roughly chopped

1 tbsp white wine vinegar or cider vinegar

3 tbsp walnut oil (or use sunflower)

½ day-old baguette or ciabatta, torn into pieces

3 tbsp olive oil

150g (5½oz) cornichons or gherkins

salt and freshly ground black pepper

SERVES 2

Vacherin is a seasonal delight: the cheeses start arriving in the shops from October. From the Jura region in France and also from Switzerland, where the rolling hills provide perfect pasture for the cattle to graze, these soft cheeses, sometimes barely able to hold their form, are girdled in wooden boxes made from spruce trees. Use a splash of white wine, preferably the same wine you will drink with the cheese, to bake the vacherin. Bread and potatoes – cornichons, too – all draped in melted cheese, this is the very definition of a treat, to eat enthusiastically, without a worry in the world.

Preheat the oven to 200°C/180°C fan/400°F/Gas Mark 6.

While the oven is heating, prepare the serving ingredients. Boil the potatoes in well-salted water for 12–15 minutes, until tender. Drain, return to the pan, cover and keep warm.

Assemble a salad by putting the lettuce leaves, apple, celery and any celery leaves and toasted walnuts in a serving bowl. When ready to serve, dress the salad with the vinegar and walnut oil and season well with salt and pepper.

Take the cheese out of the box and remove any paper wrapping. Place the cheese back in the base of the box. Score a thin ring around the top of the cheese (this will make it easier to remove the top or just to dig into the cooked cheese). Pierce the top of the cheese a few times with the point of a sharp knife, drizzle over the wine, add the thyme and replace the wooden lid of the box.

Put the bread on a baking tray and add the olive oil.

Put the bread and the cheese in the oven at the same time. Bake the bread for about 10–15 minutes, until roasted and crisp and bake the cheese for 15 minutes, until warm and molten. Remove both from the oven.

To serve, take the wooden lid off the cheese box and serve with the baked bread and boiled potatoes and cornichons or gherkins, all to dunk in. Serve the salad on the side.

Guinea Fowl with Porcini Bread Sauce & Cavolo Nero

1 guinea fowl

500ml (17fl oz) whole milk

2 cloves

1 large bay leaf, scrunched a little

⅛ nutmeg, grated (shredded), or more to taste

20g (¾oz) dried porcini mushrooms, rinsed and soaked in 100ml (3½fl oz) boiling water

60g (2¼oz) unsalted butter, plus more for the cavolo nero and rubbing the bird

1 small onion, finely diced

100g (3½oz) fresh white breadcrumbs

200g (7oz) cavolo nero, tough middle stalks discarded

salt and freshly ground black (or white) pepper

SERVES 3-4 (FOR A GUINEA FOWL)

Guinea fowl is a class meat. Once game birds, guinea fowls are now widely domesticated and available all year round. They have a flavour between chicken and their wild relative pheasant. If you're a fan of cooking chicken, I think it worth your while experimenting with cooking other birds because guinea fowl, partridge, pheasant and even quail will all reward you with a good poultry flavour, but essentially aren't all that different in appeal to a quality chicken. Good butchers should stock alternative poultry on their counters come the autumn, and even throughout the year. You might see some hanging wild birds in a brace outside the butcher's shop, complete with feathers – although don't let this put you off. Consider the challenge of cooking alternative poultry as a rite of passage, one all those interested in cooking well should tackle with enthusiasm. It's not hard and they're delicious. The porcini bread sauce is something else and will be a good match for any of these birds. I've used guinea fowl in the recipe, but note that cooking times will depend on what bird you choose (see page 260). Serve with roasted or mashed potatoes.

Preheat the oven to 200°C/180°C fan/400°F/Gas Mark 6.

Rub the bird with a bit of butter, then season all over with salt and pepper and place on a roasting tray, breast-side downward. Roast for 50 minutes, until the juices run clear and the bird is cooked through.

While the bird is roasting, in a pan over a high heat, heat the milk with the cloves and bay leaf until it is just about to come to a boil. Remove from the heat, add the nutmeg and leave the sauce to infuse for about 30 minutes.

Meanwhile, drain the porcini (reserving the liquid) and finely chop them. Melt half the butter in a saucepan over a moderate heat. Add the onion and porcini and cook for 10 minutes, until the onion is soft and translucent.

cont.

BIRDS & COOKING TIMES

Partridge: Serves 2. Roast for about 25–30 minutes, until the juices run clear, and rest for at least 15 minutes. Try not to overcook as this will make the meat dry.

Pheasant: Serves 2–3. Roast for about 30–40 minutes and rest for about 15 minutes, depending on the size of the bird. Try not to overcook the bird as this will make the meat dry; pheasant is fine to serve a fraction pink.

Quail: Serves 1. Roast for about 8–10 minutes and rest for 5 minutes. Try not to overcook the bird as this will make the meat dry; quail is fine to serve a fraction pink.

Strain the infused milk into the saucepan, stir in the breadcrumbs and the reserved porcini soaking liquid and place over a very low heat, stirring now and then, for 10–15 minutes, until the crumbs have swollen and thickened the sauce – somewhere between the consistency of porridge (oatmeal) and double (heavy) cream. Remove from the heat, stir in the remaining butter and check the seasoning, adding salt, plenty of freshly ground pepper and perhaps more nutmeg, to taste. Pour into a warm jug and keep warm.

After 50 minutes, turn the bird on to the backbone and continue to roast for 20 minutes, until golden brown and the juices run clear when the thigh is pierced with a skewer (with an internal temperature of 72°C/161°F if using a digital thermometer). Allow to rest for 15 minutes in a warm place before carving or jointing.

Cook the cavolo nero in plenty of well-salted boiling water, until tender. Drain and add a knob of butter.

To serve, carve or joint the guinea fowl and serve with the porcini bread sauce and the cavolo nero.

Carbonnade

600g (1lb 5oz) diced beef shin, ox cheek or other slow-cooking cut

2–4 tbsp sunflower oil (or use beef dripping)

3 onions, thinly sliced

2 bay leaves, scrunched a little

1 good-size thyme sprig

3 cloves of garlic, thinly sliced

30g (1oz) dark brown soft sugar

1 tbsp red wine vinegar or cider vinegar

1 tbsp Dijon mustard, plus more to taste and to serve

1 tbsp plain (all-purpose) flour (optional), to thicken

200ml (7fl oz) hot chicken or beef stock

660ml (23fl oz) dark Belgian-style beer or ale

salt and freshly ground black pepper

Use beef shin, cheek or featherblade to make this Flemish classic. Cooked in those inky-black beers of the same region, this unctuous, slow-cooked stew is brooding with meltingly soft onions, bay, vinegar and mustard. Ideally, drink the beer you have cooked the beef in when you come to eat – this way you can enjoy the alchemy of how the beer is transformed in the stew. Serve with boiled or mashed potatoes, or even piled on thick toast, spread with too much butter. It is autumnal fireside eating, a belts-and-braces sort of recipe.

Season the meat with salt and pepper. Heat some of the oil or dripping in a casserole over a high heat. Working in batches, adding more oil or dripping as necessary, brown the meat for about 10 minutes, until nicely browned and caramelized all over. Remove from the heat and put to one side on a plate, keeping the oil in the pan.

Reduce the heat to moderate and add the onions, bay leaves and thyme to the pan. Cook for 12–15 minutes, adding the garlic for the last 5 minutes of the cooking time, until the onions are meltingly soft and just beginning to brown ever-so slightly.

Add the sugar and the vinegar and cook for about 3–5 minutes, until the liquid has nearly all evaporated, then stir through the mustard and the flour (if using).

Add the stock and the beer and bring to a simmer, then return the beef to the pan and season with salt and pepper to taste. Then, reduce the heat to a gentle simmer and cook, covered, for about 2–3 hours, until the meat is very tender but not falling apart. (Alternatively, cook in the oven at 160°C/140°C fan/ 315°F/Gas Mark 2–3 for about 3 hours.)

Remove from the heat (or oven) and allow to rest for at least 10 minutes, checking once more on the seasoning and adding more salt and plenty of freshly ground black pepper to taste, if necessary. Serve with mashed or boiled potatoes, or good chunks of crusty bread, and, definitely, with more mustard on the side.

Quince with Málaga Raisins & Oloroso Sherry

100g (3½oz) caster (superfine) sugar

about 5 tbsp runny honey

juice of 1 lemon

100ml (3½fl oz) dark oloroso sherry (or any medium sherry)

4 quinces, peeled, quartered and cored

80g (2¾oz) Málaga raisins (or any big raisins, such as flame raisins)

To Spain again with quinces. I think the Spanish have a handle on these waxy, fragrant splendours. A quince cannot be hurried along as it cooks. If this happens, the fruit's flesh will disintegrate, exploding almost, and you won't get the perfect, yielding, ruby-hued interior that quinces, when cooked well, are capable of giving. Oloroso is my favourite sherry to cook with, full-bodied with notes of caramel and walnuts, also of too-dried prunes, figs and raisins. In this recipe, the sherry is simmered down along with a good handful of Málaga raisins, plumping in the liquid, turning fat once again like grapes. These are classic flavours for an autumnal dessert, serve with good vanilla ice cream to soften in the warm syrup.

Mix the sugar, honey, lemon juice and sherry with 400ml (14fl oz) of water in a large non-reactive saucepan and place over a moderate heat. Bring to a simmer.

Drop the quince quarters into the pan of simmering liquid. Cover with a round of baking paper directly on top of the quinces to prevent discoloration, then put a lid on the pan.

Simmer the quince pieces gently over a low–moderate heat for 45 minutes–1½ hours, until cooked through and tender when pierced with a knife or skewer. Remove from the heat, put the cooked quinces on a plate and keep warm.

Put the pan with the cooking juices back on the heat and turn the heat up high. Reduce the liquid until syrupy, rich and dark (about 3–5 minutes), adding the raisins as you boil it down. Add the quince back to the pan when the syrup is ready and serve warm.

Baked Fresh Borlotti

1kg (2lb 4oz) borlotti beans in their pods, podded (or use 150g/5½oz dried, soaked in plenty of cold water overnight)

3 cloves of garlic, whole and unpeeled

about 15 sage leaves (about a bunch)

3 ripe tomatoes (or use good canned, drained of juice)

about 5 tbsp good olive oil

¼–½ tsp chilli flakes (optional)

salt and freshly ground black pepper

SERVES 4–6 AS A SIDE DISH
OR ACCOMPANIMENT

I find fresh borlotti irresistible when I spot them at the greengrocer. They beat the dried or canned sort hands-down, and it's not just because with fresh you get to marvel at these pink-purple-cream-speckled beauties. Fresh borlotti beans in their fuchsia-pink pods, especially those that have been very newly picked, with the beans all plump and glossy, are a joy to cook and a treat to eat. Choose fleshy pods flecked dark with pink and with hardly any green (green indicates that they are likely to be unripe). Serve these beans simply – warm with very good olive oil as they do in Italy as an accompaniment to all number of good things to eat: mozzarella, burrata, grilled fish, roasted meats, on garlic- and rosemary-rubbed toast, also in soups, risotto and pasta dishes. Store any leftover cooked beans in the liquid, super-flavourful as the bean cooking liquor is with all that sage, garlic and olive oil.

Preheat the oven to 200°C/180°C fan/400°F/Gas Mark 6.

Put the beans, garlic, sage leaves and tomatoes in a casserole or high-sided roasting pan, big enough to accommodate the beans comfortably but that will also fit in your oven!

Add enough cold water to cover the beans by at least 5cm (2in). Add the olive oil to cover the surface with a good film. Put the pan over a high heat and bring to a boil. Remove from the heat and cover with foil or a lid.

Put the pan in the oven and bake for 45 minutes–1 hour, until the beans are tender (as much as 2 hours, if you are cooking soaked dried beans). Check the beans from time to time, topping up with more fresh water, if they need it – they should be swimming fairly freely in the water and oil and not in any way parched. When the beans are cooked, remove from the oven and season with salt, pepper and chilli flakes (if using), to taste.

Blackberry & Apple Hand Pies with Sour-cream Pastry

200g (7oz) cold unsalted butter, diced

250g (9oz) plain (all-purpose) flour

pinch of salt

3 tbsp demerara or granulated sugar, plus more to sprinkle on top

125g (4½oz) sour cream

½ punnet (about 125g/4½oz) blackberries, halved if large

1 eating apple (such as russet), peeled, cored and diced small

2 tbsp berry jam (blackberry, raspberry or strawberry, and so on, as you like)

1 squeeze of lemon juice

1 egg, beaten

MAKES 10 PIES

Sour-cream pastry is a doddle to make and roll out. Cooked, it's beautifully crisp and ever-so slightly flaky. I've suggested using a little jam in lieu of sugar in the filling for these little pastries, or hand pies as I've called them here. You could call them a pithivier, as they might in a French pâtissérie or restaurant, but I can't for a moment come anywhere close to calling myself a pastry chef, or someone capable of fine pâtissérie work, so call them hand pies and delight in their rustic appearance.

Blend the butter, flour, salt and sugar in a food processor until the mixture resembles breadcrumbs. (By hand, use your fingertips to rub the mixture together.)

Add the sour cream and pulse or mix until the dough just comes together. Form the dough into a flat disk, then wrap and chill for at least 30 minutes before using.

Meanwhile, mix the blackberries with the apple, jam and squeeze of lemon juice in a bowl and put to one side.

Preheat the oven to 210°C/190°C fan/415°F/Gas Mark 6–7. Grease a baking tray and line it with baking paper.

Roll the chilled pastry out to 2mm (¹/₁₆in) thick and use an 8cm (3¼in) circular cutter or cup to cut out as many circles as possible. Re-roll the scraps and continue cutting out circles until you run out of dough, ensuring you end up with an even number of circles. Ideally, you should have about 20.

Place half the dough circles on the lined baking tray and place 1 tablespoon of the filling on each, leaving a 1cm (½in) border around the filling. Place the reserved dough circles on top, then use a fork to crimp the edges together to seal.

Brush each pie with the beaten egg and use the tip of a sharp knife to cut two vents on the top of each one. Sprinkle the pies with an extra pinch of sugar on each.

Bake the pies for about 15 minutes, until they're golden brown and crisp. Remove from the oven and rest for at least 10 minutes before serving.

Rillettes, Remoulade & Mum's Pickled Damsons

50ml (1¾fl oz) brandy

6 cloves of garlic, very finely chopped

1½ tsp salt, plus more to season

½ tsp freshly ground black pepper, plus more to season

1 good-size thyme sprig

2 bay leaves, scrunched a little

½ tsp ground mace or nutmeg

½ tsp ground allspice

5 juniper berries, crushed a little

400g (14oz) pork shoulder, diced

400g (14oz) fatty pork belly, diced

150ml (5fl oz) dry white wine

MAKES 850G (1LB 14OZ)

FOR THE PICKLED DAMSONS

900g (2lb) damsons

275ml (9½fl oz) malt vinegar

900g (2lb) dark brown soft sugar

1 cinnamon stick

6 cloves

MAKES ABOUT 1KG (2LB 4OZ)

FOR THE REMOULADE

1 celeriac, peeled and cut into very thin matchsticks, or coarsely grated (shredded)

good pinch of salt, plus more to season

juice of 1 lemon

200g (7oz) crème fraîche

2 tbsp Dijon mustard

freshly ground black pepper

I have a soft spot for rillettes (remoulade, too). Perhaps more than any of the other charcuteries, I love the coarse texture of rillettes and all the flavour you can, quite literally, pack into a jar. I like to make mine with a mixture of pork shoulder and pork belly. As for aromatics, these are non-negotiable: plenty of black pepper, mace, juniper, allspice, thyme and bay; quite a bit of salt, for obvious reasons, and a decadent glug of brandy, and white wine, too. Sealed under fat and kept in the fridge, rillettes will keep for weeks. Once opened, they will last up to 5 days (chance would be a fine thing!) with the flavour improving day by day. Served with my mum's recipe for pickled damsons, the remoulade, a glass of Gamay and good bread, this, above all others, might well be my favourite lunch. You'll need to make the pickled damsons about 6 weeks ahead.

In a large bowl, mix together the brandy, garlic, salt, pepper, herbs, spices and juniper berries. Add all the pork to the bowl and mix to coat. Cover and refrigerate for at least 2 hours or overnight.

Preheat the oven to 120°C/100°C fan/235°F/ Gas Mark ½–1.

In a large, lidded ovenproof pan or casserole over a moderate heat, cook the pork with half of the wine for 15 minutes, stirring occasionally. This will start to render out the fat from the pork. Cover the pan and put it in the oven.

After 1 hour, add the remaining wine and give the pork a good stir to help to start to break it down a bit. Replace the lid and return to the oven for another 1–2 hours, until the pork is very, very soft and falling apart. Remove from the oven and pick out the thyme stalks, bay and juniper and discard. Set aside to cool.

Separate the pork meat from the fat and put it into a large bowl. Using your hands, or a couple of forks, shred and mash the pork meat into a very rough paste. A few small chunks still in the mixture is fine.

cont.

Using the reserved liquid, cooking juices and fat in the pan, add spoonfuls to the pork meat, mixing it in each time to make the shredded meat juicy and moist – a rough paste that is loosened by the liquid you add back in. (Use some liquid and some fat – there's no right or wrong on the proportions, but do keep some of the fat to seal the finished rillettes.) Spoon the mixture into a clean sterilized jar (one that will hold about 850g–1kg/1lb 14oz–2lb 4oz, or use two smaller jars) and pat down tightly, then seal with a layer of the fat. I like to put the bay leaf and another good grinding of ground black pepper on the rillettes, too. Screw on the lid and cool before putting in the fridge.

Prick the damsons with a fork or several times with a skewer. Put the damsons, vinegar, sugar and spices in a large saucepan and bring to a boil. Cook for 3 minutes. Remove from the heat.

Carefully spoon the still-hot damsons into clean, sterilized jars and seal tightly. Leave for at least 6 weeks before eating to let the flavours develop. Stored well, these pickled damsons will last a year or more.

When you are ready to serve everything, remove the rillettes from the fridge at least 30 minutes before you intend to serve them, and make the remoulade.

Place the celeriac into a large colander and add the pinch of salt. Mix in half the lemon juice to stop the celeriac discolouring, and leave for 10 minutes.

In a bowl, mix together the crème fraîche, mustard and remaining lemon juice with a good seasoning of salt.

Give the celeriac a good squeeze to drain it and place it in a serving bowl. Mix the dressing into the celeriac, check the seasoning, and serve with the pickled damsons and rillettes, with some cornichons, butter, mustard, more black pepper and very good bread.

Tray-baked Kebab

600g (1lb 5oz) minced (ground) beef or lamb

1 onion, finely diced

2 cloves of garlic, finely chopped

1 large red or green (bell) pepper, deseeded, ½ finely diced, ½ cut into 4 wedges

1 small bunch of flat-leaf parsley, leaves picked and finely chopped

½ tsp salt, plus more to season

1–2 tsp Turkish chilli flakes (preferably Aleppo or Urfa)

1 tsp cumin seeds, toasted and ground

4 waxy potatoes, peeled and thinly sliced into rounds

8 pickled, long, green chillies, plus more to serve

1 tomato, cut into 4 wedges

1 tbsp tomato purée

1 tbsp olive oil, plus more to grease

freshly ground black pepper

TO SERVE

natural yogurt, seasoned with a little salt and crushed garlic

lemon wedges

flat breads or cooked rice

From the southern Mediterranean to the Middle East and on through to India, there are a great many variations on the kebab. It wasn't until the research for this book that I came across this version, tray-baked and easy to cook at home. Originating from the Antakya region of Turkey, this highly flavoured, mince kebab (known as *tepsi kebabi* in Turkish) is baked as one big round. Families without a domestic oven would assemble the kebab at home and take it to the town bakery, where it was cooked and set aside ready for collection. This is a generous and convivial meal, to make and share with friends. Serve it with warm pita breads and a salad made of chopped cucumber, tomatoes, red onions and parsley, seasoned with olive oil, salt and lemon juice.

Preheat the oven to 180°C/160°C fan/350°F/Gas Mark 4.

In a bowl mix the meat with the onion, garlic, diced pepper, half the parsley, the ½ teaspoon of salt, and the chilli flakes and cumin. Knead well with your hands for a good few minutes, until thoroughly combined.

Grease a round, 25cm (10in) baking tin (or use an equivalent square or rectangular dish, if you prefer) with a little olive oil and spread the mince mixture out evenly into the tin, pressing it into the edges. Score the round into 8 triangles.

Place the sliced potatoes slightly overlapping around the outer edge, then place one pickled chilli on each triangle, and the tomato and (bell) pepper pieces on alternating triangles. Season with salt and pepper.

In a small bowl, mix the tomato purée with 100ml (3½fl oz) of water and the 1 tablespoon of olive oil, and season with salt and pepper to taste. Pour this mixture over the mince and bake the mince in the oven for about 40–45 minutes, until nicely bronzed and cooked within and the vegetables are cooked and tender.

Remove from the oven, scatter with the remaining parsley and serve with the yogurt, lemon wedges and extra pickled green chillies on the side. Warmed flat breads or steamed rice are a good accompaniment.

Bacon & Egg Tarts

about 80g (2¾oz) unsalted butter, softened

12 thin slices of day-old or more white bread, crusts removed

6 thin rashers of rindless streaky bacon, halved

6 eggs, beaten

200ml (7fl oz) whole milk

200g (7oz) cheddar cheese, grated (shredded)

salt and freshly ground black pepper

MAKES 12

My husband is a Kiwi, and in New Zealand they take their bacon and egg pies very, very seriously. This is incredibly quick to make and uses stale white bread, thinly sliced and squashed affirmatively into a muffin tin to form individual tart cases. The bread and bacon are cooked briefly for the bread to crisp and the bacon to cook, exuding fat, before the cheese, eggs and milk are added to bake. They are amazing served warm, and just as good cold in a packed lunch or picnic. Bacon and egg tarts, waving to you all in NZ.

Preheat the oven to 190°C/170°C fan/375°F/Gas Mark 5. Lightly grease a 12-hole muffin tin with some of the butter.

Butter both sides of the bread lightly and push snugly into the muffin tin, pressing right into the corners so the squashed bread forms a little tart case.

Put half a bacon rasher in each bread mould, stick the bacon tight against the wall of the mould and bake for 10–12 minutes, until the bread is crisp and beginning to brown at the edges and the bacon is crisp and golden. Remove from the oven.

Whisk the eggs with the milk and season well with salt and freshly ground black pepper, to taste.

Sprinkle the cheese equally into each bread case and pour in the egg mixture. Bake in the oven for 15 minutes, or until the egg mixture puffs up nicely and the surface is set and ever-so slightly brown.

Remove from the oven and allow to cool a little before serving, or cool and serve at room temperature, if you prefer.

Palmières with Butter-baked Tomatoes

plain (all-purpose) flour, for dusting

200g (7oz) puff pastry, from a ready-made block

50g (1¾oz) parmesan, grated (shredded)

1 small bunch of flat-leaf parsley, leaves picked and finely chopped

2 thyme sprigs, leaves picked and finely chopped

1 small bunch of oregano, marjoram or rosemary, leaves picked and finely chopped

1 egg, lightly beaten

2–3 large tomatoes, each cut into 1cm (½in) slices

2 cloves of garlic, finely chopped

large pinch of caster (superfine) sugar

1 tbsp white wine vinegar

30g (1oz) unsalted butter

salt and freshly ground black pepper

This is exactly the sort of recipe I find myself making at the weekend, as there just aren't enough hours in the day to make a palmière (come to that, any sort or tart) during the week. Palmière sounds tricky, but it really isn't. Puff pastry is a reliably easy ingredient that demands very little effort, and this recipe requires just a modicum more exertion. Palmières make a great canapé or aperitivo to serve with drinks. Tomatoes, early autumn, should still be in abundance – lightly cooked with butter and vinegar, and more herbs still, draped over the herb-and-cheese flecked pastries.

Preheat the oven to 200°C/180°C fan/400°F/Gas Mark 6. Line 2 baking trays with baking paper.

Use a little flour to lightly dust your work surface. Roll out the puff pastry until it measures about 20 x 30cm (8 x 12in) and trim the edges, if necessary, with a sharp knife. Sprinkle the parmesan and half the herbs over the puff pastry and season with salt and plenty of pepper.

With the longest side of the pastry rectangle facing you, roll up the pastry into a large Swiss roll. Brush the roll all over with the beaten egg and refrigerate for 30 minutes, reserving any remaining egg.

Place the tomato slices in a single layer on one of the lined baking trays and scatter over the garlic. Season with salt, pepper and the pinch of sugar, to taste. Drizzle over the vinegar and dot each slice with some of the butter. Roast for 5–10 minutes, until the tomatoes are tender, then remove from the oven and put to one side.

Remove the pastry roll from the fridge. Brush it all over once again with the remaining beaten egg, then use a sharp knife to cut the log into 10 equal slices.

Place the slices of pastry onto the second baking tray and bake for 10–12 minutes, or until the pastry has puffed up and is crisp and golden brown. Remove from the oven.

Top each pastry disk with a tomato slice or two and scatter with the remaining herbs to serve.

Hand-smashed Noodles with Xian-style Lamb

300g (10½oz) strong white bread flour

good pinch of salt

500g (1lb 2oz) diced lamb shoulder

5 tbsp light soy sauce

1 tbsp cumin seeds, toasted and ground

120ml (4fl oz) sunflower oil, plus more for greasing and brushing

1–1½ tsp chilli flakes, or more to taste (or more whole facing heavens)

½ tsp Sichuan peppercorns, toasted and ground (or use more freshly ground black pepper)

2 tbsp sesame seeds

2 tbsp rice vinegar (or use white-wine or cider vinegar)

3 cloves of garlic, finely chopped

1 tbsp grated (shredded) fresh ginger

½ bunch of spring onions (scallions), thinly sliced

1 tsp caster (superfine) sugar

2 tbsp Chinese rice wine or sherry

2 tsp cornflour (cornstarch)

1 black cardamom pod (optional)

2 cinnamon or cassia sticks

2 star anise

2 facing heaven chillies (or any other dried, hot, red chillies)

My stepmother comes from Chengdu in central China. I am lucky enough to have enjoyed many meals with her both in China and, home-cooked, here in the UK. The diversity of produce on offer in this massive country, and the assortment of cookery styles and techniques throughout, is astonishing. The lamb in this recipe is cooked with quite a bit of cumin, a spice I hadn't really associated with China until one trip to Xian where I ate lamb with cumin and soft, fat noodles. It just blew me away. Paring back a recipe to the fundamentals is necessary and often a blessing for busy home cooks, but just sometimes, with enough time and inclination, it's worth your while to source more esoteric produce in the name of authenticity and exploration. For example, the chillies in this recipe (short and stubby in appearance and often sold dried) are grown in the Sichuan province with their stalks up to the heavens – giving them their name, 'facing heaven'. They are a foundation, fried in oil, for so many dishes from the region and beyond. Hand-smashed noodles are fun to try: a simple dough, worked until smooth, then stretched to form long, thick fingers. Their texture in the spiced lamb is sensational – chewy and fat, and just like I remember them.

Mix the flour with 170ml (5½fl oz) of water and the salt until you have a soft dough. Knead for 5 minutes, until smooth and elastic, then cover and leave to rest on one side while you prepare the other elements.

In a bowl, mix the lamb with 2 tablespoons of the soy sauce and half the cumin and leave to marinate for at least an hour (or up to 8 hours) in the fridge.

Heat 100ml (3½fl oz) of the oil in a large saucepan over a moderate heat. Add the chilli flakes and Sichuan peppercorns and heat for 1 minute, until the chilli starts to darken in colour and the oil turns slightly red. Remove from the heat and carefully pour over the sesame seeds. Leave to one side in a heatproof bowl.

cont.

Fry the lamb in the remaining oil for 5 minutes, until well browned all over. Work in batches, adding the rice vinegar, garlic, ginger and spring onions (scallions) to the final batch. Cook for 2 minutes, until the spring onions have wilted.

Add the remaining 3 tablespoons of soy sauce, along with the sugar, rice wine or sherry, cornflour (cornstarch), the remaining ground cumin, whole spices and whole chillies. Cook for 1 minute more, then add 100ml (3½fl oz) of water. Bring to a boil, reduce the heat to a simmer and cook, covered, over a moderate–low heat for 45 minutes, until the lamb is meltingly tender. Keep warm until you are ready to serve.

Meanwhile, have a large saucepan of water ready and boiling, and a large baking tray greased with a little sunflower oil.

Knead the dough for 1 minute more on a lightly oiled surface, then divide into 2 equal pieces. Roll out one piece into a rough rectangle about 1cm (½in) thick, brush with some oil, then cut into strips 1cm (½in) wide. Repeat with the other half of the dough.

Use the heel and side of your hand to squash and flatten each strip into a wide, thick noodle about 2mm ($^1/_{16}$in) thick, a few hillocks to the texture of the noodles is good – some of the noodle thinner and some fatter. Then, give each noodle a stretch and lay each on the oiled tray so that the noodles don't touch each other.

When you're ready to eat, cook the noodles in batches in the boiling water for 2 minutes, until they float to the surface, then scoop them directly into the lamb in the pan, stirring to coat. Add enough of the chilli oil to coat the lamb and noodles in the pan, leaving the remainder to serve at the table on the side.

Sausage & Fennel Focaccia Rolls Dipped in Passata Sauce

400g (14oz) strong white bread flour

1 tsp dried yeast

3 tbsp olive oil, plus more for proving and rolling

300ml (10½fl oz) warm water

1 tsp salt, plus a good pinch more for the passata

2 sausages, meat squeezed out

1 tsp fennel seeds, toasted and lightly crushed

6 sage leaves, finely chopped

½ clove of garlic, finely crushed

about ¼ tsp freshly ground black pepper

100ml (3½fl oz) tomato passata

MAKES ABOUT 8

My friend Rachel Roddy, a brilliant writer who always makes me want to down tools and begin cooking right away, has a way with words. Her peg is food – and her adopted home of Rome, also sometimes Sicily – but I think she could pretty much write about anything... more than food, more than recipes, and her words will propel us, just as her food writing does, to stop and read whatever it is she has to say. These sausage rolls were her idea. I've tinkered with her method just a little, and I have also dipped the dough in some passata when it proves before baking. I've run this recipe past Rachel. (In fact, I was messaging her while testing them.) I'll say it like it is: with Rachel's blessing, there is a strong possibility for hilarity and innuendo while preparing these tomato-dipped sausage rolls. Steady yourselves, the outcome will be worth it. This is a recipe to make when the windows are rattling with the wind and rain outside, and the kitchen smells better for a dough that sits on the worktop proving and getting fat with its own importance.

Mix the flour, yeast, 2 tablespoons of the oil and the warm water together in a bowl – ideally in a mixer with a dough hook, but you can do it by hand. Add the salt and mix or stir to form a sticky, scruffy dough. Continue mixing with the dough hook, or stirring then kneading to combine, for at least 5 minutes, by which time the dough should be smooth and cohesive. With well-oiled hands, shape it into a neat round and leave covered with a clean, damp cloth to rise in a bowl somewhere warm for about 1–2 hours, or until doubled in size.

Meanwhile, make the filling. Put the sausagemeat into a small bowl. Add the fennel seeds, sage, garlic and plenty of black pepper and mix well to combine.

Line a baking tray with well-oiled baking paper.

cont.

With the dough doubled in size, oil the work surface or work straight onto the prepared tray. Oil your hands and pull off ping-pong-size lumps of dough. Flatten these with your hands to form a rough oblong shape, about 10–12cm (4–4½in) long by 8cm (3¼in) wide.

Using 1 teaspoon of the sausage filling at a time, roll this into a long, thin sausage to stretch the length of the dough oblong shape. Place in the centre of the dough and wrap the dough around it. Seal and lay the rolls, seam side downward, on the prepared tray. Repeat with the remaining sausage filling and dough. You should get about 8 sausage rolls – it doesn't really matter, just use up all the sausage and dough.

Put the passata in a small, shallow bowl. Add the remaining tablespoon of olive oil and a good pinch of salt. Mix well. Carefully dip the sausage rolls into the seasoned passata sauce and place back on the lined oven tray. Let the dough rest for 35 minutes. Preheat the oven to 210°C/190°C fan/415°F/Gas Mark 6–7.

Using a sharp knife, carefully slash 3 marks on top of each of the rolls, not going through to the sausagemeat, just nicking the top of the dough. Bake for 18 minutes, until the tomato passata is a good colour, the underside of the bread is crisp to tap and the sausagemeat within is piping hot and cooked through. Remove from the oven and leave to cool for at least 5 minutes before serving.

Duck & Damson Bao

FOR THE BAO BUNS

2 tbsp whole milk

1 tsp dried yeast

1 tsp caster (superfine) sugar

250ml (9fl oz) warm water

450g (1lb) plain (all-purpose) flour, plus more for dusting

1½ tsp baking powder

sunflower oil, for oiling

FOR THE DUCK & DAMSON FILLING

1 tbsp five spice

juice and 1 strip of peel (no pith) from 1 unwaxed mandarin, clementine or small orange

3 tbsp light soy sauce

1 tbsp runny honey

2 duck legs

1 tbsp rice or white wine vinegar

4 thin slices of peeled fresh ginger

16 damsons, stoned (or use 4 large, dark plums)

MAKES 16

These bao buns are irresistible. Granted, what they do have is a bit of a lengthy to-do list. But, by breaking it down into making the filling, then the dough, then assembling the bao to steam, you'll be surprised how easy they are. You'll also look like a complete boss to anyone lucky enough to be there when you come to serve them. Damsons are my favourite of the plum-tree species, all of which are a member of the rose family. A small fruit with a deep, blue-black colour, they have a fruity, sour flavour that works brilliantly with rich, fatty meats, or with quite a bit of sugar as a jam or in a pudding. At the back of my mum's house in Shropshire stands a damson tree. It looks as old as the house itself. Some time in the autumn, before the wasps can get the fruit, the slender branches are teeming, drooping with the weight of these inky gems. We pick the lot and make use of them in various ways. Cooked here, with the duck, they are brilliant. A good greengrocer should have damsons in the autumn. If not, by all means use plums, using a good deal fewer than the recipe states for diminutive damsons. Equally so, if you would rather use pork (belly) over duck, do so.

Cut a sheet of baking paper into 16 rectangles, each measuring 6 x 4cm (2½in x 1½in).

First, marinate the duck. In a mixing bowl stir together the five spice, citrus peel, soy sauce and honey. Add the duck legs and rub all over with the marinade, then refrigerate for at least 2 hours or overnight.

Preheat the oven to 180°C/160°C fan/350°F/Gas Mark 4.

Place the duck legs snugly together in a roasting tin or casserole along with the citrus peel from the marinade. Tightly cover with foil or a lid, and cook for 1 hour.

Remove from the oven and stir through the citrus juice, vinegar, ginger and damsons. Return to the oven, uncovered, reduce the temperature to 160°C/140°C fan/ 315°F/Gas Mark 2–3 and cook for a further 1 hour, until the duck is tender and falling off the bone and you have a rich and sticky sauce.

cont.

Add a tiny splash of water during cooking if the liquid in the pan dries out too much. Remove from the oven to cool slightly.

Pick the meat away from the bones, discard the citrus peel and also the ginger, and pull the meat into smaller chunks, folding it back into the rich and sticky cooking juices in the pan. Put to one side.

Make the dough. Warm the milk slightly and stir it in a small bowl with the yeast and a pinch of sugar and allow to activate for 5 minutes until foaming. Add the water and flour and mix until a dough forms. Knead on a lightly floured surface for about 3–5 minutes, until the dough is pliable, elastic and smooth to touch. Put the dough into an oiled bowl, cover and allow it to rise at room temperature for 1 hour, until doubled in size.

Add the baking powder to the dough and knead in the bowl for 30 seconds, then transfer to a lightly floured surface and flatten slightly. Cover and rest for 15 minutes.

Using your hands, roll the dough into a long 30cm (12in) sausage shape, then cut this into 16 pieces that are about 3cm (1¼in) wide. Using a rolling pin, roll out each piece of dough into a 15 x 7cm (6 x 2¾in) oval on a lightly floured work surface. Put 2 teaspoons of the filling in the centre of the oval and pull the sides together like a drawstring purse, encasing the filling in the centre of the dough. Flatten slightly and place the bao bun, seam-side downward, on a piece of baking paper. Then, put the whole thing on a large, flat baking sheet, and cover loosely with a cloth. Proceed with the remaining dough and filling, until all the bao are made. Leave to prove for about 30 minutes, until the dough is slightly risen and puffed.

Line a steamer with baking paper, fill the steamer with water and set over a moderate–high heat. Bring the water to a boil. Working in batches, carefully place the buns in the steamer, along with their baking paper pieces and so that they don't touch each other. Cover tightly with a lid and steam for about 3–5 minutes, until the buns are puffed and the dough is aerated and cooked through. Using tongs, transfer the buns to a plate, discarding the pieces of paper, and cover with a clean cloth to keep warm until you're ready to serve.

Plantain with Ginger & Tomato & Kenyan Chapati

FOR THE PLANTAIN

2 tbsp sunflower oil

1 tbsp grated (shredded) fresh ginger

4 cloves of garlic, finely chopped

1-2 green chillies, finely chopped (remove the seeds if you want less heat)

200g (7oz) chopped tomatoes (fresh or canned)

6 medium or 4 large plantains, peeled, chopped into bite-size pieces, soaked in cold water for 15 minutes and drained

1 tsp salt, plus more to season

juice of ½ lemon

freshly ground black pepper

1 small bunch of coriander (cilantro), leaves picked and roughly chopped, to serve

FOR THE CHAPATI

250g (9oz) plain (all-purpose) flour, plus more for kneading and dusting

½ tsp salt

30g (1oz) ghee or unsalted butter, melted, plus more to cook (or use sunflower oil)

150ml (5fl oz) warm water

I had plantain cooked like this in a bustling restaurant in Naivasha when my family and I were visiting Kenya a little over a year or so ago. I had seen plenty of plantain in shops here in the UK, but had not really known all that much about them or how best to use them in my cooking at home. This stew was a revelation. As is often the way when two chefs sit down to eat food cooked by another, my husband Matt and I were both quick to quiz our server about how this gingery, rich stew of plantain and tomatoes was made. Beyond the pass, in the kitchen, the waiter explained our request to about five women of different ages and statures. Cue laughing with lots of articulation – they all seemed to have something crucial to convey to us, via him. This recipe is my interpretation of that explanation.

Choose ripe plantains, yellow with some blackened blemishes on the skin. As for the chapati (very lucky to have been taught this method by a Kenyan chef called Isaac, working at El Karama Lodge out in Laikipia), roll the dough flat, into a round, then roll the round like a fat cigar before coiling it like a child might make a plasticine snail, then roll it flat again. This gives the chapati an excellent, flaky texture. Isaac had the technique well-honed – he deftly spun the chapati with his hand in the pan to cook, exerting the right amount of pressure to flatten and scorch it. Make the stew, then make the chapati, using the chapati to scoop up the plantain and sauce. Serve with plenty of coriander (cilantro) and more chopped green chilli, or use hot sauce, as you like.

Heat the oil in a saucepan over a moderate heat. Add the ginger, garlic and chillies and cook for 1 minute, until fragrant, then add the tomatoes, the soaked and drained plantains, the salt and 150ml (5fl oz) of water. Bring to a boil, then reduce the heat and simmer for 10–15 minutes, until the plantains are tender when pierced with a skewer and the sauce has thickened. Add the lemon juice, season with more salt and plenty of black pepper to taste, and once the chapati are ready serve topped with fresh coriander (cilantro).

cont.

In a large mixing bowl, combine the flour and salt, then mix in the ghee or butter (or oil) and rub the flour mixture between your hands for a few minutes to form light breadcrumbs. Add the warm water, a little at a time, mixing with your hands until you have a slightly sticky dough, then cover and rest for 10 minutes. Transfer the dough to a lightly floured surface and knead for 5 minutes, or until it becomes smooth and elastic, then allow to rest, covered with a clean, damp cloth, for 10 minutes.

Divide the rested dough into 4 balls. Roll out each dough ball into a circle and brush the entire surface with ghee, butter or oil and sprinkle with a little flour. Roll up each round like a cigar, then coil it like a snail shell into a disk. Leave the rounds to rest like this for 10 minutes, then roll each round into a flat disk about 25cm (10in) in diameter.

Heat a frying pan (skillet) over a medium heat. Lay one chapati in the dry pan and cook for a few seconds until the surface forms bubbles and bronzes slightly. Spin the chapati a few times in the pan for 10 seconds or so, then brush with a little extra ghee or butter (or oil) and flip the chapati over.

Use a cloth (to protect your hand) to spin and flatten the chapati in the pan for about 1 minute, until the chapati is spotted light golden brown all over. Place on a plate and cover with a cloth and repeat with the next 3 disks. Keep warm while you serve the plantain.

Handmade Orecchiette with Romanesco Broccoli, Fennel, Chilli & Parmesan

200g (7oz) semolina (cream of wheat), plus more for dusting

100ml (3½fl oz) warm water

1 Romanesco broccoli

3 tbsp olive oil, plus more to finish the dish

4 cloves of garlic, finely sliced

1 tsp fennel seeds, toasted and lightly crushed

1 bay leaf, scrunched a little

¼–½ tsp chilli flakes, or more to taste

juice of ½ lemon, to taste

1 small bunch of flat-leaf parsley, leaves picked and roughly chopped

salt

parmesan, grated (shredded), to serve

This is the just sort of meditative cookery task I enjoy while listening to the radio. Better still to have a pair of willing hands to help shape the dough, perhaps with a glass of wine on the side and some blather to catch up on. I've always been fascinated by orecchiette as pasta shapes go, so-called because the neat little furl of dough is said to resemble the shape of an ear. But please don't let the semantics of pasta shapes hold you back, as I don't especially think mine happen to look like anything like an ear. As with most so-called finicky recipe procedures, confidence is all. Cut the dough to size and move it assertively, and, with enough determination across the semolina-dusted work surface, I am sure your pasta will glide and shape, and as it does create a crevice, crater or pocket for the ingredients to nestle within. You can make the orecchiette and leave them to dry out overnight or through the day. Although do bear in mind that, dried, the pasta will take longer to cook than freshly rolled. Use regular broccoli for this dish if you like, but I'm a big fan of Romanesco, which is sturdier in form. Boiling the florets first to then cook again, breaking them down to become all creamy and flavoursome, some minuscule and some not, gives good contrast for the pasta here. Olive oil, salt, chilli and lemon – taste, taste and taste – and also do make use of the all-important slosh of cooking water. It's these few ingredients together with the Romanesco, parsley and parmesan that make up the sauce.

Mix the semolina (cream of wheat) and warm water together in a large mixing bowl and knead well for 5–7 minutes, until really smooth and super-supple. Add a touch more semolina if the dough seems too wet to handle. (Go easy, though, do not add too much. The dough should be smooth, firm and cohesive, like pasta dough.) Wrap and refrigerate for about 30 minutes.

Dust a tray well with semolina flour.

To shape, cut the dough into long strips about 2cm (¾in) wide. Then, cut each strip into 2cm (¾in) cubes.

cont.

Dust the work surface well with extra semolina and use your thumbs to smudge, scraping the piece of dough firmly across the surface, creating a rustic, rounded, ear-shaped curl of pasta. Put each orecchietta to one side, creating a single layer on the flour-dusted tray and sprinkle semolina over the surface.

Cook the Romanesco in well-salted boiling water until very tender (about 12–15 minutes). Remove from the heat and drain well, reserving a cup or so of the cooking water.

Put the same pan back over a moderate heat to dry briefly, then add the olive oil. When hot, add the garlic, fennel seeds, bay leaf and chilli and cook for about 2–3 minutes, until fragrant. Add the cooked Romanesco, mixing well as you do so to break the florets down into the pan. Add a splash of the reserved cooking water to moisten the mixture a little. Season well with salt and add the lemon juice to taste. Add the parsley and mix well. Remove from the heat and keep warm.

Cook the orecchiette. Bring a large saucepan of well-salted water to a boil over a high heat. Add the orecchiette and boil for about 4 minutes, until they rise to the surface. Leave them to boil there for about a further minute, then test one – it should be tender with a little resistance. When the pasta is ready, drain and mix the orecchiette through with the Romanesco in the pan.

To serve, check the seasoning, add a little more olive oil to loosen the contents of the pan, then finish with plenty of freshly grated (shredded) parmesan.

Breakfast Kofte Naan Rolls with Tomato Chutney Sauce

100ml (3½fl oz) whole milk, plus more for glazing

2 tsp dried yeast

2 tbsp caster (superfine) sugar

200g (7oz) strong white bread flour, plus more for kneading

75g (2½oz) natural yogurt

60g (2½oz) ghee, plus more to fry the kofte (or use sunflower oil)

1½ tsp salt, plus more to season

2 tsp nigella seeds, plus more to sprinkle

1 small onion, finely diced

1–3 tsp chilli flakes, to taste

3 tomatoes, roughly chopped

2 tbsp white wine vinegar or cider vinegar

400g (14oz) minced (ground) lamb

½ tsp freshly ground black pepper

1 tsp garam masala

½ cucumber, deseeded and coarsely grated (shredded)

The clue is in the name here: a breakfast naan to be cooked and served at breakfast time, which by all accounts might mean that you have to rise early to get the dough made and proved in time to bake. Call these brunch kofte naan rolls, if you prefer. Use ghee to cook the naan, make the chutney and cook the kofte. Ghee will reward you with a more luxurious and complex flavour, and especially so in the naan dough. Buy a good-size pot of ghee. Stored well it will last up to a year, and is the *de facto* fat to use when cooking recipes from India, Bangladesh, Pakistan and Egypt. Essentially, what you are making is a tomato sauce. But, crucial to complement the spiced lamb kofte and also the naan, is to make this tomato sauce with a good amount of chilli – and, yes, I do find that blending the sauce makes all the difference to the finished dish. Cook the kofte still a little pink and juicy within but nicely caramelized on the exterior. Shoved in the still-warm naan with plenty of the spiky tomato-sauce chutney, this really is some kind of breakfast (sorry, I mean brunch).

Warm the milk slightly and stir it in a small bowl with the yeast and 1 tablespoon of the sugar. Leave the mixture to one side for 5 minutes, until frothy.

In a mixing bowl, combine the flour, yogurt, half the ghee or oil, ½ teaspoon of the salt and half the nigella seeds. Add the yeast mixture and mix well to form a rough dough.

Turn out the dough onto a lightly floured surface and knead vigorously for at least 2 minutes. Place in a bowl, cover with a clean, damp cloth and leave in a warm place for about 1 hour, or until roughly doubled in size.

Heat the remaining ghee or oil in a saucepan over a moderate heat. Add the onion and the remaining nigella seeds and fry for about 5 minutes, or until soft and translucent. Add the chilli flakes (to your taste), the tomatoes, another ½ teaspoon of salt, the vinegar, 1 tablespoon of the remaining sugar and 100ml (3½fl oz) of water.

Cook for 20 minutes, or until the tomatoes have formed a thick sauce, then blend to form a smooth sauce (although you can leave it as is if you prefer).

Mix the minced (ground) meat with the remaining ½ teaspoon of salt, the ½ teaspoon of freshly ground black pepper and all of the garam masala. Divide the mince into 8 sausage-shaped kofte.

Next divide the risen dough into 4 equal pieces and roll into smooth balls. Place these on baking paper on a baking sheet and cover with a clean tea towel. Leave in a warm place for 10 minutes to prove slightly.

Preheat the oven to 220°C/200°C fan/425°F/Gas Mark 7.

Brush the buns with some extra milk to glaze, sprinkle with a few extra nigella seeds and bake for 10–12 minutes, or until risen up and a deep, golden brown. Remove from the oven and keep warm.

Heat a spot of ghee or oil in a frying pan over a moderate heat. Add the kofte and fry for 2–5 minutes, until crisp and brown on the exterior and cooked to your liking.

Split the naan buns, add 2 kofte to each and top with the tomato chutney sauce. Serve straight away.

Chard & Taleggio Empanada or Impanata

350g (12oz) strong bread flour, plus more for dusting

1 tsp dried yeast

225ml (7¾fl oz) warm water

6 tbsp good olive oil, plus more for greasing

1 tsp salt, plus more to season

300g (10½oz) waxy potatoes

150g (5½oz) chard, stalks and leaves separated, both chopped small

1 onion, finely diced

3 cloves of garlic, thinly sliced

1 tsp fennel seeds, toasted and lightly crushed

1 tbsp tomato purée

200g (7oz) taleggio cheese, thinly sliced (or use camembert, brie, vacherin or any soft cheese with a rind)

1 egg, beaten

freshly ground black pepper

As kitchen activities go, making bread dough is among one of my favourites. I love the possibility a dough presents to the kitchen as time ticks on. It's one thing to bake a loaf, and quite another to use the dough to then make an empanada, impanata, pie or stuffed flat bread (call it what you like) such as this one. As processes go, this gently unassuming assembly of ingredients, wrapped as a gift to go into the oven, is one to tackle on the weekend, or with a good amount of time on your side. Time for the dough to prove, time to cook the onions soft and glossy to mix through with the fennel seeds and chard, and potatoes too, all of which must then cool; time to arrange the taleggio crosshatch, before sandwiching the whole lot, tightly shut, like a bubble-wrap envelope, save for one or two vents, to bake until golden and crisp, burping and belching its steamy, cheesy chard vapours.

Put the flour in a large mixing bowl and add the yeast, warm water and 2 tablespoons of the olive oil. Mix until fully incorporated. Then, add the salt and mix well again, until the dough is scraggy but come together. Put the mixture in an oiled bowl, cover with a clean, damp cloth, and put to one side for 10–15 minutes somewhere warm.

Put the potatoes in a pan and cover in well-salted cold water. Place over a high heat and bring to a simmer. Reduce the heat and simmer for about 15–18 minutes, until tender and cooked through. Remove from the heat and drain well. When cool enough to handle, cut into 5mm (¼in) slices.

Bring a large pan of salted water to a boil over a high heat. Add the chard stalks and boil for 2–3 minutes, until tender, then add the leaves and boil for 2 minutes more, until they are tender too. Drain well and put to one side until cool enough to squeeze dry.

Tip out the dough onto a lightly floured or oiled work surface and give it a good and vigorous knead for at least 2 minutes, until it is smooth and elastic.

Shape into a round and place it back into an oiled bowl, cover with a clean, damp cloth and leave somewhere warm for about 1–2 hours, or until just doubled in size.

Meanwhile, make the filling. Heat another 2 tablespoons of the olive oil in a saucepan over a moderate heat. Add the onion and fry for about 10 minutes, until soft and sweet, then add the garlic and crushed fennel seeds and cook for 3–5 minutes, until the garlic is soft and the fennel is fragrant.

Add the tomato purée and cook for 30 seconds more, then add the tender chard stalks and leaves and season to taste with salt and pepper, then put to one side.

Preheat the oven to 180°C/160°C fan/350°F/Gas Mark 4. Line an approximately 40 x 30cm (16 x 12in) flat baking sheet with baking paper and grease generously with the remaining 2 tablespoons of olive oil.

Divide the dough in half. On a lightly floured work surface, roll out the first portion until it is slightly larger than the baking sheet. Place the rolled-out dough onto the baking sheet with the edges slightly overhanging.

Spoon the chard filling on top and spread it out in an even, flat layer, then distribute the cheese and potato slices on top.

Roll out the second portion of dough until it is the same size as the baking sheet and place this on top of the filling. Cut off any pastry that hangs over the sides. Seal the sides of the empanada by pressing and rolling the top and bottom layers of dough together, and then pressing the two doughs together with the tines of a fork to seal securely.

Brush the top with the beaten egg. With a sharp knife, slash a couple of small holes in the top to create a vent for the steam. Transfer to the oven and bake for about 45–55 minutes, until nicely crisp and golden on top and piping hot throughout. Remove from the oven and leave to cool slightly, before cutting into pieces to serve warm.

Caramel Apple Cake

100g (3½oz) unsalted butter

160g (5¾oz) light brown soft sugar

175g (6oz) plain (all-purpose) flour

1 tsp ground ginger

1 tsp ground cinnamon

1 tsp baking powder

big pinch of salt

3 large eating apples (such as russet): 1 coarsely grated (shredded); 2 peeled, cored and cut into 8 wedges

3 eggs

200g (7oz) caster (superfine) sugar

150ml (5fl oz) sunflower oil

crème fraîche, cream or ice cream, to serve

This is a simple cake, which in my eyes makes it a great cake, one that anyone can make. Choose an interesting variety of apple if you can. With it being autumn, this shouldn't be all that difficult. I especially love russet apples, to eat and also to use in cakes and desserts. Russets, with their matt yellow and golden-brown colour and almost sandpapery skin, are the ugly duckling of the apple world, until you bite into one. With a firm, dry texture, they are less juicy, although definitely more crunchy, and the chomp of a russet apple can be heard from a mile off. Russet apples have the best flavour of all, fragrant like a pear, slightly nutty, and beautifully sweet. Baked here in the toffee and caramel sauce, the apples turn fudgy and glossy when up-ended as the topping to this cake.

Preheat the oven to 180°C/160°C fan/350°F/ Gas Mark 4. Line an approximately 25cm (10in) cake tin with baking paper.

Put the butter and the brown sugar in the prepared cake tin in the oven for 5 minutes to melt and combine. Remove from the oven and give the mixture a gentle stir to distribute.

In a large mixing bowl add the flour, ginger, cinnamon, baking powder and salt. Set aside.

Arrange the apple slices attractively on the bottom of the pan in the buttery, sugary syrup.

In a jug, whisk together the eggs, caster (superfine) sugar, grated apple and sunflower oil, then mix this into the dry ingredients in the bowl, stirring well to combine. Pour the batter over the apples in the cake tin, then bake for 40 minutes, or until a skewer inserted into the centre of the cake comes out clean.

Place the tin on a wire rack to cool the cake for at least 10 minutes, then invert the cake onto a serving plate. Serve warm or at room temperature.

Blackberry & Bay Brownies made with Rye

200g (7oz) 70% dark (bittersweet) chocolate, broken into small pieces

125g (4½oz) unsalted butter at room temperature, plus more for greasing

3 eggs, beaten

250g (9oz) light brown soft sugar

3 tbsp cocoa powder

100g (3½oz) rye flour (or use spelt or plain/all-purpose flour, if you like)

200g (7oz) blackberries

5 bay leaves, scrunched a little

More than just a pretty picture, these are flavours that flatter one another very well; sweet and bold, as if the blackberries and rye are meant to be together. Add the aromatic, spicy menthol notes of bay leaves and fruity, dark chocolate, both of which bring with them an intensity that suits very well these flavours of the earth, of autumn, and of wild brambly hedgerows (poetic licence, pick your own or buy the blackberries), and these are remarkably good brownies. As with all brownies, the trick is to almost under-bake them, leaving the brownies to firm up in the tin, with the chocolate then dreamily recalibrating with the blackberries from a melted mass to a dense and deeply rich form. They are neither redolent of cake, nor of chocolate, but something so wickedly good you'll have to limit the number of times you bake them. A child of nine has proclaimed these as 'the best thing you have ever made' – her young years make it no less a compliment.

Preheat the oven to 180°C/160°C fan/350°F/Gas Mark 4. Line a 20cm (8in) square cake tin or 25 x 15cm (10 x 6in) rectangular tin with baking paper.

Melt the chocolate and butter in a bowl set over a pan of simmering water or in a microwave on low (the defrost setting), gently stirring every now and then.

Put the eggs and sugar together in the bowl of a stand mixer fitted with the beater attachment and beat together until light and fluffy, then, using a spoon, fold in the cocoa powder and flour, until combined. Carefully stir in the melted chocolate mixture and half the blackberries.

Pour the cake batter into the prepared tin, dot with the remaining blackberries and the bay leaves and bake for 20–25 minutes, or until just firm to the touch and cracks have appeared at the edges. Remove from the oven and leave the brownies to cool to room temperature in the tin, until they have set. Cut into squares and serve.

PIEDMONTESE FEAST

Antipasti of Gnocco Fritto with Charcuterie, Anchovy Polenta Fritters & Piedmontese Peppers

Bresato al Nebbiolo with Baked Polenta, Carrots Dada & Cavolo Nero

Ricotta and Chocolate Tart with Hazelnuts & Grapes

FEEDS 6-8

To northern Italy for this autumnal supper feast – to Piedmont, if I'm going to be really specific. A rural area in northwest Italy, renowned for its quality of produce and, in particular, its wine, the region is dominated by agriculture and has rolling hills that are dense with vines and mountainous pastures for livestock to graze. All of this makes Piedmont home to some of the best producers of meat and dairy in all of Italy, with some enormously prestigious wines to boot. With a bucolic, hardworking reputation, Piedmont is much less ritzy than other areas of Italy. Its identity as an industrious farming community means that it also has great affinity with feasting and festivity. When it comes to food and wine and the commemoration of authentic gastronomy, perhaps of all the regions in Italy, Piedmont is it.

I've come up with a menu that celebrates the best of Piedmont. One that will give you enough of a culinary workout as to call it a feast, but not so much as to overwhelm you. If you're a stickler for authenticity, try to use produce typical to the area and its neighbours. While olive oil is now commonplace throughout Italy, beef dripping, lard, walnut or hazelnut oil would be the traditional cooking fat of the region. Choose charcuterie from northern Italy to serve with the gnocco fritto (fried bread dough, simply delicious). Although coastal, anchovies are also synonymous with the region and customarily used in bagna cauda (see page 64), which is often served after the grape harvest is in. Here, the anchovies are stuffed in a polenta crust, then fried as a fritter and are devastatingly good. Piedmontese peppers are a legendary antipasti dish. I've halved them here and served them on bruschetta to finish the trio. Eat all the antipasti standing up with a glass of white wine from the region – Gavi or Arneis, for example, although you could skip across to the Veneto and pour Prosecco, no one's really going to mind (although, better even still might be to source a dry Asti, a jolly pouring fizz and classic to the region).

For the main course, here is brasato – beef short ribs braised in a full-bodied red wine. I've used a Nebbiolo; look for Barbaresco or Nebbiolo Langhe or Nebbiolo D'Alba, all from same area and from the same (Nebbiolo) grape, and all wines with silky fruit, firm tannins and good acidity that will help to make the beef ribs extraordinary. I cannot bring myself to suggest cooking this dish with a more expensive wine than any of the above, though there are some that do, and should you find a sensibly priced substitute with similar characteristics – a Chianti, for example, that has good acidity and similar flavours. Go for it. You could use an inferior or cheaper wine to cook the beef in, but I think Nebbiolo does have the right muscle and structure to stand up to this rich, unctuous cut, and also the long, slow cooking time.

And finally, to Turin, the only city in all of Piedmont, said to be the place where chocolate was first introduced to Europe. I've given a nod to the region's longstanding association with chocolate and hazelnuts in a tart that I've also studded with grapes – full circle, here's to the harvest.

Antipasti of Gnocco Fritto with Charcuterie, Anchovy Polenta Fritters & Piedmontese Peppers

FOR THE ANCHOVY POLENTA
FRITTERS

big pinch of salt

40g (1½oz) fine polenta

40ml (1¼fl oz) whole milk

1 tsp dried yeast

150g (5½oz) plain (all-purpose)
flour, plus more for coating

sunflower oil, for deep-frying

6 salted anchovies, halved

MAKES 12

Heat 250ml (9fl oz) of water with the big pinch of salt in a saucepan over a moderate–high heat. Gradually add the polenta in a steady stream, whisking all the while. Keep whisking until the polenta starts to thicken and begins to bubble vigorously. Watch out, the bubbles of polenta can scald.

Reduce the heat to low (the polenta should now have a gentle blip-blip and not be bubbling too wildly) and continue to cook, stirring often, for 30 minutes, until cooked. Leave to one side to cool completely.

Transfer the polenta to a bowl and, using a fork, mash until broken down, then add the milk and yeast. Stir through the flour and mix well with a spoon to form a soft dough. Cover with a clean, damp cloth and leave for 45 minutes somewhere warm to rise.

Heat a high-sided saucepan with at least 5cm (2in) of sunflower oil to 180°C/350°F (if you pop a teaspoon of the batter in the oil, the oil is ready when the batter immediately turns golden and crisp).

With a spoon, scoop ping-pong-ball-size spoonfuls of the polenta batter and push half an anchovy fillet into the centre of each. Sprinkle some flour on a plate and roll briefly to coat. Working in batches, deep-fry the polenta fritters for about 3–5 minutes, until crisp and golden brown all over. Take care to ensure the oil remains at a steady temperature throughout frying. Remove with a slotted spoon and set aside to drain on paper towels. Serve warm.

cont.

FOR THE GNOCCO FRITTO OR FRIED BREAD DOUGH

250g (9oz) type '00' flour, plus more for dusting

1 tsp dried yeast

1 tbsp melted unsalted butter

pinch of salt

½ tsp baking powder

125ml (4fl oz) whole milk

sunflower oil, for deep-frying

assortment of charcuterie (such as prosciutto, mortadella and salami), to serve

Put the flour in a large mixing bowl and make a well in the centre. Add the yeast, butter and pinch of salt. Mix together vigorously, giving the contents a good knead in the bowl or on the work surface for at least 2 minutes. Cover with a clean, damp cloth and leave to rest for 30 minutes somewhere warm.

Knead again for another 2 minutes, then roll out the dough on a lightly floured surface to a thickness of 3mm (⅛in) and cut into 10 x 12cm (4 x 4½in) rectangles. (You could use a pasta machine for the rolling, if you like.)

Heat a high-sided saucepan with at least 5cm (2in) of sunflower oil to 180°C/350°F (see page 297 for how to test the oil). Working in batches, fry the pieces of dough, turning them over as they puff and crisp on one side, for about 2 minutes, until crisp all over and a nice golden colour. Take care to ensure the oil remains at a steady temperature throughout frying. Remove with a slotted spoon and set aside to drain on paper towels. Serve warm with the assorted charcuterie.

FOR THE PIEDMONTESE PEPPERS ON BRUSCHETTA

4 red (bell) peppers, halved and deseeded

about 8 tsp olive oil, plus more for the tomatoes and bread

2 cloves of garlic, thinly sliced

8 basil leaves

8 anchovy fillets, torn in half lengthways

8 tomatoes, halved (or use 16 red or yellow cherry tomatoes)

4 slices of good bread

salt and freshly ground black pepper

Preheat the oven to 180°C/160°C fan/350°F/Gas Mark 4.

Place the (bell) peppers cut sides upward on a baking tray and drizzle each with olive oil, about 1 teaspoon into each pepper half. Season each pepper half with salt and freshly ground black pepper, add a couple of slices of garlic, a basil leaf and 2 halves of anchovy. Finally, squash in 2 tomato halves (or 2 cherry tomatoes). Season the tomato with a little salt and pepper and a drizzle more of the olive oil.

Place the peppers snugly together on the baking tray and bake for 30–35 minutes, until the peppers are softened and even slightly charred in places. Remove from the oven and set aside to cool a little.

Rub the bread all over with olive oil and bake on a tray in the hot oven for about 10–12 minutes, until golden and toasted. Cut each slice into smaller, antipasti-size pieces. Slice each pepper in half and place on the bruschetta to serve.

Brasato al Nebbiolo
(Beef Short Ribs Braised in Nebbiolo)

1.5kg (3lb 5oz) beef short ribs, cut into 8cm (3¼in) pieces

2 tbsp olive oil

150–200g (5½–7oz) pancetta (or use diced streaky bacon)

50g (1¾oz) unsalted butter

2 onions, finely diced

2 celery sticks, chopped into small dice

2 carrots, finely diced

6 cloves of garlic, finely chopped

2 tbsp tomato purée

30g (1oz) plain (all-purpose) flour

½ bottle Nebbiolo wine (or use another full-bodied Italian red wine)

500ml (17fl oz) hot beef or chicken stock

2 bay leaves, scrunched a little

2 rosemary sprigs, leaves picked, or about 6 sage leaves, finely chopped

200g (7oz) baby onions or small shallots, peeled then left whole

salt and freshly ground black pepper

Preheat the oven to 150°C/130°C fan/300°F/Gas Mark 2.

Season the beef all over with salt and plenty of freshly ground black pepper. Heat the olive oil in a large casserole over a high heat and, working in batches without overcrowding the pan, brown the beef until nicely caramelized all over. Using a slotted spoon, remove the beef from the heat and set to one side on a plate. Add the pancetta to the pan and cook for about 1–2 minutes, until crisp and golden.

Reduce the heat to moderate and add the butter and the diced onions, celery and carrots and cook for 10 minutes, or until the vegetables are soft. Add the garlic and cook for a further 2 minutes, until fragrant. Add the tomato purée and cook for a further 5 minutes, then add the flour and stir well to combine. Add the wine, whisking as you do so to prevent lumps, then add the beef or chicken stock, continuing to whisk a little.

Add the beef back to the pan along with the herbs and increase the heat to high again. Bring to a boil, skim away any froth that rises to the surface and remove from the heat. Place the casserole in the oven and braise for 2–3 hours, adding the baby onions or small shallots about 1 hour into the cooking time. Check on the pot midway through cooking, adding a slosh more stock or water if the liquid level has reduced too much below the line of the beef ribs – they should be just about fully submerged in the cooking liquid throughout. When the meat is ready, it should be extremely tender and you'll be able to easily pull free the bone.

Remove from the oven, check the seasoning, adding salt and plenty of freshly ground black pepper to taste before serving.

Baked Polenta

1.5 litres (52fl oz) hot chicken stock or water

1 tsp salt, plus more to season

250g (9oz) fine polenta

50g (1¾oz) unsalted butter, plus more to bake

50g (1¾oz) parmesan, grated (shredded), plus more to serve

olive oil, for oiling

freshly ground black pepper

Put the stock or water and the salt in a good-size saucepan over a high heat and bring to a boil. Gradually add the polenta in a steady stream, whisking all the while as you pour. Keep whisking until the polenta starts to thicken and begins to bubble vigorously. Watch out, the bubbles of polenta can scald.

Turn the heat to low (the polenta should now have a gentle blip-blip and not be bubbling too wildly) and continue to cook, stirring often until the polenta grain is tender and has formed a thick, almost creamy, mass. This should take about 45 minutes.

Stir in the butter and parmesan and cook for a further 1 minute. Check the seasoning, adding more salt and plenty of freshly ground black pepper to taste. Remove from the heat and pour into an oiled, shallow dish or tray that has a lip of at least 2cm (¾in). (You can make the polenta ahead up to this point and store it in the fridge to cook the next day.)

Preheat the oven to 190°C/170°C fan/375°F/ Gas Mark 5. Line a baking tray with baking paper and lightly oil it all over.

Slice the polenta into pieces and place it on the prepared tray. Dot with a few knobs of butter all over. Bake for 20 minutes, until lightly browned and crisp on top, then remove from the oven and grate over a little more parmesan to serve.

Carrots Dada
(Carrots Cooked with Vinegar & Garlic)

80ml (2½fl oz) olive oil (enough to cover the base of the pan)

800g (1lb 12oz) baby carrots, trimmed (or use small carrots, sliced 1cm/½in thick)

6 cloves of garlic, peeled and halved

1 tbsp red wine vinegar

salt and freshly ground black pepper

½ bunch of flat-leaf parsley, leaves picked and finely chopped, to serve

Heat the oil in a saucepan (make sure you cover the base of the pan) over a moderate heat. Working in batches, add the carrots and garlic to the pan in an even layer, cooking for 3–4 minutes, until nicely caramelized, reserving each batch to a plate while you cook the next.

Return all of the cooked carrots and garlic to the pan and season to taste with salt and plenty of freshly ground black pepper, then add the vinegar and cook for 2 minutes, until the vegetables are coated in a vinegary syrup. Stir through the parsley to serve.

Cavolo Nero

1kg (2lb 4oz) cavolo nero, tough middle stalks discarded, leaves roughly chopped

20g (¾oz) unsalted butter or 20ml (¾fl oz) olive oil

Cook the cavolo nero in plenty of well-salted boiling water for about 6–8 minutes, until tender. Drain and add the butter or oil to serve.

Ricotta and Chocolate Tart with Hazelnuts & Grapes

120g (4¼oz) plain (all-purpose) flour

60g (2¼oz) cold unsalted butter, diced

150g (5½oz) light brown soft sugar, plus 2 tbsp to sprinkle

2 tbsp cocoa powder

150g (5½oz) ricotta cheese

1 egg and 1 egg yolk, beaten together

½ tsp baking powder

100g (3½oz) black grapes

50g (1¾oz) hazelnuts, roughly chopped

double (heavy) cream or crème fraîche, to serve

Preheat the oven to 180°C/160°C fan/350°F/ Gas Mark 4. Grease and line a 20–22cm (8–9in) tart tin with baking paper.

Using a food processor, pulse together the flour with the butter, sugar and cocoa powder until the mixture resembles fine, sandy breadcrumbs. Spread one third of this mixture into the prepared cake tin, pressing down slightly to form an even base.

In a mixing bowl, beat the ricotta with the eggs and baking powder, then stir in the remaining flour mixture, mixing well to combine. Pour this mixture over the base in the prepared cake tin. Sprinkle the top with the grapes and the hazelnuts.

Bake for 35–40 minutes, until golden on top and a skewer inserted into the centre comes out clean. Remove from the oven and sprinkle with the 2 tablespoons of brown sugar. Serve with lightly whipped double (heavy) cream or crème fraîche.

FAT OF THE LAND – A FEAST FOR AUTUMN

Squash Baked with Beer, Cheese, Cream & Pretzels

Grilled Gem Lettuce with Ranch Dressing

Apple & Custard Doughnuts with Maple Syrup & Vanilla Ice Cream

SERVES 6–8

This menu is reliably stress-free to achieve, but nonetheless still a good one for showing off, should you be that way inclined. (Aren't we all? Or, at the very least, don't we all want to exert ourselves in the kitchen beyond the remit of everyday cooking, occasionally?)

Broadly speaking, I'm looking to North America for the flavours and ingredients used in this meal. Swollen great things, squash (and pumpkins) are the prize jewel of autumn, practically toppling supermarket and greengrocer fruit and veg stands. Always choose the variety (whether squash or pumpkin) that are superior in taste and provenance. Avoid the juggernauts set aside for Halloween, as these are produced specifically for sculpting and are usually pretty tasteless. Look for sensibly sized, ripe, firm varieties of squash: medium-size squash, like the blue-grey skinned Crown Prince, or the dark green Kabocha; or any of the smaller varieties, such as sweet Uchiki Kuri or Acorn. Lopping the top off and pouring in beer, three types of cheese (some hard, some soft) and also cream to bake like a fondue makes this a hugely impressive centrepiece, fitting of a feast. It might be nice to serve the same beer to drink, so choose a good one – something dark and malty would be ideal.

The salad of grilled (broiled) gem lettuces with ranch dressing is a classic combination, with the charred leaves turning extra juicy and flavoursome.

And as for pudding... well, it had to be doughnuts, didn't it? A well-made, super-fresh doughnut will hands-down be the best doughnut you will ever eat, so making them at home is so worthwhile if fresh doughnuts are a top priority, which I am suggesting they should be (unless you live close to a stand-out bakery). The hardest thing about making doughnuts is to fry the dough at the correct temperature and for the temperature to remain consistent throughout the cook time. Too low and the dough will soak up the oil, turning the doughnuts flaccid and greasy; too high and the doughnut will colour too much before the centre is cooked, leaving you with a highly coloured, yet ultimately, raw doughnut. I've said it before, buy a digital cooking thermometer. They are an inexpensive piece of kit and one of the most useful kitchen utensils. The oil should be at 180°C/350°F to deep-fry the doughnuts. No more, no less. And, finally, you can buy a good-quality jar of apple sauce for your doughnut filling, but if you want to make it, you just need to put some peeled cooking or dessert apples, a splash of water and some sugar to taste in a lidded pan over a moderate heat and cook until the apples are softened and broken down. Likewise, you can buy the custard or make it, as you like. This is a special-occasion meal that should consume a bit of forethought, money and organization – buying one or two things to alleviate the pressure when you come to cook it will give the same outcome and is simple common sense. Something we all need to keep in mind when it comes to home cooking.

Squash Baked with Beer, Cheese, Cream & Pretzels

1 x 1.5–2kg (3lb 5oz–4lb 8oz) squash (such as Crown Prince), or use 2 smaller squash (such as acorn)

100g (3½oz) aged gruyère cheese, grated (shredded)

100g (3½oz) emmental cheese, grated (shredded)

100g (3½oz) reblochon cheese, finely chopped (or use taleggio, fontina, raclette or camembert)

1–2 cloves of garlic, very finely chopped

2 tsp plain (all-purpose) flour (optional, to stabilize the cheese)

150g (5½oz) pretzels, bashed into large crumbs

100ml (3½fl oz) ale or beer (such as amber ales, Belgian beers, not too hoppy)

100ml (3½fl oz) double (heavy) cream

salt and freshly ground black pepper

Preheat the oven to 180°C/160°C fan/350°F/Gas Mark 4.

Cut the top off the squash to make a lid, then hollow out the seeds. Season the inside cavity with salt and plenty of freshly ground black pepper and place on a baking tray. Replace the lid loosely and bake the medium-size squash for about 1–1½ hours or small squash for 30–45 minutes, until tender when skewered.

Meanwhile, mix the cheeses together in a bowl and combine with the garlic, and the flour (if using).

Increase the oven to 200°C/180°C fan/400°F/Gas Mark 6. Remove the squash from the oven and put to one side, leaving it (or them) in the baking tray and removing the lid(s). Scape any cooked flesh off the lid(s) and place it in the squash cavity along with a few of the pretzel pieces.

A little at a time, add in the cheese mixture, beer, pretzels and cream (a little of one, then another, then the next, and so on – and repeat), finishing with a good sprinkling of pretzel pieces and cheese. Put the lid(s) back on the squash. Carefully put the squash back into the hot oven on the tray and bake for 20–30 minutes, or until the fondue is melted and bubbling within.

Grilled Gem Lettuce with Ranch Dressing

1 clove of garlic, finely crushed

200ml (7fl oz) buttermilk

75g (2½oz) soft blue cheese
(such as roquefort)

2 tbsp white wine vinegar
or cider vinegar

2 tbsp good olive oil, plus more
to serve

4 little gem lettuces, halved
lengthways

1 red onion, finely sliced into rings

1 small bunch of chives, finely
chopped

50g (1¾oz) pecans, roughly
chopped (optional)

salt and freshly ground black pepper

Whisk the garlic, buttermilk, cheese, 1 tablespoon of the vinegar, and 1 tablespoon of the oil in a medium bowl until you have a smooth dressing. Season the dressing with salt and plenty of freshly ground black pepper.

Toss the lettuce and onion in a bowl with the remaining oil and 1 tablespoon of vinegar and season well with salt.

Heat a grill (broiler) pan or cast-iron frying pan (skillet) to very hot and grill (broil) the lettuce, cut sides downward, and the onion for 2–3 minutes, until the lettuce is slightly wilted and both the lettuce and onion are charred in places.

Put the grilled lettuce on a large serving plate and spoon over the dressing. Add the chives and the pecans, if using, and a splash more olive oil to serve.

Apple & Custard Doughnuts with Maple Syrup & Vanilla Ice Cream

1 tsp dried yeast

2 tbsp caster (superfine) sugar, plus more to coat the doughnuts

120ml (4fl oz) whole milk

280g (10oz) strong white bread flour, plus more for dusting

pinch of salt

45g (1½oz) unsalted butter, melted

1 egg, beaten

sunflower oil, for deep-frying and greasing

about 4 tbsp apple sauce (shop-bought or homemade)

about 4 tbsp custard (shop-bought or homemade)

maple syrup, to serve

MAKES 6-8

Stir the yeast and sugar into the warm milk. Set to one side for 10 minutes and allow the mixture to activate and become frothy.

In a mixing bowl or in a stand mixer fitted with the dough hook, add the flour, pinch of salt, melted butter and beaten egg and mix well for at least 2 minutes to form a soft and sticky dough. Cover with a clean, damp cloth and rest the dough for 10 minutes.

Hand-knead the rested dough or mix in the mixer with a dough hook for a further 2–3 minutes, until it becomes smooth and supple. Cover and rest again for 20–30 minutes, or until increased in size by about half.

Tip out the dough onto a lightly floured work surface and roll it out to about 1.5cm (⅝in) thick. Cut out six to eight 8cm (3¼in) circles and place each round on greased baking paper, reserving the offcuts. Cover the doughnuts with a clean tea towel and allow to prove for 30 minutes–1 hour, until doubled in size.

Fill a deep-sided saucepan two thirds full with oil (do not overfill). Heat it to 180°C/350°F, or until a little piece of dough sizzles and rises to the surface and browns immediately.

Working in batches, fry each doughnut for about 1½ minutes on each side, until golden all over, then carefully remove with a slotted spoon and transfer to a wire rack. Coat with extra sugar while still warm.

Put the apple sauce into a piping bag fitted with a medium, round piping nozzle, or use the corner of a small, sturdy plastic bag with the tip cut off. When the doughnuts are cool enough to handle, push the piping nozzle (or use the tip of a knife to make a hole so that you can push in the plastic bag) into the centre of each doughnut and fill with the apple sauce, then repeat with the custard.

Put all the doughnuts on a large serving plate and drizzle liberally with the maple syrup to serve.

WINTER

Pot Roast Chicken with Prunes & Potato

8 large bone-in, skin-on chicken thighs

800g (1lb 12oz) small charlotte potatoes, peeled (or another waxy potato)

1 leek, sliced into 1cm (½in) rounds

2 onions, finely sliced

2 cloves of garlic, sliced

120g (4¼oz) pitted prunes

2 bay leaves, scrunched a little

1 thyme sprig

250ml (9fl oz) white wine (or use a medium sherry, water or chicken or vegetable stock)

salt and freshly ground black pepper

I really like prunes – as a dried fruit snack, in so many puddings and also stewed for breakfast on porridge. But, if I'm honest, where I love prunes best of all is in savoury cooking. Dried plums, jet-black prunes bring a fruity intensity to main-course dishes and I adore how they start out firm and wrinkly, then swell in the cooking juices of a braise or casserole, all deep and treacly, and bloated with a plummy savouriness. The prunes here make an everyday chicken casserole really rather special. You could use pork chops and cook in the same style, but I would brown the chops off in a pan to begin with. Some watercress or spinach on the side would be good.

Preheat the oven to 200°C/180°C fan/400°F/Gas Mark 6.

Mix all the ingredients in a bowl, then tip them into a large casserole. Cover with a lid (or thick foil) and bake for 10 minutes.

Lower the heat to 180°C/160°C fan/350°F/Gas Mark 4, and cook for 1 hour, giving everything a good stir halfway through cooking and removing the lid for the final 20 minutes, until the chicken is cooked through.

Remove from the oven and rest, with the lid on, for 15 minutes before serving.

Mushroom Meatballs with Pearl Barley

3 tbsp olive oil, plus more for greasing

2 onions, finely diced

4 cloves of garlic, very finely chopped

100g (3½oz) pearl barley

800ml (28fl oz) hot chicken or vegetable stock

1 bay leaf, scrunched a little

250g (9oz) shiitake mushrooms, coarsely grated (shredded)

250g (9oz) chestnut mushrooms, coarsely grated (shredded)

1 small bunch of flat-leaf parsley, leaves picked and finely chopped

50g (1¾oz) rolled oats

50g (1¾oz) dried breadcrumbs

2 eggs, beaten a little

40g (1½oz) parmesan, finely grated (shredded), plus more to serve

1 tsp salt, plus more to season

½ tsp freshly ground black pepper, plus more to season

Honestly, these sound so virtuous I can fully understand why a particular sort of cook, or mealtime recipient, might well want to dodge this dish altogether. My job as a food writer, however, involves encouraging you to follow these instructions and make these mushroom (meat)balls. They are delicious. Better, says my 12-year-old daughter Grace, than real meatballs. Be under no illusion, this recipe is a corker. Tender and savoury, the meatballs wallow in the barley with some parsley and parmesan. I used chicken stock to cook the barley, because I am not vegetarian, but use vegetable stock or bouillon if you like – it will be equally enjoyable.

Preheat the oven to 200°C/180°C fan/400°F/Gas Mark 6. Line a baking tray with baking paper and brush it with oil.

Heat the oil in a saucepan over a moderate heat. Add the onions and cook for about 10 minutes, until soft and translucent. Add the garlic and cook for a further 2 minutes, until fragrant, then remove from the heat and set aside half the mixture in a mixing bowl.

Add the barley to the onion mixture left in the pan and add the stock and the bay leaf. Season with salt and pepper to taste and bring to a boil. Cover, and cook over a low heat for 18–20 minutes, until the barley is tender. Remove from the heat and keep warm in the liquid.

Meanwhile, add the grated (shredded) mushrooms, half the parsley, and the oats, breadcrumbs, eggs and parmesan to the onion mixture in the bowl. Add the teaspoon of salt and ½ teaspoon of black pepper and mix the ingredients together very well. Form into meatballs, each about the size of a ping-pong ball, and place on the prepared baking tray.

Bake the meatballs for 15–20 minutes, or until they are firm and have taken on a bit of colour. Remove from the oven.

Put the barley and the juices in a large serving dish and top with the mushroom meatballs, adding the remaining parsley on top. Sprinkle with extra parmesan to serve.

Soft Polenta with Chard, Sausage & Chilli

400g (14oz) chard, stalks sliced small, leaves roughly chopped

120g (4¼oz) polenta

40g (1½oz) unsalted butter, diced small, or use 40ml (1½fl oz) olive oil

400g (14oz) sausages (about 6), meat squeezed out

2 cloves of garlic, finely chopped

1 tbsp chopped thyme, rosemary or sage leaves

½ tsp chilli flakes, plus more to taste, if you like

salt and freshly ground black pepper

about 40g (1½oz) parmesan, grated (shredded)

This is a sort of desert-island dish for me. No frills, just comfort and flavour, like the sorts of dishes your mum might have made you; ones that you recognize so well, you feel a deep sense of contentment at the prospect of sitting down to eat them. There is nothing demanding in this sort of food: you eat it and you feel replenished, and all is well with the world. Buy good sausages with a high meat content and not too much rusk – you want the broken sausagemeat to brown and caramelize in the pan with some larger, succulent pieces and some scrappy and crisp. Serve this on top of the chard and the polenta, with chilli flakes and parmesan the easy go-to.

Bring 1 litre (35fl oz) of well-salted water to a boil over a high heat and cook the chard stalks for 5 minutes, until tender, then remove but keep the cooking water. Put the pan back on the heat and whisk in the polenta. Reduce the heat to low and simmer, stirring often, for about 20–25 minutes, until thick and smooth and the polenta is cooked.

While the polenta is cooking, melt half the butter in a medium saucepan over a moderate heat. Add the sausagemeat and fry, stirring occasionally, for about 5 minutes, until nicely browned. Some larger, some smaller sausage bits are nice, and all the scraps, too. Transfer to a plate, reserving the fat in the pan.

Add the cooked chard stalks and the leaves to the pan along with the garlic, herbs and chilli flakes and cook for 2 minutes, or until the leaves are well wilted and any liquid has cooked away. Check the seasoning, adding more if necessary.

When the polenta is ready, remove from the heat and stir in the parmesan and the remaining butter, adding salt and pepper to taste. Serve the polenta topped with the chard, then the sausages and add more chilli to taste, if you like.

Carrot, Ginger & Goat Cheese Fritters

150g (5½oz) self-raising flour

3 eggs, beaten

80ml (2½fl oz) whole milk

1 tbsp coriander seeds, toasted and ground

1 tbsp grated (shredded) fresh ginger

½ bunch of spring onions (scallions), thinly sliced

1 small bunch of coriander (cilantro), leaves roughly chopped

350g (12oz) carrots, peeled and coarsely grated (shredded)

100g (3½oz) soft, fresh goat cheese

sunflower oil, for frying

salt and freshly ground black pepper

lemon or lime wedges, to serve

natural yogurt or sour cream, seasoned with salt, to serve

A super-quick midweek meal, and a striking combination of goat cheese, carrot, ginger and coriander, all flavours that work brilliantly together in these fritters. You want a fresh goat cheese for this recipe, light and acidic, and don't mix the cheese too much into the batter – ideally aim for lumps of the cheese that go soft and creamy with the heat as the fritters cook. If you don't want to use goat cheese, you could use a full-fat soft cheese or some feta instead. Serve with yogurt or sour cream seasoned with a pinch of salt.

Put the flour in a mixing bowl and whisk in the eggs, milk and ground coriander. Fold through the ginger, spring onions (scallions), and half the chopped coriander (cilantro) and, finally, all the carrots. Season with salt and pepper to taste. (Fry a little amount in advance to check that you've got the seasoning right.)

Add the goat cheese to the batter in small teaspoons and very gently fold though.

Add enough oil to a large non-stick or cast-iron frying pan (skillet) to coat the base. Place over a moderate heat, and when the oil is shimmering hot, add tablespoons of the batter. Fry for about 2 minutes, until the fritters have formed a crust and you can then flip and fry on the other side for a further 2 minutes. Work quickly in small batches until you have used up all the mixture, keeping the cooked fritters warm on a plate lined with paper towels.

Scatter the fritters with the remaining chopped coriander, then serve with the lemon or lime wedges and the seasoned yogurt at the table.

Miso & Mustard Butter Baked Potato

4 baking potatoes

2 tbsp white miso (also known as shiromiso)

120g (4¼oz) unsalted butter, at room temperature

2 shallots, thinly sliced

1 large leek, split lengthways and finely sliced

1 tbsp Dijon mustard

1 small bunch of chives, finely chopped

salt and freshly ground black pepper

Baked potatoes are immensely satisfying: crisp, salty skins with a soft and fluffy interior. Granted, they are in the oven for a wee while, but not all midweek dinners need to be fast. Some can just be simple, giving you ample time to get the 'things' done, which in my house, is never-ending on the weekdays. As for the miso, it's an ingredient I often get quizzed on: 'What else can I use miso for apart from soups and such?' Use it as a baste or marinade for grilled meat, fish or vegetables (particularly good for aubergines/eggplants). Miso lends a salty, savoury tang that comes from the fermentation process. I like the white variety best, enjoying its mellow, sweet flavour. Mixed through with the butter and mustard here, the miso forms an unbeatable assembly that melts into the hot potato along with the leek and shallot for pure comfort food. Some watercress or a green salad on the side would be ample.

Preheat the oven to 180°C/160°C fan/350°F/Gas Mark 4.

Prick the potatoes and wash them, then while they are still wet roll each in a sprinkling of salt to coat. Place them in the oven on a tray or directly on the rack and bake for 50 minutes–1¼ hours, until crisp-skinned and tender throughout. Remove from the oven.

While the potatoes are baking, mix the miso with the butter and put to one side.

Heat one quarter of the miso butter in a pan over a moderate–low heat. Add the shallots and the leek and cook for 10 minutes, until soft, then season with salt and pepper to taste and put to one side.

Add the mustard and the chives to the remainder of the miso butter and stir to combine.

Cut a deep cross into each cooked potato and divide the cooked leek and shallot mixture between each. Next, divide the butter with the miso, mustard and chives between each of the baked potatoes and pop them back in the oven for a couple of minutes to warm through before serving.

Crumpets with Eggs Arnold Bennet

300ml (10½fl oz) whole milk

150ml (5fl oz) double (heavy) cream

1 bay leaf, scrunched a little

¼ tsp freshly ground black pepper, plus more to season

⅛ nutmeg, grated (shredded), or to taste

400g (14oz) smoked, skinless haddock fillets or other firm smoked white fish

80g (2¾oz) unsalted butter

40g (1½oz) plain (all-purpose) flour

9 eggs

40g (1½oz) parmesan, grated (shredded)

1 small bunch of chives, finely chopped

8 crumpets

salt

An enterprising chef at London's Savoy Hotel famously created the omelette Arnold Bennet in 1929 for the eponymous writer. Mr Bennet didn't eat his omelette with crumpets – more's the pity, because he missed out. Crumpet pockets provide crevices for the delectable juices to pool.

Put the milk and 100ml (3½fl oz) of the cream in a small saucepan with the bay leaf, the ¼ teaspoon of freshly ground pepper and the grated (shredded) nutmeg. Place over a high heat and bring to a simmer, then add the fish. Take the pan off the heat, cover and leave the fish to cook as the milk and cream cool, about 5–8 minutes.

Using a slotted spoon, transfer the fish to a plate and flake it into large chunks. Set aside. Strain the poaching liquid and return it to the pan to keep warm.

Melt 50g (1¾oz) of the butter in a pan over a moderate heat, then whisk in the flour and cook for 1 minute. Gradually add the poaching liquid to the pan, whisking well to prevent lumps forming. Cook for 5 minutes, until thickened, then mix in the remaining cream and one of the eggs. Mix well and remove from the heat. Stir in the flaked fish, adding salt and pepper to taste.

Preheat the grill (broiler) to high.

Beat together the remaining eggs. Heat the remaining butter in a cast-iron frying pan (skillet) or omelette pan over a moderate–high heat, then pour in the beaten eggs, shaking the pan to distribute the eggs and giving it a stir with a spatula. Leave to set for a few seconds and repeat a couple of times, shaking the pan to redistribute.

When the omelette is still a little runny in the middle, take the pan off the heat and pour over the fish and sauce, then sprinkle over the parmesan and half the chives. Place the omelette under the grill and cook until golden brown and bubbling.

Meanwhile, toast the crumpets.

Remove the omelette from the grill, add the remaining chives, and spoon onto the crumpets to serve.

Pappardelle with Leek & Pancetta

50g (1¾oz) unsalted butter

4 leeks, white and pale green parts only, finely sliced

4 rashers of pancetta, roughly chopped (or use streaky bacon)

2 cloves of garlic, finely sliced

120g (4¼oz) crème fraîche

1 small bunch of flat-leaf parsley or chives, leaves picked and finely chopped

300g (10½oz) pappardelle (or another long, flat pasta)

salt and freshly ground black pepper

parmesan, grated (shredded), to serve

Leeks cooked down to a silky tangle in butter along with some pancetta and crème fraîche makes for a wonderful sauce for the pasta here. When you come to drain the pappardelle, make sure you keep back a cup of the cooking water, well-salted and a little viscous with the starch from the pasta. You can add it to the sauce if the mixture is too thick. You want the sauce to cling to the pasta just so, and not form an enormous clump of cooked pasta in a bowl. Parmesan, freshly grated (shredded) at the table and plenty of freshly ground black pepper are essential.

Melt the butter in a deep, cast-iron frying pan (skillet) over a moderate heat and add the leeks and pancetta. Cook for 10 minutes, until the leeks are very soft but without any colour. Add the garlic and cook for another minute, then add the crème fraîche and parsley or chives and remove from the heat.

Meanwhile, cook the pappardelle to al dente according to the packet instructions, reserving a little cooking liquid when you come to drain.

Check the seasoning of the leek mixture, adding salt and pepper to taste, and stir in the cooked pasta to coat. If the mixture is too thick, add a few tablespoons of the reserved pasta cooking water to loosen. Serve with plenty of freshly grated (shredded) parmesan at the table.

Tagliatelle with Brown Butter & Shrimps

400g (14oz) tagliatelle (or another long, flat pasta)

40g (1½oz) unsalted butter

100g (3½oz) spinach leaves, roughly chopped if large

2 tbsp capers (desalinated if necessary), rinsed and drained

100g (3½oz) potted shrimps

zest and juice of ½ unwaxed lemon

Tiny brown shrimps, potted in butter and seasoned with a little mace or nutmeg and sometimes cayenne pepper, are altogether a winning ingredient. You can make your own potted shrimps, but you might find it difficult to source the shrimps and, in any case, the shop-bought versions are very good and a bit of a stealth, one-pot wonder ingredient. All you need is just six ingredients for this very quick supper: tagliatelle, spinach, capers, butter and lemon all mixed through with the sweet shrimps. No parmesan necessary; it would be odd with the shrimps.

Cook the pasta to al dente according to the packet instructions, reserving a little cooking liquid when you drain.

Melt the butter in a pan over a moderate heat and add the spinach, cooking for 2–3 minutes, until wilted. Stir in the capers and potted shrimps, adding the lemon zest and juice, and seasoning with salt and pepper to taste.

Toss through the cooked pasta, adding a little of the cooking water, if required, to loosen. Serve immediately.

Black-eyed Pea Dal Makhani

200g (7oz) small black urad lentils (or use dark brown or green lentils)

1 cinnamon stick

3 green cardamom pods, squashed slightly

1 bay leaf, scrunched a little

½ tsp salt, plus more to season

50g (1¾oz) ghee or unsalted butter

1 small onion, finely diced

1 tbsp grated (shredded) fresh ginger

2 cloves of garlic, finely chopped

1 tbsp tomato purée

1 tbsp garam masala

150ml (5½fl oz) double (heavy) cream or natural yogurt

1 x 400g (14oz) can of black-eyed peas, drained and rinsed

freshly ground black pepper

green chillies, thinly sliced, to serve (optional)

Makhani dal is fantastically rich, a dal to fill you with warmth and sustenance when the weather is at its most cold and bleak. Use ghee to make the dal – it will bring terrific flavour, and buy *urad* (also known as *urid*) lentils, as they blossom best with a long cooking time. The black-eyed peas, called *chawli*, are there for added texture and I like the creamy weight a bean brings to the mass of lentils. Good garam masala brings with it a beautiful fragrance when sprinkled directly on the finished dish, perfuming the air as you sit down to eat. Serve this with chapati or roti (you can buy very good versions of either from southern Asian grocery stores or larger supermarkets, or you could make the chapati on page 281). Steamed rice would also be good.

Put the lentils, cinnamon, cardamom, bay leaf and 800ml (28fl oz) of water in a pan over a moderate heat and cook the lentils for 45 minutes–1 hour, or until cooked through. Add the ½ teaspoon of salt toward the end of the cooking time. When the lentils are tender, remove from the heat.

While the lentils are cooking, melt half the ghee or butter in a pan over a moderate heat. Add the onion and cook for about 10 minutes, until softened, then add the ginger, garlic, tomato purée and half the garam masala. Cook for 1 minute, until fragrant.

Transfer half the lentil mixture to a blender or food processor and blitz to a smooth purée, then return the purée to the pan. (Or, use a stick blender if you prefer – blending the mixture in pulses so that you leave plenty of texture.) Add 100ml (3½fl oz) of the cream and the remaining ghee. Stir through, then add the lentil mixture to the onion mixture. Add the black-eyed peas and season to taste with salt and pepper.

To serve, spoon over the remaining cream, top with the remaining garam masala, and sprinkle over some slices of green chilli, if using.

'Nduja Hot Dogs with Fried Bitter Greens

400g (14oz) cime di rapa, cavolo nero or kale, tough middle stalks discarded, leaves roughly chopped

about 1 tbsp good olive oil

50g (1¾oz) 'nduja

1 shallot, finely chopped

75g (2½oz) unsalted butter, softened

4 best-quality hot dogs

4 hot-dog buns, split down the middle

salt, for cooking the greens

'Nduja is a spreadable, spicy pork paste from Calabria, Italy, and is widely available from larger supermarkets and also Italian delis. It is dangerous stuff, because (without fail) if you enjoy cured pork and you like chilli, 'nduja makes most dishes unapologetically delicious, melting as it does in contact with heat and giving off a fiery, salty and silky spiciness. With the bitter greens here, the spice, fat and seasoning complement the earthy, inky greens beautifully. I used Italian cime di rapa, but cavolo nero or kale would work, as would chard, or cooked treviso, endive or radicchio – it's the bitter quality of the cooked leaf that is so crucial in this recipe. Without that, the 'nduja (and the extra butter) and hot dog together might well just finish you off. We ate these for breakfast on the shoot for this book. Not an awful lot else was eaten that day. Full, all four of us.

Boil the greens in well-salted water for anywhere between 8 and 15 minutes (depending on the leaf), until completely tender. Remove from the heat, drain and squeeze out any excess water. Drizzle with the olive oil and keep warm.

Put the 'nduja and shallot into a small, cold frying pan over a moderate heat and break up the 'nduja with the back of a spoon until its fat has rendered and it is fairly smooth and the shallots have bubbled in the fat briefly. Remove from the heat and cool a little.

Put the 'nduja and shallot in a bowl with the softened butter and beat together well. Cool slightly to firm up again if needed.

Heat the hot dogs according to the packet instructions.

Butter the buns with the 'nduja butter, then toast them, buttered sides downward, in a dry frying pan over a moderate heat, until lightly toasted and coloured.

To serve, fill each toasted bun with a hot dog and pile in the bitter greens.

Banana & Dulce de Leche Crumble

80g (2¾oz) plain (all-purpose) flour (or use wholemeal or spelt)

40g (1½oz) light brown soft or demerara sugar

pinch of salt

100g (3½oz) cold unsalted butter, diced

30g (1oz) rolled oats

4 large ripe bananas, peeled and thickly sliced

120g (4¼oz) dulce de leche

30g (1oz) roasted hazelnuts, roughly chopped (optional)

double (heavy) cream, ice cream or crème fraîche, to serve

Possibly lurking around the same territory as Elvis's fatal banana, bacon and peanut butter sandwiches, this is most definitely a pudding to eat in wintertime; a rib tickler and by no means one for those who don't have a sweet tooth. It appears in the midweek cookery section, because it is so easy to put together. I really like how the banana slumps into sweet obliteration as it cooks with all the dulce de leche. You could use wholemeal or spelt flour in lieu of the plain (all-purpose) white, if you wanted to salvage any sense of nutritional credibility.

Preheat the oven to 180°C/160°C fan/350°F/Gas Mark 4.

Make the crumble topping. Combine the flour, sugar, pinch of salt and butter in a large bowl. Rub in the butter with your fingertips until the mixture resembles breadcrumbs, then stir in the oats (alternatively, pulse the mixture in a food processor until just combined).

In an ovenproof dish, combine the banana, dulce de leche, and the nuts (if using). Scatter with the crumble topping, then sprinkle over a few drops of water.

Bake for 30 minutes, or until the crumble is golden brown and the mixture beneath is bubbling at the sides. Remove from the oven and serve warm.

Orange Zest Ricotta on Rye with Dark Chocolate

250g (9oz) ricotta cheese

50g (1¾oz) caster (superfine) sugar (or use icing/confectioner's sugar)

zest of 1 unwaxed orange

4 slices of dark rye bread

50g (1¾oz) 70% dark (bittersweet) chocolate, grated (shredded)

Not really a recipe, more a casual assembly of good-tasting, complementary ingredients; and less a pudding, more a decent snack at 11 (a.m. or p.m. – I don't think either time slot would mind). I am a huge fan of good rye bread – the really dark kind, that goes a little bit chewy when toasted. If it has some caraway in the mixture, I'm sold. Work quickly, and have the chocolate already grated (shredded) to scatter over the hot toast, to melt before piling on the ricotta mixture, all stippled with the orange zest.

Put the ricotta in a bowl and mix in the sugar and orange zest.

Toast the bread and immediately add half the grated (shredded) chocolate to the hot toast to melt a little.

Pile on the ricotta mixture and sprinkle over the remaining chocolate to serve.

Mushroom & Smoked Tofu Ciabatta Buns with Aioli & Watercress

12 large flat mushrooms, stalks removed and reserved

4 tbsp olive oil or about 60g (2oz) unsalted butter, plus a little more for grilling (broiling)

2 small red onions, finely diced

2 cloves of garlic, finely chopped

1 small bunch of flat-leaf parsley, leaves picked and finely chopped

200g (7oz) smoked tofu or smoked cheese, cut into 2cm (¾in) pieces

1 large ciabatta cut into 4 (or use buns or rolls)

4 tbsp mayonnaise or aioli (see page 52)

1 bunch of watercress, rocket (arugula) or lettuce

salt and freshly ground black pepper

Don't throw away the stalks on your mushrooms. In this recipe they go into the stuffing, along with some smoked tofu (or use smoked cheese, if you like). The result is a gargantuan fungi burger that will dribble down your chin and have your guests grovelling in the presence of such mighty culinary wizardry.

Preheat the oven to 180°C/160°C fan/350°F/Gas Mark 4.

Rub 8 of the mushrooms all over with half the olive oil or butter, then season with salt and plenty of freshly ground black pepper and place on a baking tray. Roast for 8–10 minutes, until softened but still holding their shape. Remove from the oven and put to one side.

Heat the remaining olive oil or butter in a pan over a moderate heat. Add the onions and cook for 10 minutes, until soft and translucent. Add the garlic and cook for a further 2 minutes, until fragrant.

Meanwhile, coarsely grate/shred (or use a food processor) the remaining 4 mushrooms and all the stems, then add this to the cooked onions and garlic in the pan and cook for about 5 minutes, until the mushrooms have softened and released their liquid. Increase the heat and cook until all the liquid has completely evaporated.

Stir in the parsley and tofu (or smoked cheese) and season well with salt and pepper to taste. Use this mixture to fill 4 of the cooked, whole mushrooms and place another on top to enclose the filling.

Place the stuffed mushrooms back into the oven to heat through for around 5–8 minutes, or until piping hot. Remove from the oven,

Cut each chunk of ciabatta in half through its middle to create a top and bottom (or slice the buns or rolls). Toast the ciabatta halves (or buns or rolls), spread the bottom halves with mayonnaise or aioli. Add the salad leaves and carefully place on top a stuffed mushroom. Top with the remaining half of the bread and serve.

Fried Chilli Butter Sesame Eggs with Kale on Toast

2 tbsp sunflower oil

1 tsp sesame oil

4 cloves of garlic, thinly sliced

250g (9oz) curly kale, stems discarded

2 tbsp light soy sauce

90g (3¼oz) softened unsalted butter

1 tsp–1 tbsp chilli flakes (such as Turkish Aleppo; or use finely chopped red chilli)

4 eggs

2 tbsp sesame seeds

4 slices of good bread

Minutes. That is what this lunch or supper should take you to assemble. Stir-frying the kale in sesame, garlic and a splosh of soy to soften is delicious. Once cooked, the leaves will sit quite happily warm in a pan as you fry the eggs. There's quite a bit of butter to cook the eggs. I enjoy cooking eggs in butter because I like how it foams and caramelizes around the egg whites as they cook, although you could just as well use oil, if you prefer. Chilli. Again, quite a bit because the eggs can take it, and I like Turkish Aleppo chilli flakes for a sweet, hot heat that suits the nutty, molten butter so well. Cavolo nero would be just as good as the kale, again, if you prefer.

Heat both oils in a large pan or wok over a high heat, then add the garlic and stir-fry for 30 seconds, until fragrant. Add the kale along with the soy sauce and 1 tablespoon of water, and cook to wilt down, until the kale is cooked through but still has texture. Remove from the heat and keep warm.

Heat the butter and chilli in a non-stick or cast-iron frying pan (skillet) over a moderate–high heat until foaming. Crack open the eggs one at a time and slip each into the pan, one at a time, immediately reducing the heat to low and sprinkling over the sesame seeds. (Work in batches to cook the eggs, if you prefer.)

Cook until the edges of the eggs have set and the whites are opaque (about 2–5 minutes), then baste the eggs with the chilli butter in the pan until the yolk is cooked to your liking.

Toast the bread, add the softened kale to the toast and top with the eggs, spooning over the chilli butter from the pan.

Clay Pot Rice

2 boneless, skinless chicken thighs, cut into bite-size pieces

2 cloves of garlic, finely chopped

1 tbsp finely grated (shredded) fresh ginger, unpeeled is fine

2 tbsp light soy sauce

2 tbsp oyster sauce

2 tbsp rice wine or sherry

1 tbsp light brown soft sugar

350g (12oz) jasmine rice, or another long grain rice

5 dried shiitake mushrooms, soaked in warm water for at least 20 minutes

3 tbsp sunflower oil

100g (3½oz) streaky bacon, chopped

1 bunch of spring onions (scallions), trimmed and finely sliced

800ml (28fl oz) hot chicken or vegetable stock or water

salt and freshly ground black pepper

Clay pot rice is a southern Chinese, Malaysian or Singaporean rice dish. Traditionally, as the name suggests, the rice is cooked in a clay pot, and I am absolutely sure there are many, many versions of how it's done in rice-eating countries the world over. In a clay pot, rice can achieve its much-vaunted crust, with the rice singeing and sticking to the sides of the pot as the liquid evaporates. A heavy-based, cast-iron casserole will work, too – it just won't have exactly the same effect. Of course, you can't then call it clay pot rice, either, but you could call it cast-iron-pot rice and no one's really going to mind, are they? Use a small amount of meat for this recipe: chicken thighs and streaky bacon, also a few inexpensive-to-buy dried shiitake mushrooms. The rice swells to feed four, with not an awful lot of money spent.

Mix the chicken with the garlic, ginger, soy, oyster sauce, rice wine or sherry and sugar. Leave to marinate for at least 30 minutes.

Rinse the rice in cold water and drain well, then drain the mushrooms, slice thinly and put to one side.

Heat the oil in a casserole over a high heat. Add the chicken and stir-fry for 2 minutes, or until lightly browned all over. Add the mushroom slices, bacon and half the spring onions (scallions) and stir-fry for 2 minutes, then remove from the heat and pile onto a plate.

Add the rice and chicken stock to the pan and place it back over a high heat with the lid on. Bring to a boil, then immediately reduce the heat to a low simmer and steam the rice for 15 minutes, until nearly cooked through.

Spread the cooked chicken mixture on top of the rice and replace the lid. Continue to steam over a low heat for another 15 minutes, until the chicken and rice are both cooked. There should be no liquid left in the pan and the bottom of the pot might even have formed a slight crust (if you're lucky) with the rice. Remove from the heat and top with the remaining spring onions to serve.

Boston Baked Beans

350g (12oz) dried cannellini beans, soaked overnight in plenty of cold water

1 bay leaf, scrunched a little

5 cloves of garlic, 1 whole and unpeeled, 4 peeled and finely chopped

3 tbsp olive oil

1 onion, finely sliced

1 x 400g (14oz) can of chopped tomatoes

2 tsp English mustard powder

60g (2¼oz) dark brown soft sugar

20g (¾oz) black treacle

300g (10½oz) piece of pork belly, cut into 5 pieces

salt and freshly ground black pepper

Shamelessly hearty, these beans are cooked with pork belly, black treacle and English mustard powder, among other aromatics. They are the sort of meal that should keep its consumer well-nourished for hours, and hours later still. I've suggested cannellini beans, although I also like haricot, borlotti or butter (lima) beans. The quantity of pork belly you need is not large – not just because of budget, but also because the long, slow cooking time renders it melting and soft. It is easily broken down, with plenty enough to share around. This is robust and sensible cooking; and economical in that a little goes a long way. Serve these on toast, of course.

Drain and rinse the soaked beans. Put them in a large saucepan with plenty of fresh water, the bay leaf and whole garlic clove. Place over a high heat and bring the liquid to a boil. Skim off any froth, reduce the heat to a simmer and cook for 40 minutes–1 hour, until just tender and no longer chalky.

While the beans are cooking, make the tomato base. Heat the olive oil in a saucepan over a moderate heat. Add the onion and cook for 10 minutes, until soft and translucent. Add the chopped garlic and cook for a further 2 minutes, until fragrant. Add the tomatoes, mustard powder, sugar and treacle and season with salt and pepper to taste. Simmer for 2 minutes, then remove from the heat and blend until smooth.

Preheat the oven to 140°C/120°C fan/275°F/Gas Mark 1.

Drain the beans, reserving the liquid. Tip the beans into a casserole and stir in the sauce and the pork, topping up with a little of the bean liquid to just cover. Put a lid on the pan and cook in the oven for 2–3 hours, until the pork is melting and tender. Uncover the beans for the final 30 minutes of the cooking time and increase the temperature to 180°C/160°C fan/350°F/Gas Mark 4 for the final 10 minutes to get a bit of colour over the top. Remove from the oven and check the seasoning, adding more salt and pepper to taste, if necessary.

Sardine Pasty

250g (9oz) plain (all-purpose) flour, plus more for dusting

1 tsp salt

125g (4½oz) cold unsalted butter, diced

2 large eggs, beaten separately

2 tbsp olive oil

1 onion, finely diced

1 leek, thinly sliced

4 cloves of garlic, finely chopped

200g (7oz) potatoes, peeled and cut into 3cm (1¼in) cubes

100g (3½oz) swede, peeled and cut into 3cm (1¼in) cubes

150ml (5fl oz) hot chicken or vegetable stock or water

about 100g (3½oz) sardine fillets, drained and flaked a little

freshly ground black pepper

MAKES 4 LARGE PASTIES

On holiday in Cornwall most summers, as a family of five we get through quite a few pasties. We used to live down there, so we also know where to buy the best. I'll never forget the one summer my mum came on holiday with us and asked in one of the bakeries in Newlyn for a 'par-sty'. The children and I, also the shopkeeper, fell about laughing: 'It's a pasty mum, pronounced paaaasty.' The Cornish take their pasties incredibly seriously, and I can see why. They are the best sort of portable lunch, or hand-warmer for when the sea is cold and the weather is rough (which is often enough in my experience). I've yet to see a fish pasty on the menu of the bakery shop we most often visit, and I've got a hunch I never will. The Cornish are sticklers for the traditional mixture of steak, swede and potato, with plenty of black pepper (and for cheese and onion for any vegetarians), so I'm braving controversy here with a canned fish version (sardine or mackerel). And I'm doing so from the safety of land-locked Somerset. Forgive me Cornwall, and the lady who works in the Newlyn bakery, canned fish in a pasty is excellent and surely not all that unconventional given the Cornish connection with canned fish (pilchards, in particular)? We like to eat these pasties with a good dollop of Dijon mustard (again, not entirely canonical... I'll get my coat...).

Make the pastry. Mix together the flour and ½ teaspoon of the salt in a large bowl until combined. Using your fingertips, rub in the butter until the mixture resembles breadcrumbs. (Alternatively, pulse the mixture in a food processor until just combined.)

Add 1 egg and knead it into the dough, then add 1 tablespoon of water, and knead again. Keep adding a further 2–4 tablespoons of water, a tablespoon at a time, kneading between each addition until a smooth dough forms. Cover with a clean, damp cloth and refrigerate for at least 30 minutes.

cont.

Make the filling. Heat the oil in a saucepan over a moderate heat. Add the onion and leek and cook for about 10 minutes, until soft and translucent. Add the garlic and cook for a further 2 minutes, until fragrant. Add the potatoes and swede and stir well to combine. Turn down the heat to moderate–low and cook for about 10 minutes, stirring often, until the potatoes are cooked. Add the stock or water and the remaining ½ teaspoon of salt. Season with a generous amount of black pepper and stir to combine. Cook the mixture for 10–15 minutes, until the liquid has evaporated and the potatoes have nearly (but not completely) cooked through. Remove from the heat and set aside to cool. Stir in the fish and mix well.

Preheat the oven to 190°C/170°C fan/375°F/Gas Mark 5.

Lightly dust your work surface with flour and line a baking tray with baking paper. Roll out the chilled dough until it is about 5mm (¼in) thick. Using a 15cm (6in) round cutter (or a similar-size plate), cut out the dough into 4 rounds, re-rolling as necessary.

Spoon one quarter of the filling onto the bottom half of each round. Dip your finger into water and run it around the edge of the top half. Fold each top half over its bottom half and press the edges together to seal tightly. Put the pasties on the lined baking tray.

Brush the pasties with the second beaten egg to glaze. Bake for 25–30 minutes, until puffed and golden, then remove from the oven and allow to cool for 10 minutes before serving.

Chicken Liver Rice with Allspice

3 tbsp sunflower oil

250g (9oz) minced (ground) pork

200g (7oz) chicken livers, finely chopped

700ml (24fl oz) hot chicken stock or water

1 large onion, finely diced

3 celery sticks, finely chopped

5 cloves of garlic, finely chopped

½–1 tsp chilli powder,

1 tsp paprika (sweet or hot, as you like)

1 tsp cumin seeds, toasted and ground

1 tsp ground allspice

1 tsp dried oregano

1 tsp salt, plus more to season

1 bunch of spring onions (scallions), thinly sliced

1 small bunch of flat-leaf parsley, leaves picked and finely chopped

300g (10½oz) long grain or basmati rice

freshly ground black pepper

There are quite a few herbs and spices listed for this rice dish, but none too esoteric or difficult to find, and they will make all the difference. Granted, this dish is not a looker, and I've seen similar versions go by the name of 'dirty rice', a Creole and Cajun term for cooking rice with livers and sometimes gizzards – the meat muddies the rice to give the signature name. Chicken livers are a frugal ingredient that delivers masses of flavour. Most supermarkets and many good butchers should stock them – you'll be surprised how little money they cost. The minced (ground) pork I've used is a tiny quantity, with the rice providing the main bulk of the meal.

Heat 2 tablespoons of the oil in a wide frying pan over a high heat. Add the minced (ground) pork and chicken livers and fry until they are beginning to brown (about 5–10 minutes). Add 100ml (3½fl oz) of the chicken stock or water to the pan and heat until evaporated, then fry for a further 5 minutes, until the pork is completely browned. Remove to a plate.

Heat the remaining 1 tablespoon of oil in the same pan over a moderate heat. Add the onion and celery and cook for 10 minutes, until soft and translucent. Add the garlic and cook for a further 2 minutes, until fragrant. Add the spices, the oregano and the 1 teaspoon of salt. Stir well, then add the pork mince and livers back into the pan along with a further 100ml (3½fl oz) of the chicken stock or water and cook until all of the liquid has evaporated (about 3–5 minutes).

Add the spring onions (scallions), half the parsley and all the rice, then add the remaining 500ml (17fl oz) stock or water. Cover the pan and leave the rice to cook for about 20 minutes, then turn off the heat and rest with the lid on for 10 minutes, until the rice is tender.

Fluff up the rice with a fork, seasoning with more salt and pepper, if needed. Top with the remaining parsley to serve.

Red Lentil & Roasted Carrot Soup with Za'atar

500g (1lb 2oz) carrots, peeled and roughly chopped

1 onion, finely sliced

2 tbsp olive oil, plus more to serve

big pinch of salt, plus more to season

1 tsp cumin seeds, toasted and ground

1 tsp coriander seeds, toasted and ground

250g (9oz) split red lentils

freshly ground black pepper

4 tbsp za'atar, to serve

I make soups often through the colder months of the year. Their ingredients are chiefly determined by whatever vegetables I have to hand and (more often than not) some thrifty lentils or beans, which will muscle their way into the pan. At that point, I'll be eyeing up the spice shelf – a vast medley of jars and cans with labels written in masking tape that stretches tightly around their midriffs. With most soups I like to include base spices and, often, if appropriate, a bay leaf or two – flavours that will swell and resonate as the soup cooks. Then, to finish a soup, I might also include something like a za'atar, various spice condiments or blends of spices, or just a standalone spice, such as chilli flakes or ground sumac, to serve at the table for everyone to sprinkle for themselves. This recipe is a frugal one with the za'atar and the olive oil being the costliest ingredients on the list. I am never without lentils – of all different sorts – but it's red split lentils that are among the cheapest and quickest to cook.

Put the carrots and onion into a roasting tin. Add the olive oil and big pinch of salt, and season with a good grinding of black pepper. Add the ground spices, mixing well to coat. Cover the roasting tin tightly with foil and roast the carrots and onion for about 35 minutes, until tender.

Rinse the red lentils well in cold running water and place in a saucepan with 1 litre (35fl oz) of water. Place over a moderate heat and bring to a boil. Skim off any froth that rises to the surface, then reduce the heat and simmer for 15–20 minutes, until cooked and very soft.

Blend the lentils until smooth. Add the roasted carrots and onion and process to a texture of your liking (either coarse or smooth – up to you). Check the seasoning, adding more salt and pepper to taste. You can thin with additional water if you prefer the soup to be a little looser.

To serve, slick each bowl of soup with a little more olive oil and sprinkle over the za'atar.

Trinidad Doubles (or Fried Flat Breads with Spiced Chickpeas & Tamarind Chutney)

250g (9oz) self-raising flour, plus more for dusting

½ tsp ground turmeric

½ tsp cumin seeds, toasted and ground

½ tsp salt, plus more to season

180ml (6fl oz) whole milk

2 tbsp sunflower oil, plus more for deep-frying

1 onion, finely diced

1 tbsp finely grated (shredded) fresh ginger

2 cloves of garlic, finely chopped

2 tsp Trinidadian or Jamaican curry powder (or use hot curry powder)

500g (1lb 2oz) cooked or canned (and drained) chickpeas (garbanzos)

1 small bunch of coriander (cilantro), leaves picked and finely chopped

freshly ground black pepper

hot sauce of your choice, to serve

FOR THE TAMARIND CHUTNEY

200g (7oz) block of tamarind (or 100g/3½oz deseeded tamarind paste)

300ml (10½fl oz) boiling water from a kettle

80–100g (2¾–3½oz) dark brown soft sugar, or more to taste (the chutney can be very sweet)

½ tsp cumin seeds, toasted and ground

at least ½ tsp salt, to taste

big pinch of chilli powder or flakes (optional)

This recipe goes by the name of Trinidad Doubles. Actually Indian in origin, it is a popular street food served on the Caribbean islands of Trinidad and Tobago. The fried flat bread is called a *bara* and it is filled with a *chana*, spiced curried chickpeas (garbanzos). Low-cost to produce, this is a perfect recipe to make use of storecupboard faithfuls: spices, pulses and flour. The flat breads are quick to make and use self-raising flour as the gravitational hike in the bread dough. Fried, the flat breads puff, turning golden and crisp in the oil. They are delicious swooped though the curried chickpeas. I like to eat my doubles with tamarind chutney and also some fiery hot sauce – hot enough to take my breath away.

First, make the tamarind chutney. If you're using a block, break the tamarind into pieces and soak it in the boiling water for about 20 minutes, until softened. Mash the tamarind into the water using the back of a spoon, then pass this mixture through a sieve into a heatproof bowl, leaving behind the pips and fibrous pulp. Discard the contents of the sieve.

Place the mixture (or the ready-made tamarind paste) in the bowl in a small saucepan over a moderate–low heat and add the sugar and cumin, gently cooking to dissolve the sugar. Add the salt (at least ½ teaspoon) and chilli, if using, to taste, then remove from the heat and put into a bowl to serve with the doubles. (If you have any extra, you can store it in a clean jar or container in the fridge for up to 2 weeks.)

Make the flat breads. Mix the flour with the turmeric, cumin, ½ teaspoon of salt and milk to form a soft dough. Turn out onto a lightly floured work surface and knead until very smooth. Cover with a clean, damp cloth and leave to rest for 10 minutes.

Meanwhile, heat the oil in a saucepan over a moderate heat. Add the onion and cook for 10 minutes, until soft and translucent. Add the ginger, garlic and curry powder and cook for a further 2 minutes, until fragrant. Add the chickpeas (garbanzos) and just cover with cold water. Simmer for about 15 minutes, until rich and thick. Season with salt and pepper to taste, then remove from the heat and keep warm.

Heat 5cm (2in) oil in a deep-sided pan until it reaches 180°C/350°F on a digital thermometer.

While the oil is coming up to temperature, cut the dough into 8 equal pieces, then roll each out into a 10cm (4in) circle about 2–3mm (1/16–1/8in) thick.

Working in batches of 2 or 3 breads at a time, fry each bread in the hot oil for 1 minute, or until puffed up and golden on both sides. Set each batch aside to drain on paper towels while you cook the next.

To serve, add the coriander to the chickpeas and serve with the fried bread, tamarind chutney and hot sauce on the side.

Brussels Sprout Galette with Pancetta & Chestnuts

40g (1½oz) unsalted butter

1 large leek, thinly sliced

200g (7oz) Brussels sprouts, thinly shredded

75g (2½oz) parmesan, aged gruyère, or gouda cheese, finely grated (shredded)

1 tsp chopped fresh thyme leaves

350g (12oz) shortcrust pastry (make your own or use shop-bought)

1 egg, beaten

3 or 4 slices of streaky bacon or pancetta (optional)

10 peeled chestnuts, coarsely grated/shredded (optional)

Despite ongoing and voracious food press relating to key seasonal ingredients, Brussels sprouts continue to have an abysmal reputation. I just can't fathom it. People apparently loathe them, largely, I suspect, because these diminutive brassicas are so often boiled to death, turning all soggy and wrinkly, and smelling... well, you are no doubt aware of the rumours. In season, sprouts are super-cheap to buy. Picked when they are fresh, and cooked soon afterward, they have extraordinary flavour. Far better than boiling is to fry or roast them so that their natural sugars caramelize, turning sweet and nutty as the leaves cook. I've snuck some chestnuts into this recipe – they are not entirely budget, but you can omit them or seek them out when pouches of prepared chestnuts are on offer in supermarkets and greengrocers.

Melt the butter in a pan over a moderate heat. Add the leek and fry for 5 minutes, until softened. Then add the Brussels sprouts and cook for a further 2 minutes, until the sprouts have softened slightly. Season to taste, remove from the heat and leave to cool.

Preheat the oven to 180°C/160°C fan/350°F/Gas Mark 4.

Mix half the cheese and all the thyme into the leek and sprout mixture. On a sheet of baking paper, roll out the pastry into a large circle about 3mm (⅛in) thick. Spread the leek and sprout mixture on top, leaving a 4cm (1½in) border around the edge.

Brush the edge with egg and fold the sides of the round back toward the centre around the filling. Press down gently to form a crust. Brush the edges with egg again. Top with the reserved cheese, and the slices of pancetta and grated (shredded) chestnut, if using.

Bake on the baking paper on a baking tray for 25–35 minutes, until the pastry is crisp golden-brown and the sprout and leek filling has taken on a bit of colour. Remove from the oven and rest for at least 5 minutes before serving.

Sausage Paprikash

2 tbsp sunflower oil (or use unsalted butter)

400g (14oz) sausages, plain with a high meat content

1 large onion, finely diced

2 cloves of garlic, finely chopped

1 tbsp unsmoked paprika (sweet or hot, but Hungarian, if possible)

½ tsp caraway seeds

400g (14oz) sauerkraut, drained, liquid reserved

250ml (9fl oz) hot chicken or vegetable stock or water

150g (5½oz) sour cream or crème fraîche, plus more to serve

salt and freshly ground black pepper

Paprikash is Hungarian in origin and needs Hungarian paprika to become the best possible (authentic) version of this dish. Paprika has a short shelf life and deteriorates relatively quickly, so use quickly and replenish it often. Made using dried and ground peppers, Hungarian paprika is rich and full-flavoured and generally considered to be sweeter and more intense than Spanish varieties. Sauerkraut is an incredible ingredient and a storecupboard staple in my kitchen. Sauerkraut, sausages and a good tablespoon of paprika, stirred through with sour cream, makes for wholesome winter cooking that will pair well with either boiled potatoes or egg pasta, both glossy with a good amount of butter.

Heat the oil in a casserole over a moderate heat. Add the sausages and brown for a few minutes on each side. Remove the sausages to a plate, and leave the pan on the heat.

Add the onion to the pan and cook for 10 minutes, until soft and translucent. Add the garlic and cook for a further 2 minutes, until fragrant, then add the paprika and caraway and cook for 1 minute, until aromatic. Stir in the sauerkraut and nestle in the sausages. Add the stock, topping up with a little of the sauerkraut liquid, if needed, and season with salt and pepper to taste. Increase the heat and bring the liquid to a boil, then cover and reduce the heat to moderate again and cook for 18–20 minutes, until the sausages are cooked through. Uncover and cook for a further 5 minutes, until nicely reduced.

Finally, stir through the sour cream, but don't let the liquid boil as it will split the cream and turn it grainy. Remove from the heat and serve.

Quick Pickled Red Cabbage
with Butternut Squash & Giant Couscous

½ red cabbage, cored and very thinly sliced

1 red onion, very finely sliced

1 tsp salt, plus more to season

200ml (7fl oz) red wine vinegar or cider vinegar

1 tbsp caster (superfine) sugar

1 large butternut squash, peeled, deseeded and cut into about 3cm (1¼in) dice

3 tbsp olive oil, plus more to serve

300g (10½oz) giant couscous (wholewheat is especially nice)

1 small bunch of flat-leaf parsley, leaves picked and roughly chopped

freshly ground black pepper

40g (1½oz) walnuts, finely chopped, to serve

I am keen on using pickles in salads. Especially these sorts of salads – a great big assortment of flattering ingredients. Pickled, the cabbage will keep well in the fridge for up to a month. Although, used as an ingredient in salads such as this, and also as a condiment for rice dishes such as pilafs, or stuffed in a sandwich or roll with cheese or leftover roast meat, I don't suppose it will really need to last all that long. Use pumpkin or squash, diced small and roasted until soft and caramelized. Likewise, use mint, dill or coriander (cilantro) in lieu of the parsley, if you wish.

Put the cabbage and onion in a large bowl and mix in ½ teaspoon of the salt, rubbing it in well to soften the vegetables.

In a saucepan combine the vinegar with 100ml (3½fl oz) of cold water, the sugar and the other ½ teaspoon of salt and bring to a boil. Stir until the salt and sugar have dissolved, then remove from the heat. Add the sliced cabbage and onion, ensuring they are submerged, and leave for at least 2 hours before using. (Use a small plate to hold the cabbage and onions beneath the surface of the liquid in the pan if required.)

Preheat the oven to 200°C/180°C fan/400°F/Gas Mark 6.

Mix the squash with 2 tablespoons of the olive oil and season well with salt. Roast for 20–25 minutes, or until well softened and browned at the edges. Remove from the oven and set to one side.

Boil the couscous in well-salted water according to the packet instructions (usually about 8–10 minutes), until just cooked but still al dente. Drain and refresh under cold running water. Drain again and stir through with the remaining 1 tablespoon of olive oil. Then, add the parsley and also the cooked squash. Mix well and add more salt and freshly ground black pepper to taste.

Spread the pickled cabbage over a large platter, dress with a little olive oil to coat, then spoon over the couscous and squash. Top with the walnuts, to serve.

Burmese Fried Egg Salad with Cabbage, Shallots & Toasted Chickpea Flour

8 eggs

2 tbsp chickpea (garbanzo) flour

1 tsp ground turmeric

sunflower oil, for frying

400g (14oz) shallots, very thinly sliced

½–1 white cabbage, depending on size, thinly shredded

juice of 2 limes (or 3 if they aren't so juicy), plus more to taste

1 tbsp fish sauce, plus more to taste

1 tsp light brown soft sugar, plus more to taste

chilli flakes, to taste

salt

This salad is a cracker. It has relatively few ingredients, and boiling the eggs, then frying them until the whites turn golden, is astonishingly good practice. You need quite a few shallots, some fried and some dressed with lime and fish sauce, giving you two different textures. Do taste and test the seasoning in this recipe, getting it just so for you and your guests.

Bring a saucepan (large enough to fit the eggs in a single layer) of water to a boil. Gently add the eggs and cook for 6 minutes, remove from the heat, drain and cool under cold running water. Peel and put to one side.

In a small, dry frying pan over a moderate heat, toast the chickpea (garbanzo) flour with the turmeric for about 1–2 minutes, until toasted and nutty. Remove from the heat and put in a bowl to serve at the table.

Carefully heat 3cm (1¼in) of oil in a deep-sided frying pan over a high heat. The oil is ready to use when you drop in a piece of shallot and it sizzles immediately (or when the oil reaches 180°C/350°F on a digital thermometer).

Add half the shallots to the oil and fry for 3–5 minutes, until golden brown and crisp. Using a slotted spoon, remove the shallots from the oil and set aside to drain on paper towels. Then, sprinkle well with a little salt.

Fry the peeled eggs in the same oil for a few minutes, until the whites turn golden brown all over. Remove from the oil and then set aside to drain on paper towels. Cut each egg in half when cool enough to handle.

Mix the cabbage with the remaining shallots, and the lime juice, fish sauce and sugar. Add chilli flakes to your taste (I use about ½ teaspoon), and more lime, sugar and fish sauce if you like.

To assemble the salad, place the cabbage and shallot mixture on a platter, top with the eggs and the fried shallots and sprinkle with the toasted chickpea and turmeric powder to serve.

Brown Rice, Mushroom & Roasted Kale with Oyster Sauce

300g (10½oz) short-grain brown rice

200g (7oz) kale, leaves stripped and roughly chopped

1 tbsp sunflower oil

1 tbsp sesame seeds (black or white)

2 tbsp oyster sauce

1 tbsp runny honey

1 tbsp rice vinegar

1 tbsp sesame oil

300g (10½oz) oyster mushrooms, sliced

1 bunch of spring onions (scallions), cut into 3cm (1¼in) lengths

salt and freshly ground black pepper

Roasting the kale with sesame seeds and sesame oil transforms this hardy winter leaf into something very moreish indeed. I suggest using oyster mushrooms, but you could just as well use any kind. I love the floppy, fleshy feel of oyster mushrooms, even more so when they cook down in a pan, turning slippery with heat. They are a good foil for the nutty, brown rice and roasted kale. A simple dressing of oyster sauce and rice vinegar is sweet, salty and sharp. I could happily eat this all winter long.

Boil the rice with twice its volume of cold water and a good pinch of salt for 40–45 minutes. Make sure it doesn't boil dry, adding a bit more boiling water, if required. Remove from the heat, drain and put to one side.

Preheat the oven to 150°C/130°C fan/300°F/Gas Mark 2.

Using your fingertips, rub the kale with a pinch of salt and the sunflower oil, then sprinkle with the sesame seeds, place in a single layer on a baking tray and bake for 15–20 minutes until crisp.

In a bowl, whisk together the oyster sauce, honey and vinegar and put to one side.

Heat the sesame oil in a pan over a moderate heat. Add the mushrooms and spring onions (scallions) and fry for 5 minutes, until soft and wilted, then season with salt and pepper and remove from the heat.

To serve, mix together the mushrooms and spring onions with the cooked rice and transfer the mixture to a serving platter or plate. Add the kale and top with the oyster sauce and rice vinegar dressing.

Apple & Endive with Smoked Mackerel & Roasted Buckwheat

80g (2¾oz) raw buckwheat groats

2 tbsp olive or sunflower oil

good pinch of salt, plus more to season (use smoked salt, if you like)

80g (2¾oz) mayonnaise (shop-bought or homemade)

3 tbsp sour cream or crème fraîche

4 celery sticks with leaves: sticks very thinly sliced, leaves roughly chopped

1–2 sweet, tart apples (such as russet), unpeeled, cored and thinly sliced

1 endive, leaves separated and halved (or use radicchio, treviso, watercress or gem lettuce)

4 smoked mackerel fillets, skin and bones removed, pulled into smaller pieces

1 small bunch of flat-leaf parsley, leaves picked and roughly chopped

1 tsp white wine vinegar or cider vinegar

freshly ground black pepper

I owe a thanks to Paris for introducing me to roasted buckwheat groats. Up until that Parisian lunchtime last autumn (celebrating my 40th birthday with my very best friend, Isabel, 24 hours, beaucoup de food, wine and chat), I'd only ever used buckwheat as a flour in baking or eaten it in noodle or pasta form. Widely available in larger supermarkets and health-food stores, buckwheat is considered something of a superfood – and I use that term very, very lightly. (After all, all food is super; it's just that some ingredients are more virtuous than others.) High in protein, buckwheat is not a wheat, and unlike many other grains does not require cooking in liquid to render it edible. Fried or roasted, buckwheat seeds are delightfully addictive, all crunchy and nutty when strewn over salads. The combination here of bitter leaves, sweet apple and smoked fish with a creamy mayonnaise dressing and a scattergun of roasted buckwheat is a good one.

Preheat the oven to 180°C/160°C fan/350°F/Gas Mark 4.

Put the buckwheat into a baking tray, sprinkle over the oil and good pinch of salt and toss to coat. Roast for about 10–15 minutes, until slightly darkened in colour and crisp. Stir the groats and rotate the tray halfway through the cooking time. Remove from the oven and set to one side.

Mix the mayonnaise with the sour cream or crème fraîche and thin with a splash of cold water until you have a dressing consistency. Check the seasoning, adding more salt and plenty of pepper as necessary.

In a large bowl or on a serving platter, toss together the celery and leaves, the apples and the endive (or other leaves) with the pieces of smoked mackerel, the chopped parsley and the vinegar. Check the seasoning, adding a little more salt and some pepper, if necessary.

Spoon the dressing over the salad, mixing well to coat, then sprinkle with the roasted buckwheat to serve.

Radicchio with Comté & Prunes

1 tight or 2 loose radicchio heads, cored and leaves roughly torn or chopped (or use treviso or castelfranco lettuces)

60ml (2fl oz) red wine vinegar

1 tbsp runny honey

1 small red onion, very finely diced

1 tbsp Dijon mustard

100ml (3½fl oz) sunflower oil

100g (3½oz) pitted prunes

1 small bunch of flat-leaf parsley, leaves picked and roughly chopped

150g (5½oz) comté or aged gruyère cheese, peeled and finely sliced

salt and freshly ground black pepper

Using a hard cheese as a component in a salad can seem a little outdated – remember cheddar and celery with salad cream? However, I feel it is an oversight to be reliant, as so many of us seem to be, on just mozzarella, feta and halloumi (and increasingly burrata) as the acceptable face of cheese in salads. What you get with an aged cheese such as a comté, older gruyère, hard goat and even some cheddar cheeses, is a deep, creamy, salty savouriness, and incredible flavour when matched with bitter, sweet and tart, such as in this salad. Comté is a wonderful cheese from the Jura region in eastern France. Aged for a minimum of four months, and often more, comté is made from cow's milk. Depending on the season in which the cattle have grazed, the cheeses can vary in flavour from creamy and buttery through to nutty, tasting intensely of the earth; even, some say, of the location in which the cattle grazed. Bitter salad leaves come into season in the wintertime and, given the right accompaniments, work beautifully in a salad to serve as an appetizer, getting the taste buds working in anticipation of the meal you are about to eat. This salad is a real beauty.

Soak the radicchio in well-salted, cold water for 15 minutes, then drain and leave on a cloth to dry (or use a salad spinner). Salting will reduce excess bitterness and make for super-crunchy salad leaves.

In a small bowl make a dressing by mixing together the vinegar, honey, onion and mustard and seasoning with salt and pepper to taste, then gradually add the oil, stirring all the time. Put to one side.

On a large plate or in a salad bowl, toss the radicchio leaves with the dressing, then add the prunes, parsley and cheese and serve straight away.

Kohlrabi & Parsnips with Dates, Honey & Yogurt

3-4 large parsnips, peeled, woody cores cut out, and coarsely grated (shredded)

1 kohlrabi, peeled and finely sliced

juice of 1 lemon

good pinch of salt, plus more to season

100g (3½oz) mixed seeds (pumpkin, sunflower and sesame, say)

1 tbsp runny honey, plus more to taste

300g (10½oz) natural yogurt

50g (1¾oz) pitted dates, finely chopped

2 tbsp good olive oil

½-1 clove of garlic, crushed to a smooth paste with a pinch of salt

4 spring onions (scallions), finely sliced

1 small bunch of mint, leaves picked and roughly chopped

freshly ground black pepper

1 tsp sumac, to serve (optional)

I use quite a bit of yogurt in my savoury cooking. I like to season it with some salt, and often some raw garlic, adding lemon juice and olive oil to form a dressing to spoon over soups, cooked vegetables and rice dishes, among other things. In this salad, the sharpness of yogurt brings all the ingredients together with the earthiness of the vegetables, plump sweet dates, bracing mint and the toasted, nutty seeds. Kohlrabi is the vegetable I am most often quizzed on by people who receive vegetable boxes and the like. It is not a root vegetable; rather, it is a brassica, dense and crunchy with a sweet, vegetable flavour. Use as you would raw cabbage for a slaw or as broccoli stalks in cooked dishes. In this salad, this quirky, knobbly, 'I-don't-know-what-to-do-with-it' vegetable is transformative.

Put the parsnips and kohlrabi into a bowl and mix through with half the lemon juice and a good pinch of salt.

Put the seeds into a dry, non-stick frying pan over a moderate heat and toast for about 2–3 minutes (depending on the seeds), until they begin to crackle. Tip into a bowl and put to one side.

In a serving bowl, mix the remaining lemon juice with the honey, yogurt, dates, olive oil and garlic, seasoning with salt and pepper to taste.

Add the grated (shredded) parsnip and kohlrabi along with the spring onions (scallions) and chopped mint. Check the seasoning once again, adjusting as necessary with salt, pepper and more honey to taste.

Put the salad on a serving platter or individual plates and scatter over the toasted seeds, and the sumac, if using.

Roasted Cauliflower with Red Onion & Preserved Lemon

1 cauliflower, cut into bite-size florets

1 red onion, cut into thin wedges

4 tbsp good olive oil

2 tsp coriander seeds, toasted and ground

2 tsp nigella seeds

3 preserved lemons, flesh discarded

1 clove of garlic, crushed to a smooth paste with a pinch of salt

juice of 1 lemon

1 small bunch of coriander (cilantro) and/or flat-leaf parsley or dill, leaves picked and finely chopped

salt and freshly ground black pepper

Come wintertime, when the citrus bounty begins to arrive in the shops, I make it a priority to preserve some lemons; also oranges and, recently, some Seville oranges, too. Salted citrus fruit is a gorgeous ingredient to have to hand when you want to inject some dazzle, a hard-to-pinpoint piquancy, into your cooking. I've included recipes on preserving citrus in my previous books, but I am sure there are a good many recipes online. I would urge you to use them, as buying ready-made preserved citrus is certainly the more costly option. The salting process takes about 3 months, tenderizing and seasoning the skin of the fruit. Sealed in a clean, sterilized jar, the fruits will last well up to a year or more. To use, discard the flesh, which will have turned into an inedible salty gunk, then slice or chop the peel, which will taste intensely of citrus fruit, but also have a delightful savoury saltiness, with a similar profile to capers and olives I suppose.

Preheat the oven to 200°C/180°C fan/400°F/Gas Mark 6.

Toss the cauliflower florets in a large bowl with the red onion wedges, half the olive oil, the ground coriander and the nigella seeds, along with a generous seasoning of salt and plenty of freshly ground black pepper.

Spread out the coated cauliflower and onion mixture evenly on a large baking tray and roast for 20–25 minutes, until tender, even slightly charred in places. Remove from the oven and put to one side to cool for a bit.

While the cauliflower is cooling, coarsely blend the preserved lemon with the remaining olive oil, and the garlic and lemon juice, then stir through with the chopped herbs.

Transfer the cooked cauliflower and onion mixture to a serving platter and drizzle with the dressing to serve.

Risotto with Prosciutto, Vermouth & Quite a Bit of Butter

120g (4¼oz) unsalted butter, diced

1 onion, finely diced

400g (14oz) risotto rice (ideally, arborio, carnaroli or vialone nano)

150ml (5fl oz) white vermouth

1.5–1.75ml (52–60fl oz) hot chicken stock

70g (2½oz) prosciutto, cut into fat ribbons

70g (2½oz) parmesan, grated (shredded), plus more to serve

salt and freshly ground black pepper

I can't quite fathom how risotto has become one of those default, easy midweek recipes that so many people seem to rely on. Risotto is not a dish to throw together, clock ticking, everyone hungry. In my view, risotto is a treat, because a good one needs good rice, good stock, a good amount of butter and best-quality parmesan. A generous slug of good wine or vermouth will also boost flavour. Think: some for the rice and some in a glass with ice and a slice, topped up with a spritz. Cook's treat. Bring on the butter.

Melt one quarter of the butter in a heavy-based casserole over a moderate–low heat. Add the onion and cook gently for 10 minutes, until soft and translucent, then increase the heat and stir in the rice, mixing well to coat in the butter and onions.

Add the vermouth and stir until evaporated, then start adding the hot chicken stock, 2 ladlefuls at a time, while stirring continuously. Add more stock once almost all of the previous addition of stock has been absorbed and continue like this until you have used half the stock.

Reduce the amount of stock you add each time to 1 ladleful, until you've been cooking the risotto for about 10–12 minutes. After that time, start to test and taste the rice. Ideally, it should still have quite a bit of bite without being chalky in the middle at all. Remember, you will rest the rice with a lid on before serving it and the rice will continue to cook during that time, so do err on the leaner side of cooking time. Once the rice is cooked, with a creamy semi-liquid texture, add a tiny bit more stock (the rice will continue to absorb liquid and you don't want a claggy, stiff risotto).

Add half the prosciutto and stir well, then follow with the remaining butter and the parmesan and stir well until all of the butter and cheese have melted and emulsified into the rice. Check the seasoning, adding more salt and pepper as necessary.

Cover and allow to rest for 5 minutes, then divide between 4 serving plates and serve topped with the remaining slices of prosciutto and some extra grated parmesan and freshly ground black pepper.

Ray with Crème Fraîche & Leek Mashed Potatoes & Caper Butter

600g (1lb 5oz) floury potatoes, such as Maris Piper, peeled and cut into 4cm (1½in) cubes

1 leek, white part only, thinly sliced

6 cloves of garlic, peeled then left whole

200g (7oz) crème fraîche

100g (3½oz) plain (all-purpose) flour, to dust the fish

1 tsp salt, plus more to season

4 x 150–200g (5½–7oz) ray wing portions

120g (4¼oz) unsalted butter, plus more if necessary

30g (1oz) capers (desalinated, if necessary), rinsed and drained

½ bunch of flat-leaf parsley, leaves picked and finely chopped

freshly ground black pepper

lemon wedges, to serve

Ray and skate species are generally sold collectively as skate, although you should completely avoid true skate because stocks are at catastrophically low levels. Instead, look for spotted ray, whose stocks are thought to be in healthier supply. Don't buy small fish, as these won't have had time to breed, and, lastly, look for fish caught on boats that encourage sustainable fishing practice. Your fishmonger or supermarket fish counter should know and be able to tell you the origin of your fish. Ray is a gorgeous fish to cook with. This is the sort of dish that I associate with restaurant cooking, but don't let that put you off; this meal is terribly easy to achieve.

Put the potatoes, leek and garlic in a large saucepan of cold, salted water, cover and bring to a boil. Cook for 15–20 minutes, until the potatoes are tender and the leeks and garlic are very soft. Drain and return to the pan, adding the crème fraîche and mashing the mixture together. Season well and keep warm.

Meanwhile, preheat the oven to 140°C/120°C fan/275°F/ Gas Mark 1.

Next, cook the fish. Season the flour with the 1 teaspoon of salt and plenty of freshly ground black pepper. Lightly dust each fish wing in the seasoned flour.

Melt the butter in a large, non-stick or cast-iron frying pan (skillet) and fry the fish over a moderate heat. Work in batches of 2 wings at a time, if you like, and fry for 5 minutes on each side, making sure the butter doesn't burn. Add a touch more butter if it looks like it might, as this will help to reduce the temperature in the pan.

Remove the wing portions to a baking tray lined with baking paper and keep them warm in the oven. Add the capers and parsley to the butter in the pan and heat through.

To serve, spoon some of the crème fraîche and potato mixture onto each plate. Add a ray wing, plenty of the caper butter and serve with lemon wedges on the side.

King Prawns with Orange, Garlic & Tomato

4 tbsp good olive oil, plus more to serve

1 red onion, finely diced

6 cloves of garlic, thinly sliced

1 tbsp tomato purée

250ml (9fl oz) tomato passata, or use canned (or fresh) chopped tomatoes

½ tsp smoked paprika (sweet or hot, as you like)

1 pinch–½ tsp chilli flakes

2 bay leaves, scrunched a little

2 strips of zest from 2 sweet or Seville unwaxed oranges, remainder cut into wedges

600g (1lb 5oz) raw prawns

1 small bunch of flat-leaf parsley, leaves picked and finely chopped

salt and freshly ground black pepper

On holiday in Porto in Portugal a few years ago, we ate lunch in a restaurant recommended by a Portuguese wine-merchant friend. We sat at a table outside, under an umbrella – sun fierce, not a cloud in the sky – with a view of the elegant *rabelo* boats (once used as cargo ships for the city's extensive wine trade, now mostly used for tourists). I had been told that we must order the prawns. So, we did. Prawns cooked in tomato and garlic, beautifully arranged and surrounded with lots of orange quarters. The mountain of prawns still sizzled in the dish as the waiter put it on the table. I smiled and asked 'Why all the oranges?' The waiter just winked and squeezed his hands like castanets, scooting off to the next table. On the side was a basket of bread and a green salad with very thinly sliced white onion and good olive oil. This lunch was epic – and very messy, with piles of prawn shells and orange skins, and trails of smudgy red fingerprints on the white tablecloth (best-laid plans, napkins and water bowls). It was undoubtedly the best meal we ate on that holiday. Buy sustainably sourced prawns. Winter is peak orange season – use sweet or Seville oranges as they both suit the prawns, tomatoes and garlic so well.

Heat the olive oil in a wide, high-sided frying pan (skillet) or casserole. Add the onion and cook for 10 minutes, until well softened and translucent. Add the garlic and cook for a further 2 minutes, until fragrant, or even just beginning to turn a bit golden brown.

Add the tomato purée, then the passata, paprika, chilli, bay leaves and strips of orange zest. Add a splash of water and simmer for 10 minutes, until rich and thick. Check the seasoning, adding salt and pepper to taste.

Add the prawns and stir well to combine. Cook over a moderate heat for 2–3 minutes, until the prawns have turned opaque and pink and have fully cooked through. Remove from the heat, add the parsley and a slick more olive oil and serve with the orange wedges on the side.

Oysters with Muscadet Butter Sauce & Brown Bread

100ml (3½fl oz) Muscadet wine

1 large shallot, finely chopped

30ml (1fl oz) double (heavy) cream

150g (5½oz) unsalted butter, cubed, plus more for the bread

1 lemon, cut into wedges

3 or 4 (or more) oysters per person (you decide how many you can eat)

salt and freshly ground black pepper

good bread, to serve

To Paris, to Bastille Market, where you can buy and eat oysters from the stallholders who will stand and wait as you tip your head back, chew and swallow, then pour a slug of Muscadet into your spent oyster shell. This wine variety, mineral and thirst-quenching, is the most perfect chaser to the fleshy, saline oyster. Here, I've used a cheat-method beurre blanc, adding a splosh of cream to stabilize the butter – do away with it if you feel confident in your ability to monté butter successfully. And, why not serve some oysters as they do on that fish stand in the market: as they are, washed down with Muscadet. Buy a good baguette to serve, or make the soda bread on page 59.

Finally, a word (or two) on oysters. Buy only oysters whose shells are firmly shut. They are best eaten on the day you buy, but they will keep for about 5 days if properly stored in the fridge, covered with a clean, damp cloth, with the deep shell facing downward and never sitting in water. Once opened, oysters should smell fresh, like the sea. There should still be seawater contained in the shell and the meat should be opaque. If in doubt, don't consume. Be careful when skewering open the shells – there is a knack: dig into the hinge and crank up swiftly in one movement. And do wrap a tea towel tightly around your hand, to protect your palm from the oyster knife.

Pour the wine into a small saucepan over a high heat. Add the shallot and a good grind of black pepper and boil, reducing until there is almost no liquid left.

Add the cream, reduce the heat to low and gradually whisk in the cubes of butter, piece by piece, never allowing the sauce to boil. Add a squirt of lemon juice, seasoning to taste with more black pepper and a pinch of salt, if necessary. Keep warm, without allowing it to get too cold or too hot, lest the sauce splits.

Meanwhile open the oysters, dislodging the oyster from the ligament that attaches it to the hinge in the shell, but still leaving the oysters in the shells.

To serve, spoon the warm Muscadet butter sauce over the oysters in their shells, with the remaining lemon wedges on the side and with bread and butter to mop as you eat.

Aguachile with Seville Oranges, Avocado & Blue Corn Tortilla Chips

200g (7oz) raw prawns, halved lengthways and deveined

½ tsp sea salt, plus more to season

3 Seville oranges: 2 juiced, 1 cut into wedges to serve (or use orange and grapefruit and add some extra lime)

½ small red onion, very finely sliced

1–2 jalapeño or fresh habanero chillies, roughly chopped

1 small bunch of coriander (cilantro), leaves picked and roughly chopped

juice of 1 super-juicy lime

1 small clove of garlic, finely chopped

1 purple or green kohlrabi, peeled and thinly sliced (or use ½ cucumber)

freshly ground black pepper

tortilla corn chips or soft tortillas, to serve

1 or 2 avocados, stoned and sliced, to serve

SERVES 4 AS A STARTER

Aguachile, or 'chilli water', is a Mexican dish made of prawns or shrimp immersed in a highly seasoned liquid comprising citrus juice, salt, chilli, coriander (cilantro) and finely sliced onion. The prawns are 'cooked' in the acidulated liquid (no heat required), making this a pretty easy starter to assemble, but I'll be honest and tell you – this dish lives or dies by its seasoning. You want a flawless balance between salty, sour, fragrant and hot. You can use other raw, firm seafood (bass or scallops, for example) and switch the name to ceviche. As ever, buying the best, freshest fish from sustainable sources is important. The Mexicans may use cucumber to mix through with the prawns and onion, but I think kohlrabi – crunchy, sweet and in season in the winter – does the job brilliantly, even if it is a little nonconformist. Seville oranges are an intoxicating ingredient, and not just for marmalade. These gnarly citrus excel as a juice to season all number of dishes (savoury included). More fruity than lemons, less sweet than oranges, Seville oranges are perfect to use in dishes when you want a juicy, bitter and sour burst of citrus sunlight.

Put the prawns in a bowl and mix with the ½ teaspoon of salt. Refrigerate to rest for 20 minutes, then squeeze over the Seville orange juice and put to one side.

Sprinkle the red onion with a good amount (a big pinch should do) of salt and toss together in a bowl, leaving the onions to sit for 5 minutes, then rinse in cold water, drain well and put to one side.

Use a mortar and pestle or food processor or blender to blend the chillies with the coriander (cilantro), 50ml (1¾fl oz) of water, and the lime juice, garlic and another good amount of salt to form a coarse purée.

In a mixing bowl, toss together the prawns with the chilli purée. Add the onion and the kohlrabi. Check the seasoning, adding more salt and pepper if appropriate. Serve immediately, along with the tortillas, avocado and extra Seville orange wedges.

Good Vanilla Ice Cream
with New Season Olive Oil & Pink Salt

good vanilla ice cream

new-season olive oil, such as
arbequina (especially grassy and
aromatic)

pink salt flakes or rock salt, to grind

SERVES AS MANY AS YOU HAVE
SCOOPS OF ICE CREAM

Let me explain. Beside my hob there is a large litre bottle of olive oil – perfectly ordinary and used for everyday cooking, it does the job and more. In my storecupboard, however, hidden away from too much light and heat, there are quite a few other bottles of oil, all with very different characters from one another – some grassy, some nutty, some fruity – depending on vintage and variety. They have very different applications. Some work well for dressing salads and just-cooked vegetables; others are more robust in flavour, to slick over grilled meat or fish; and some are there to dress cooked dishes of beans, pulses or pasta. Some have been there longer than others – their potency, their freshness of fruit changes the longer the oil has been harvested and stored in the bottle. Rather like wine, olive oil shares what the French call *terroir* – the complete natural environment of where an ingredient is produced, taking into account soils, geographical location and weather patterns. Farmers harvest their olives in the autumn, pressing, bottling and selling them as 'new vintage' olive oil – with its marked vibrancy, there's nothing else like it. At a cookery school in Sicily last autumn, with the olives just pressed, I was served this ice cream for pudding. I was speechless; it was so good. The oil was grassy, sweet and fresh-tasting. The cold of the ice cream solidified it ever so slightly as it was poured over, and there was an assertive grind of crunchy pink salt to finish. The treat here is purchasing some new-season olive oil. The vanilla ice cream is an unbelievably good canvas and pink salt is its giddy sidekick.

For each serving, put 1 scoop of ice cream in a bowl and pour over 1 teaspoon of olive oil. Top with a pinch of pink salt to serve.

Vincisgrassi

FOR THE PASTA

500g (1lb 2oz) type '00' pasta flour or strong white bread flour

2 eggs

4 egg yolks

1 tsp salt

olive oil, for greasing

FOR THE SAUCE

150g (5½oz) unsalted butter, plus more for greasing and assembling the dish

60g (2¼oz) plain (all-purpose) flour

1.2 litres (40fl oz) hot whole milk

4 tbsp good olive oil

400g (14oz) porcini, sliced (or use any wild mushroom, such as chanterelle, morel or girolle)

200ml (7fl oz) single (light) cream

150g (5½oz) parmesan, grated (shredded)

150g (5½oz) prosciutto or Parma ham

salt and freshly ground black pepper

1 black or white truffle (optional), to serve

This dish is very much an extravagance, a true seasonal treat. I couldn't – and wouldn't for the sake of my arteries and also my wallet – eat it more than once a year. It is porcini and prosciutto sandwiched between layers of fresh egg pasta, slathered in a béchamel sauce enriched with cream, more butter and parmesan. And, while I say the truffle is optional, I don't really mean it. This baked pasta dish comes from the Marche region in Italy and lore has it that it is customary to add offal to the mixture, making a lasagne of sorts. But this is not really my story to tell, because I'll be honest and say I've never eaten or even seen a vincisgrassi made with offal. I have, however, heard many, many people (chefs and food writers among them) squeal, sigh, then gush with tangible delight about the vincisgrassi they once ate cooked by Franco Taruschio, the enigmatic Italian chef at his celebrated restaurant The Walnut Tree, near the Welsh town of Abergavenny. I've met Franco and his wife, Ann, a few times. They have a legendary reputation, and while Franco no longer cooks in the restaurant, his vincisgrassi is the only version anyone is really interested in.

I have made few amendments to Franco's list of ingredients. I have kept the prosciutto in slices rather than cutting it into ribbons, left out the parsley, and grated (shredded) black truffle over the dish instead of using truffle oil. The béchamel is quite a loose one and the dish is cooked in a very hot oven for a short burst of time, so let the vincisgrassi rest out of the oven for at least 15–20 minutes before serving. That way, the béchamel and layers of mushrooms, prosciutto and pasta meld together, but are still hot enough so that when you come to grate the truffle, the scent will send you and your lucky guests reeling. Make the pasta if you have time, otherwise use good shop-bought fresh (not dried) egg pasta sheets.

Make the pasta dough. In a bowl mix together the flour, eggs and egg yolks with the 1 teaspoon of salt to form a dough.

cont.

Tip out the dough onto a lightly oiled work surface and knead for at least 8 minutes, until smooth and shiny. (Or use a food processor with a pasta blade.) Refrigerate to rest for at least 1 hour, then roll into sheets through a pasta machine, stopping when you have sent each sheet through the second-to-thinnest setting. Cut the pasta into lengths about 12.5cm (4¾in) long.

Bring a large saucepan of well-salted water to a boil and have a bowl of cold water to the side. Working in batches, boil a few sheets of pasta at a time for 1–2 minutes, to soften. Remove from the pan and immediately plunge the sheets into the cold water, then set aside to drain on a clean cloth. Repeat for all the pasta sheets, leaving them on the cloth while you make the sauce. (If you're using shop-bought fresh sheets of pasta, you still need to blanch them in boiling water.)

To make the sauce, melt the butter in a pan over a moderate heat until foaming. Add the flour and mix well with a wooden spoon. Using a whisk, gradually beat in the milk, beating well between each addition. Reduce the heat to moderate–low and let the béchamel putter away for 15–20 minutes, stirring often with the wooden spoon. Season well with salt and pepper.

Preheat the oven to 220°C/200°C fan/425°F/Gas Mark 7 and grease a gratin dish with butter.

While the béchamel is bubbling away, heat the oil in a small frying pan over a moderate heat. Add the porcini and cook for about 5 minutes, until soft and fragrant, then season with salt and pepper. When the béchamel is ready, add in the mushrooms, then the cream. Bring the mixture briefly to a boil, then remove from the heat.

Cover the bottom of the gratin dish with a layer of cooked pasta, then spread over a layer of béchamel, dot with a little extra butter and sprinkle with some parmesan. Add a slice or two of prosciutto or Parma ham. Continue the process, layer after layer, until you've used up all the ingredients and can finish with a layer of béchamel and a final sprinkling of parmesan. (Aim for three or so layers, depending on the size of your dish.)

Bake the vincisgrassi in the hot oven for 20–30 minutes, until golden brown and the pasta is tender. Remove from the oven and leave to rest for 15–20 minutes before serving. Serve the truffle whole at the table for your guests to grate over themselves, if they wish.

Fried Fruit Cake in Marsala Butter

60g (2¼oz) unsalted butter

40g (1½oz) icing (confectioner's) sugar

2 tbsp sweet Marsala, or oloroso or other sweet sherry

400g (14oz) fruit cake, or Christmas cake or pudding, cut into slices

crème fraîche or thick double (heavy) cream, to serve

Fruit cake (indeed, Christmas cake or pudding, too) has a good shelf life, especially if it has been doctored with enough alcohol. Should your family be anything like mine, cake does not hang around that long – whatever the festivity, once the first slice is gone, its demolition is swift. This method is a good one for those of you with family members or friends who view fruit cake with suspicion and might not tackle it with such gusto, leaving you with a cake in its tin that has seen better days. This recipe adds a little razzle-dazzle and is dangerous – you have been warned. Frying fruit cake in butter sweetened with icing sugar, then laced with Marsala is foolhardy. It cannot – must not – be everyday eating.

Cream the butter and sugar together in a bowl or use a food processor until combined, then beat in the Marsala or sherry.

Melt the laced butter in a large, non-stick or cast-iron frying pan (skillet) over a moderate heat. Working in batches, add the slices of fruit cake 2 at a time and fry, turning every 2–3 minutes, until fragrant and hot all the way through.

Remove from the heat and serve with crème fraîche or thick cream.

Pumpkin Dhansak with Brown Rice

800g (1lb 12oz) peeled and deseeded pumpkin or squash (prepared weight), cut into bite-size pieces (or use sweet potato)

4 tbsp sunflower oil

2 onions, finely sliced

4 cloves of garlic, finely chopped

1 tbsp finely grated (shredded) fresh ginger

1 tbsp tomato purée

1 tsp salt, plus more to season

1–2 tsp chilli powder

2 tbsp garam masala

100g (3½oz) split red lentils, rinsed in cold water and drained

1 cinnamon stick

2 bay leaves, scrunched a little

30g (1oz) tamarind purée (see page 342) or shop-bought tamarind paste, or the juice of 1 lemon

juice of ½ lemon

1 tsp light brown soft sugar

300g (10½oz) brown rice

1 tsp dried fenugreek leaf (optional)

freshly ground black pepper

1 small bunch of coriander (cilantro), leaves roughly chopped, to serve

Dhansak is a sweet, sour and hot curry that is Parsi (or Parsee) in origin. While chicken and lamb dhansak are commonplace, as curries go dhansaks are well suited to a vegetarian and vegan diet, because, conventionally, they must always include lentils. A good dhansak must be hot with chilli, sweet with the spices, and sour with the tamarind. Balance is everything in this dish.

Preheat the oven to 200°C/180°C fan/400°F/Gas Mark 6.

Toss the pumpkin or squash in half the oil, tip into a roasting tin and roast for about 20 minutes, until tender and beginning to brown at the edges, then remove from the heat and put to one side.

While the pumpkin or squash is roasting, heat the remaining oil in a large saucepan over a moderate heat. Add the onions and cook for 10–12 minutes, until soft and translucent, even just beginning to brown at little. Add the garlic and ginger and cook for a further 2 minutes, until fragrant. Add the tomato purée and the teaspoon of salt, along with the chilli powder and half the garam masala and cook for 1 minute, until fragrant.

Add the lentils, cinnamon stick and bay leaves along with 600ml (21fl oz) of water, then cover and cook for 25 minutes, stirring occasionally to prevent sticking, until the lentils have completely broken down. Add the cooked pumpkin, along with the tamarind, lemon juice and sugar and cook for 5 minutes to allow the flavours to meld. Add a splash of hot water, if required, to loosen the curry a little. Then check the seasoning, adding salt and plenty of black pepper to taste.

Meanwhile cook the rice according to the packet instructions (usually about 40–45 minutes) in a saucepan of well-salted boiling water.

Sprinkle the remaining garam masala and the fenugreek leaf all over the curry and serve immediately, allowing the fragrance from both to warm in the heat of the curry, permeating the air as you serve. Serve with the brown rice and the chopped coriander on the side.

Whole Fish Wrapped in Paper & Baked with Chermoula

4 portions of whole sea bream or bass, equal in size, scaled, gutted and cleaned, and slashed 3 times on each side

4 slices of lemon (cut the remaining lemon into wedges, to serve)

4 large bay leaves, scrunched a little

chermoula (see below)

salt and freshly ground black pepper

FOR THE CHERMOULA

1 small bunch of coriander (cilantro), roughly chopped

1 small bunch of flat-leaf parsley, roughly chopped

50ml (1¾fl oz) olive oil

juice of ½ lemon

2 tsp smoked paprika (sweet or hot, as you like)

1 tsp ground cumin

2 cloves of garlic, peeled then left whole

1 small red chilli, stem removed

The French call this cooking method *en papillote*; the Italians call it *al cartoccio*. Wrapping fish in greaseproof paper is a great hack for anxious fish cooks, as it guarantees the fish cooks well, remaining moist, and it gives you a decent window of flexibility in the cooking and serving times. The fish, sealed in with its steamy vapours, can't dry out too terribly if your mealtime organization slips up. The liquid that seasons and cooks the fish within the parcel can be as little as some olive oil or butter and a slosh of white wine or some citrus juice (among other things), but the real drama of a fish baked in a parcel comes when you and your guests unwrap the paper at the table: you are each walloped in the face with such a fiercely fragrant steamy belch, it's all anyone can talk about. The chermoula here is a case in point.

First, make the chermoula. Use a food processor to blend all the chermoula ingredients together to form a smooth sauce. Season with salt and pepper and put to one side.

Preheat the oven to 180°C/160°C fan/350°F/Gas Mark 4. Place a large, flat baking sheet in the oven to heat up, too.

Cut 4 large sheets of baking paper and fold each in half – each folded piece should be big enough to fit a whole fish. Season the fish inside and out with salt and pepper. Place 1 lemon slice and a bay leaf inside the cavity of each fish. Spoon over 1 tablespoon of chermoula per fish.

Put the fish in the centre of each piece of folded baking paper, then fold up the sides and fold over the top to create a seal, roughly like an envelope. Put the fish parcels on the baking tray, evenly spaced in a single layer. Bake for 18–20 minutes, until cooked through.

To serve, place a parcel on each plate and let your guests unwrap their portion at the table. Serve with the additional chermoula for everyone to help themselves.

Leek Tarte Tatin

350g (12oz) puff or shortcrust pastry

plain (all-purpose) flour, for dusting

5 leeks, white and pale green parts cut in half lengthways

2 tbsp good olive oil

½ tsp salt, plus more to season

½ tsp freshly ground black pepper, plus more to season

50ml (1¾fl oz) cider vinegar or white wine vinegar

1–2 tsp caster (superfine) sugar

40g (1½oz) unsalted butter, plus more for greasing

2 tbsp Dijon mustard

½ small bunch of thyme, leaves picked

Leeks are an unsung hero in the kitchen and deserve more attention than to be simply sliced and diced, then lost in a mixture. As dishes go, this one is really something to take your time over. You don't get to see the beauty of your tarte until it is cooked and turned out; it's nerve-racking stuff, so arrange those leeks like a work of art, then cross your fingers that you've got your masterpiece just right.

Preheat the oven to 200°C/180°C fan/400°F/Gas Mark 6. Grease about a 25cm (10in) cast-iron skillet or frying pan that will fit in your oven with a little butter.

Roll out the puff pastry on a lightly floured work surface to a circle that matches the size of your pan, then chill the round of pastry on a plate in the fridge.

Put the leeks in a baking tray with the oil and gently coat (so they don't fall apart) and season with the ½ teaspoon each of salt and pepper. Roast the leeks, cut side downward, for 10–15 minutes, until tender and just beginning to turn golden brown.

Boil the vinegar and sugar in the prepared skillet or frying pan over a high heat for 2 minutes, until reduced by half, then whisk in the butter, mustard and half the thyme. Remove from the heat and put to one side.

Arrange the leeks, cut sides downward, in the butter mixture in the pan, making sure they fit attractively and snugly together, then cover with the pastry round, pushing the sides of the pastry down into the bottom of the pan to encase the leeks tightly. Slash the top of the pastry right through to the leeks a couple of times to allow steam to escape during cooking.

Bake for 35–40 minutes, until the pastry is golden brown, then allow to cool for at least 5 minutes in the pan before placing a large plate over the top and flipping the pan to invert the tart out onto the plate. Take care you don't burn yourself with any of the hot juices escaping out of the sides. Rearrange any leeks that might have stuck in the pan and sprinkle with the remaining thyme leaves, adding a final seasoning of salt and freshly ground black pepper to taste.

Kimchi

500g (1lb 2oz) Chinese cabbage, daikon, radish or kohlrabi, finely sliced

1 tsp salt

½ tsp caster (superfine) sugar

2 cloves of garlic, finely sliced

25g (1oz) fresh ginger, peeled and finely sliced

4 tbsp light soy sauce

4 tbsp fish sauce

1 tbsp Korean chilli flakes or other medium-hot chilli flakes

MAKES ABOUT 600G (1LB 5OZ)

This one's for you especially, Grace, my bright and ever-curious eldest daughter. Quizzed as to why she loves kimchi so very much, she tells me, 'It's the salty, chilli tang that crunches and pops in your mouth.' And she's right, it does. Kimchi is one of the world's best table condiments. Served with steamed rice and vegetables, a mound of kimchi sprinkled with sesame seeds provides knee-jerk cooking later in the week, when your brain is too tired to think all that much more of an evening. Refrigerated in clean, sterilized jars, kimchi should last and last, although do check on it – it should taste good and sour, but not be fizzy.

Put the sliced cabbage (or alternative) in a large mixing bowl and rub in the salt and sugar. Do this until the vegetables begin to release some of their liquid, then sit the mixture in a colander overnight, with a plate sat on top of them, pressing down to release more liquid.

The following day wash the vegetables briefly in cold running water and drain well in a colander again.

In a separate bowl, combine the garlic and ginger with the remaining ingredients. Rub this mixture thoroughly into the drained vegetables.

Pack the mixture into sterilized jars, pressing down firmly to push out as much air as you can. If the neck of the jar can fit one, place a small, clean plate or weight on top of the vegetables to weigh them down in the liquid, submerging them for fermentation; if not, a small freezer bag filled with water will work. Leave 1cm (½in) clear at the top of the jar for any fermentation gases to linger, and not explode the jar!

Ferment at room temperature for 5 days, after which time taste the kimchi: it should taste salty with a good sour flavour. Refrigerate and leave well alone for a further 3–5 days before using. The longer you leave it, the sourer the kimchi will get.

Katmer

4 sheets of filo pastry, thawed
if frozen

80g (2¾oz) unsalted pistachios,
crushed to a coarse powder, plus
more to serve

2 tbsp light brown soft sugar
or runny honey

100g (3½oz) clotted cream or
mascarpone (or Turkish kaymak)

30g (1oz) unsalted butter, melted

runny honey, to serve (optional)

This is a good recipe for using up leftover sheets of filo. If you buy filo especially, a whole packet will make many (you need only one sheet per katmer), so just increase the remaining quantities accordingly. Katmer is a lot less bother to make than baklava, with its many layers and large quantity of honey. I've used clotted cream, though I am sure Turkish cooks and bakers do not use that – look for Turkish kaymak if you prefer, but clotted cream gives a good approximation and will be easier to find. You want a thick, creamy consistency to daub on the filo along with some of the pistachio before folding and cooking the parcel until crisp, then drizzling over with honey and yet more pistachios (in a blizzard of bright green).

Preheat the oven to 230°C/210°C fan/450°F/Gas Mark 8 and place the filo under a damp cloth. Brush a baking sheet with melted butter.

Mix the pistachios and sugar or honey together and, on a plate, separate the mixture into four piles.

Place 1 filo sheet at a time on a dry work surface (keeping the rest of the filo sheets well covered). Spoon little dabs (amounting to about 1 tablespoon) of the clotted cream over the top half of the square and sprinkle with half of one of the four piles of pistachio. Then fold the filo sheet in half and repeat over one half of the pastry rectangle, folding over the other half to create a square. Brush with a little melted butter and place onto the prepared baking sheet. Repeat with the remaining filo sheets and filling.

Bake for 10–15 minutes, until crisp and just beginning to turn golden. Remove from the oven, transfer to a serving plate and drizzle with honey, sprinkling over the extra crushed pistachios.

Croque Monsieur Bread & Butter Pudding

60g (2¼oz) unsalted butter, softened, plus more for greasing

1 day-old baguette, cut into 1cm (½in slices)

2 tbsp Dijon mustard, plus more to serve

150g (5½oz) sliced ham, roughly chopped

350ml (12fl oz) whole milk

300ml (10½fl oz) double (heavy) cream

6 eggs

100g (3½oz) gruyère, cheddar, comté or emmental cheese, coarsely grated (shredded)

freshly ground black pepper

cornichons, to serve (optional)

green salad, to serve

Translated into English, *croque monsieur* means 'Mr Crunch'. It's safe to assume, then, that way back when the croque monsieur was first conceived – crunchy on the outside, dripping with cheese and slices of ham within – the intended audience might well have been a masculine one. A croque madame is a Mr Crunch with a fried egg on top, the egg being a gratuitously floozy accessory to this hunk of a sandwich. In this recipe, using the same croque components, I'm suggesting you do away with the béchamel and forget about sandwich as form entirely, instead baking the lot much as you would for a bread and butter pudding. Soaked in the egg emulsion, the bread takes on a custardy wobble, with the top turning crunchy and brown. Same, same, and equally so altogether very different.

Preheat the oven to 160°C/140°C fan/315°F/ Gas Mark 2–3. Grease a 25cm (10in) baking dish with a little butter.

Butter the slices of bread on one side and spread a thin layer of mustard on the other side. Stick a bit of ham to the mustard on most of the pieces of bread. Arrange the bread, buttered sides upward, in an overlapping pattern in the dish.

In a bowl, whisk together the milk, cream and eggs, then season with plenty of freshly ground black pepper, remembering the cheese and ham will bring salt to the dish. Pour this mixture over the bread and ham in the dish and sprinkle over the cheese. Allow the dish to soak in the liquid for 15 minutes before baking.

Bake for 35–40 minutes, until the custard is set and the bread and cheese are golden brown, then remove from the oven and allow to rest for 10 minutes before serving warm, or even at room temperature, with extra mustard and some cornichons on the side, if using. And, of course, a green salad.

Fried Cheese Empanadas
(Empanadas de Viento)

250g (9oz) plain (all-purpose) flour

½ tsp salt

½ tsp baking powder

75g (2½oz) cold unsalted butter, diced

1 egg, beaten

200g (7oz) cheddar cheese, coarsely grated (shredded)

½ small red onion, very finely diced

sunflower oil, for frying

caster (superfine) sugar, to serve

Serve these Ecuadorian appetizers hot with drinks at a party, or when guests arrive for supper. Something small, fried and salty suits fizz or bitter aperitif drinks especially well – one bite leads to a sip and then to another, thank you very much. The sugar sprinkled on the pastry might sound a little wacky at first glance, but it shouldn't do. Serving cheese alongside something sweet is a classic combination. Here, the cheese melts obediently with the onion in the fried pastry. The sprinkle of sugar is a perfect finish.

Put the flour, salt and baking powder in a food processor or bowl. Add the pieces of butter and pulse until mixed and resembling breadcrumbs. If you're using a bowl, rub the mixture together with your fingertips.

Add the egg and 4 tablespoons of cold water and mix to form a soft dough (adding a bit more if it is too dry, or a bit more flour if it is sticking – you want a smooth and pliable dough). Knead until smooth, then place in a bowl, cover with a damp, clean cloth and allow to rest for at least 30 minutes.

Meanwhile, in a separate bowl, mix the cheese and onion together.

Roll out the dough to about 3mm ($^1/_8$in) thick and cut into disks 15cm (6in) in diameter. Spoon the cheese and onion filling onto the centre of each disk. Fold the disks in half and seal the edges, pressing gently with your fingertips, then using a fork to press down and firmly seal. Ensure the empanadas are sealed well – twist the ends together, too, if necessary. They must not leak when you come to fry them. Refrigerate the empanadas for at least 30 minutes.

Working in batches of 2 empanadas at a time, fry them in about 3cm (1¼in) of oil, at 180°C/350°F, for about 1–2 minutes per side, until they are golden and crisp. Drain on paper towels and sprinkle generously with sugar. Serve immediately.

Deep-fried Whole Artichoke

2 lemons, halved

4 large artichokes

1.5 litres (52fl oz) sunflower oil

50ml (1¾fl oz) white wine

salt and freshly ground black pepper

I wanted to include this recipe because, in winter, globe artichokes are readily available from greengrocers and market stalls, and yet I suspect that many shoppers do not quite know what to do with them. As a chef, I have prepped many of these vegetables (in fact, a thistle) with a paring knife, dropping the trimmed artichokes into bowls of cold water with lemons to stop them from discolouring. Take your time in the preparation and enjoy the enormously agreeable and satisfying results.

Squeeze the juice from 2 of the lemon halves into a large bowl of cold water. Add the squeezed lemon halves to the water too. Leave to one side.

Cut away the tough, dark, outer leaves of one of the artichokes, until you get to the softer, paler internal leaves, then use a sharp knife to cut away the top, leafier purple part. Peel the stem to remove the tough skin, then put the artichoke into the lemony water while you prepare the others in the same way.

Pour the sunflower oil into a deep pan and heat it to 140–150°C/275–300°F.

Remove the artichokes from the water, drain them and give them a good shake to dislodge any water stuck within them, then dry thoroughly with a clean tea towel. Working in batches of 2 at a time, fry the artichokes in the hot oil for 10 minutes, until just tender at the base, then remove from the oil with a slotted spoon.

Drain the artichokes upside down in a colander. When cool enough to handle, prise open the leaves with your fingers and sprinkle with the white wine and some salt.

Heat the oil again, this time to 180°C/350°F. Cut the remaining lemon halves into wedges.

Again working in batches, deep-fry the artichokes for 1–2 minutes, until golden and beginning to brown and crisp up at the edges. Remove from the oil and drain upside down on paper towels.

Season the artichokes with salt and pepper and serve immediately with the lemon wedges on the side.

Banana & Maple Granola

1 tsp ground cinnamon

3 tbsp coconut or sunflower oil

50g (1¾oz) light brown soft or demerara sugar

2 tbsp maple syrup (or use runny honey)

1 very ripe banana, mashed

250g (9oz) rolled oats

75g (2½oz) walnuts, roughly chopped

75g (2½oz) hazelnuts or almonds, roughly chopped

50g (1¾oz) sunflower seeds

200g (7oz) pitted dates, roughly chopped (or use raisins)

75g (2½oz) dried or semi-dried banana chips, crushed or chopped into small pieces

salt, to taste

MAKES 1 LARGE JAR

Making granola is one of those weekend tasks you will thank yourself for on a frantic weekday morning. Smugness can be a nice feeling when you are the beneficiary. For this recipe you will need a very, very ripe banana, one that is well freckled, where, with the skin peeled back, the banana has a strong, candied aroma. These are the bananas that mash the best (the green ones just do not mash obligingly). Mixed with the oil, maple and sugar, the banana coats the oats to bake. My top tip for making really good granola is to not disturb the oats at all when cooking and cooling the granola. As the oats cool, all coated with the sugars and fat, they clump and crust together. When the granola is completely cool, you should then be able to break the mixture up, giving you decent boulder-y chunks. Stored in an airtight jar, the granola will last a month or more.

Preheat the oven to 150°C/130°C fan/300°F/Gas Mark 2. Line a baking tray with baking paper.

Warm the cinnamon, oil, sugar and maple syrup together in a pan over a low heat, until the sugar has melted (about 2–3 minutes). Remove from the heat and stir through the mashed banana.

Add the oats, nuts and seeds and stir well until completely coated, then spread this mixture out evenly onto the lined tray, sprinkling over a little salt to taste.

Bake the granola for 25–30 minutes, until the mixture is golden brown and crisp throughout, rotating the tray halfway through cooking, so that the mixture bakes evenly. Do not stir or disturb the granola on the tray while baking and cooling.

Remove the tray from the oven and allow the granola to cool completely before adding the dried fruit and banana chips to the mixture. Store in a large airtight jar.

Gnocchi with Cavolo Nero Sauce

700g (1lb 9oz) floury potatoes

1 tsp salt

¼ nutmeg, freshly grated (shredded)

1 egg, lightly beaten

100g (3½oz) type '00' flour (or use plain/all-purpose flour), plus more if needed and for rolling

400g (14oz) cavolo nero, tough middle stalks discarded, leaves roughly chopped

3 cloves of garlic, peeled then left whole

butter or olive oil, for frying

parmesan, to serve

Deep, dark green – even purply-black sometimes – cavolo nero leaves, when boiled with whole garlic cloves, then blitzed, will give you a tender and glossy sauce that tastes sublimely of bitter, of sweet and of the greenest of greens. A silky puddle of seasoned green, with plump gnocchi, fat with purpose, given the obligatory snowstorm of parmesan to serve.

Preheat the oven to 200°C/180°C fan/400°F/Gas Mark 6.

Bake the potatoes for 45 minutes–1 hour, until cooked through and tender when pierced with a skewer. Remove from the oven and leave until cool enough to handle.

Halve the potatoes and scoop out the flesh. Using the back of a spoon, push the flesh through a sieve, or use a potato ricer, so that the potato is completely smooth.

Place the mashed potato on a clean work surface and mix through the salt and nutmeg. Add the egg and scatter over the flour. Mix together to form a soft dough, adding just a touch more flour if the mixture is too sticky. Very gently knead for about 1 minute, taking care not to overwork the dough. Leave for 5 minutes to rest.

Cut the dough into four equal pieces. On a lightly floured surface, roll each into a long sausage shape about 3cm (1¼in) in diameter. Cut each sausage into pieces about 4cm (1½in) long, placing the cut gnocchi on a lightly floured chopping board.

Cook the gnocchi in plenty of well-salted boiling water for 2–3 minutes, or until they float to the surface. Scoop them out using a slotted spoon and place them onto a lightly oiled tray. Allow to cool, reserving the water.

Boil the cavolo nero and the garlic in the gnocchi water for 10–15 minutes, until tender, then drain, reserving a little of the water. Blend the cavolo nero and garlic, adding a little reserved liquid if required, to a thick, verdant sauce. Check the seasoning and keep warm.

Heat a little butter or oil in a pan over a moderate heat. Add the gnocchi and fry for about 2–3 minutes each side, turning gently, until lightly browned on all sides. Serve in the cavolo nero sauce, sprinkled with parmesan.

Buttermilk Fried Cauliflower with Jalapeño & Lime Dressing

1 cauliflower, cut into bite-size florets

400ml (14fl oz) buttermilk (or use natural yogurt)

1 small clove of garlic, finely chopped

1–2 jalapeño chillies, roughly chopped

1 lime (or 2 if your limes aren't especially juicy), halved

1 small bunch of coriander (cilantro), leaves picked and roughly chopped

½–1 tsp chilli powder

1 tsp cumin seeds, toasted and ground

½ tsp salt, plus more to taste

100g (3½oz) self-raising flour

50g (1¾oz) cornflour (cornstarch)

sunflower oil, for frying

SERVES 4 AS A SNACK OR APPETIZER

One of my favourite recipes in the book, this is so good. Watch as a whole cauliflower is devoured in minutes – it's so delicious, you might even want to think about tackling two heads of cauliflower. Use half the buttermilk to drench and flavour the cauliflower before frying and the other half to blitz with some chilli, garlic, coriander (cilantro) and lime to make the dressing. When they are fried, heavens above, cauliflower becomes so unbelievably good, this will be your favourite way to eat it forevermore.

Bring a large pan of well-salted water to a boil. Add the cauliflower florets and boil for 2 minutes, until just tender, then drain well and allow to cool at little.

In the meantime, blend half the buttermilk with the garlic, chilli, salt to taste, juice from half the lime and all the coriander to make a smooth dressing and put to one side.

Mix the remaining buttermilk with the chilli powder, cumin and a ½ teaspoon of salt, then mix the drained cauliflower florets into the buttermilk mixture until fully coated.

In a separate bowl, mix the flour and cornflour (cornstarch) together with a big pinch of salt.

Coat the cauliflower in the flour mixture and place on a baking tray so that the pieces aren't touching each other. Pour at least 3cm (1¼in) of oil into a wide, deep pan and heat to 180°C/350°F. The oil is ready for frying when you drop in a piece of cauliflower and it sizzles and floats to the surface immediately.

Working in batches of about 6–8 pieces at a time, fry the cauliflower florets for a few minutes, or until golden on all sides. Remove each batch with a slotted spoon and set aside to drain on paper towels while you fry the remainder. Season well with salt.

Serve the fried cauliflower immediately along with the dressing and with the remaining half of the lime cut into wedges for squeezing over.

Marmalade

900g (2lb) Seville oranges

3 lemons

2kg (4lb 8oz) granulated sugar

MAKES 2.5KG (5LB 8OZ)

One of my favourite kitchen tasks, marmalade-making has the advantage of filling your house with the smells of citrus and sunshine. I find this is especially welcome during the cold, dank months of January and February when Seville oranges come into season. In my recipe you boil the oranges and a few lemons whole, then leave them to cool (overnight is best) in the bright, bitter liquid before scraping out the pith and pips, then cutting the skin to size. I like my marmalade thick cut, a jagged and chaotic jigsaw of orange skin – a million, trillion miles away from thin and straggly. Buy a digital thermometer to take the indecision and heartache out of marmalade-making (among other cooking tasks). Boiled for 1 minute when the marmalade reaches 105°C/221°F, the marmalade will set with a tender, covetous wobble.

Put the oranges and lemons in a large saucepan and pour over 2 litres (70fl oz) of water. Bring to a boil over a high heat, then reduce the heat and simmer for 2 hours. Remove from the heat and leave the fruit to sit in the liquid in the pan for at least 6 hours, or overnight.

Remove the fruits, leaving the liquid in the pan, and spilt them in half, scooping out the flesh and pips and reserving these in a bowl. Chop the orange and lemon skins however you like – into fat or thin strips.

Tie the fruit flesh and pips tightly in cheese cloth or muslin (or use any clean cloth).

Add the sugar and the chopped skins to the pan with the liquid, along with the cloth tied with the flesh and pips. Bring the pan to a rapid boil over a high heat – be careful it will boil volcanically, so keep a watchful eye – then boil steadily until the marmalade reaches the magic setting point of 105°C/221°F. When you get to this temperature, boil the marmalade for a further 1 minute.

Remove the pan from the heat and leave the marmalade to stand and settle for at least 30 minutes before spooning into clean, sterilized jars and sealing tight. The marmalade can last for anything up to a year or more.

Stout & Chocolate Cake with Toasted Oats

250ml (9fl oz) stout

230g (8½oz) unsalted butter

70g (2½oz) unsweetened cocoa powder

50g (1¾oz) rolled oats, plus 2 tbsp more to sprinkle

200g (7oz) plain (all-purpose) flour

250g (9oz) caster (superfine) sugar, plus 1 tbsp more to sprinkle

1½ tsp bicarbonate of soda (baking soda)

big pinch of salt

2 eggs, beaten

150g (5½oz) sour cream, plus more to serve

My daughter Ivy was born on 23 December. We arrived home with her on Christmas morning, shell-shocked, loved up and thoroughly knackered – just as many parents of newborns are. Christmas that year, not surprisingly, was a little different from others. I can't quite remember how we even got through the day to be honest. On Boxing Day, or shortly afterwards (time takes on a curious quality when you're relentlessly sleep-deprived), a baker friend dropped round with a cake (disclaimer: dropping round on somebody post-birth can elicit joy, but also visceral horror at the thought of having to greet anyone from the outside world, so do get permission first). 'It's got stout in it,' she said, and with that she was gone. The rumour goes, although I think it's considered a bit of an old wives' tale these days, that drinking stout is good for new mothers, improving iron and stimulating milk supply. I have no idea whether stout does help, but I do know that good cake is a salve and makes the world go round, especially for bleary-eyed new parents. This one is also incredibly easy to bake.

Preheat the oven to 180°C/160°C fan/350°F/Gas Mark 4. Line a 24cm (9½in) cake tin with baking paper.

Bring the stout and butter to a boil in a saucepan over a moderate heat. Add the cocoa and oats and whisk well until smooth. Remove from the heat and cool a little.

Whisk the flour, sugar, bicarbonate of soda (baking soda) and big pinch of salt together in a large mixing bowl. Whisk the eggs and sour cream into the stout and cocoa mixture, mixing thoroughly to combine. Add the flour mixture to the egg mixture and fold together until the batter is completely combined.

Pour the batter into the prepared tin and sprinkle with the extra sugar and oats. Bake for about 45 minutes, or until a skewer inserted into the centre comes out clean. Remove from the oven and cool in the tin a little, then turn out onto a wire rack to cool completely. Serve with extra sour cream.

Parsnip, Ginger & Date Loaf

150g (5½oz) parsnip, peeled and grated (shredded), woody cores cut away as necessary

150g (5½oz) light brown soft sugar

250ml (9fl oz) sunflower oil

3 eggs

300g (10½oz) self-raising flour

1 tsp bicarbonate of soda (baking soda)

1 tbsp ground ginger

1 tsp ground cinnamon

pinch of salt

50g (1¾oz) pitted dates, finely chopped

MAKES 2 LOAVES

This is a doddle to make and terrific for packed lunches. Parsnips are an ancient vegetable, a plant of the parsley family. They were grown for their medicinal value in Greek and Roman times. Parsnips have been especially favoured for their hardiness through the winter, and their high sugar content, which unsurprisingly made them a favourable ingredient to use in wine making, jam and cakes, too. Sweet and fudgy, the parsnip in this recipe cooks in the cake crumb and makes for a moist cake that keeps very well. In fact, I think it is better eaten on the day after it is baked. This cake also freezes well.

Preheat the oven to 160°C/140°C fan/315°F/ Gas Mark 2–3. Grease and line 2 x 500g (1lb 2oz) loaf tins with baking paper.

In a mixing bowl, beat together the parsnip, sugar, oil and eggs. Sift in the flour, bicarbonate of soda (baking soda), ginger, cinnamon and pinch of salt. Stir well and add the chopped dates.

Pour the batter equally into the 2 loaf tins and bake for 45 minutes–1 hour, or until a skewer inserted into the centre of each loaf comes out clean. Remove from the oven and leave to cool in the tins before turning out to cool completely.

THE MEXICAN ONE

Seville Orange Cantaritos

Pork & Seville Orange Carnitas
served with Tortillas, Oaxacan
Mushrooms, Refried Black Beans,
Guacamole, Pink Pickled Onions
& Fried Cumin Pumpkin Seeds

Buñuelos with Spiced Pineapple
& Chilli, Bay & Cinnamon Syrup

SERVES 6–8

Feast like you mean it with this Mexican-inspired menu. A table laid with a generous Mexican spread is one of the most vibrant and commanding of eating prospects, often with many different dishes to scoop and pile up into warm tortillas, no one taco ever tasting quite the same as the previous one. I guarantee that you will always tend to overfill your first taco, eyes bigger than your stomach can ever realistically be. And you will eat it with a joyful gusto, pledging that yes, you will eat at least six, possibly more, such is your hunger and so delicious is the food. Struggling at four, you push on through with a fifth, but six... you've got to be kidding. I've used soft wheat tortillas in this recipe to wrap as tacos. They are readily available, but please (in fact, I urge you to) try at least once to make your own soft corn tortillas. They are a wholesome and authentic backdrop to much Mexican cuisine.

I've used quite a few Seville oranges. To kick off the meal, and to get your taste buds working, is a Seville orange cantarito (a kind of margarita traditionally served in a clay pot, but here a tall glass will do). It's thought that these bitter Seville oranges were introduced to Europe via Sicily (from Asia) in the 11th century. Then, the following century, they were first cultivated in Seville, Spain, from where they take their name. Eventually, Spanish explorers took the bumpy, bitter-skinned fruits with them on their voyages, in turn introducing them to England, Scotland and further afield – to Brazil and Mexico some time around the late 15th and 16th centuries. To this day, although Seville oranges are primarily grown in Spain for European markets, some parts of Mexico (mostly in the Yucatán) also grow them and they have become integral to Mexican cuisine. The word for orange in Spanish is *naranja*, which in Mexico refers specifically to the Seville orange rather than the sweet orange. Many associate Mexican cooking with lime juice, but if you want to be authentic, use Seville oranges instead.

cont.

Get well ahead with this busy menu, making the carnitas a day ahead and reheating when you're ready to serve. The flavour will only get better. Use lard if you like – pork fat would be the cooking fat of choice in Mexico and will lend good depth of flavour. You could make the spiced pineapple ahead, too, perhaps on the morning of your feast, leaving you with just the mushrooms and smaller dishes to serve alongside the tortillas, and the *buñuelos*. These are deep-fried wheat dough balls or flat rounds and are served flecked with sugar and drenched in spiced, sweet syrup. I've used pineapple for the syrup, but you could just as well use mango, banana, papaya or guava – or any tropical fruit, it's up to you.

If you really want to get a handle on Mexican cooking, the chillies are where you should probably start. The variety of chillies now available, both fresh and dried, is astounding. My storecupboard would fall short if not for the dry, wrinkled black and deep-red beauties of ancho (earthy, dried fruit, liquorice, hot heat) and chipotle (smoky, sweet cherries, hot heat), which I like to first fry in a dry pan to toast then rehydrate in water or a slow braise. When it comes to fresh chillies, jalapeño and habanero are perhaps my favourite of all. Jalapeños are sweet, juicy and grassy; habaneros have more tropical flavours and a tremendous depth of heat. Finally, buy some good hot sauces. We have quite an assembly on the shelf here at home – from those that you can shake and splash from the bottle (too much, too little, who cares?) to those little cans of chipotle in adobo, chillies packed in a swampy and slightly sweet sauce of vinegar and tomatoes. Mexican cooking has it all, and while chilli might lead the pecking order as vital seasoning, salt, fat, sugar and acid all combine to make this one of the greatest cuisines in the world (sharing the pedestal with Italian, if you ask me).

Seville Orange Cantaritos

½ bottle of tequila or mezcal

100ml (3½fl oz) Seville orange juice (or use sweet oranges and limes), plus more juice to rim and a few slices to garnish

sugar syrup or gomme (shop-bought or homemade; see method)

1 tbsp coarse salt, crushed

1 tsp dried chilli flakes

lots of ice

soda water (optional)

Make your own sugar syrup, if you like, using a ratio of 50:50 water to sugar. Boil the sugar in the water until dissolved, then cool completely before using.

In a big jug or pitcher, mix the tequila with the Seville orange juice and add sugar syrup to your taste.

In a separate bowl, mix the salt and chilli together to form a coarse dust. Use 4 tall glasses. Dip the rims of the glasses in a little extra Seville orange juice. Dip the wet rims of the glasses in the chilli salt and add lots of ice to each glass. Pour the tequila mixture into each glass and top with extra soda water, if you like.

Pork & Seville Orange Carnitas

600g (1lb 5oz) diced pork belly or fatty pork shoulder

juice of 2 Seville oranges (or use sweet oranges with a splash of red wine vinegar), plus more to serve

2 bay leaves, scrunched a little

1 tsp salt, plus more to season

4 dried ancho chillies, stems removed and deseeded

boiling water from a kettle

3 tbsp sunflower oil or lard

1 onion, finely diced

4 cloves of garlic, finely sliced

½ tsp cumin seeds, toasted and ground

1 tsp dried oregano (Mexican if possible)

freshly ground black pepper

TO SERVE

selection of side dishes, opposite

flour or soft corn tortillas, warmed

1 bunch of coriander (cilantro), leaves picked and roughly chopped

sour cream

hot sauce of choice – chipotle, habanero, jalapeño (up to you)

Seville oranges, or limes, quartered, to squeeze

Place the pork in a heavy-based saucepan or casserole with a tight-fitting lid. Add the Seville orange juice, the bay leaves, 200ml (7fl oz) of cold water and the salt and bring to a boil over a high heat. Reduce the heat to moderate and simmer with the lid on for 40–45 minutes, or until the pork is tender, then remove the lid and cook for 10–15 minutes, until the liquid has mostly evaporated and the meat has rendered most of its fat into the sauce, giving tender meat.

Meanwhile, toast the dried chillies in a dry frying pan over a moderate heat, then place in a bowl and cover with boiling water. Leave to soak for at least 10 minutes.

Heat half the oil or lard in a saucepan over a moderate heat. Add the onion and cook for 10 minutes, until soft and translucent. Add the garlic and cook for a further 2 minutes, until fragrant. Add the cumin and oregano and cook for 30 seconds–1 minute, until very aromatic. Remove from the heat and put to one side.

Put the cooked onion mixture, the soaked chillies and 200ml (7fl oz) of the chilli soaking liquid into a blender and blitz until smooth. Put to one side.

Heat the remaining oil or lard in a frying pan over a moderate heat. Add the onion and chilli purée and cook for 3–5 minutes, until thickened. Remove from the heat and stir this mixture into the slow-cooked pork.

Cook the pork over a moderate heat for another 10 minutes or so, until the meat has absorbed most of the sauce and the dish is rich and thick and highly seasoned. Remove from the heat and check the seasoning, adding more salt, freshly ground black pepper and Seville orange juice to taste, as necessary.

Serve the pork as it is or, if you prefer, use two forks to pull and shred any remaining larger pieces of meat. Serve with the side dishes, warmed tortillas, chopped coriander (cilantro), sour cream, hot sauce and orange or lime quarters for guests to assemble themselves.

Side Dishes for the Carnitas

OAXACAN MUSHROOMS

1 tbsp sunflower oil or lard

1 onion, finely diced

2 cloves of garlic, finely chopped

1 tsp ground cumin

1 tsp dried oregano

1 tbsp tomato purée

1-2 tsp chipotle paste, to taste

250g (9oz) chestnut mushrooms (or other mushrooms), thinly sliced

salt and freshly ground black pepper

Heat the oil or lard in a saucepan over a moderate heat. Add the onion and cook for 10 minutes, until soft. Add the garlic and cook for a further 2 minutes, until fragrant. Add the cumin, oregano, tomato purée, chipotle paste and ½ teaspoon of salt. Cook for a further 1 minute, scraping the pan to coat the onions well.

Add the mushrooms to the pan and cook over a moderate heat for 10 minutes, or until the mushrooms are cooked through and most of the liquid has evaporated. Remove from the heat and check the seasoning, adding more salt and some pepper to taste.

EASY REFRIED BLACK BEANS

1 tbsp sunflower oil or lard

1-2 x 400g (14oz) cans of cooked black beans, drained and blended

¼ tsp ground cumin

salt and freshly ground black pepper

Heat the oil or lard in a saucepan over a moderate heat. Add the blended beans and fry for 2 minutes, then stir in the cumin, and add enough water for a thick pureé consistency. Season with salt and pepper to taste.

GUACAMOLE

2-3 ripe avocados, stoned and peeled

lime juice, to taste

salt

Mash the avocados with enough lime juice to taste and season with salt.

PINK PICKLED ONIONS

1 red onion, very finely sliced

boiling water from a kettle

¼ tsp salt

juice of ½ lime

Put the sliced onion in a small bowl and cover with boiling water. Leave to sit for 5 minutes, then drain and cool. Add the salt and lime juice, mixing well to combine.

FRIED CUMIN PUMPKIN SEEDS

1 tsp sunflower oil

50g (1¾oz) pumpkin seeds

pinch of salt

pinch of ground cumin

Heat the oil in a pan over a moderate heat. Add the pumpkin seeds with the salt and cumin until popping and crackling in the pan (about 2–3 minutes). Remove from the heat and place in a bowl to serve.

Buñuelos with Spiced Pineapple & Chilli, Bay & Cinnamon Syrup

FOR THE BUÑUELOS DOUGH

125g (4½oz) self-raising flour, plus more for dusting

4 tbsp caster (superfine) sugar

pinch of salt

1 tsp ground cinnamon

1 tsp ground allspice

1 egg, beaten

2 tbsp whole milk

20g (¾oz) unsalted butter, melted

sunflower oil, for frying

FOR THE SYRUP

200g (7oz) caster (superfine) sugar

100ml (3½fl oz) dark rum

½ small ancho chilli, deseeded and cut into very thin strips (or use ½ a mild red chilli)

2 bay leaves, scrunched a little

1 cinnamon stick

1 large ripe pineapple, peeled and cut into small dice

Begin by making the buñuelos dough. In a mixing bowl mix together the flour with 1 tablespoon of the sugar, and the pinch of salt and ground spices. Make a well in the centre and add the egg, milk and melted butter, mixing thoroughly to form a rough dough.

Tip out the mixture onto a lightly floured work surface and knead assertively for a good few minutes until smooth and slightly elastic. Cover with a damp, clean cloth and put to one side.

Next make the syrup to spice the pineapple. Put the sugar in a heavy-based saucepan and warm through, without stirring, over a moderate heat. When the sugar starts to melt at the edges of the pan, give the pan a good shake, then continue to heat, until it begins to form a caramel. This can take 5 minutes or so.

When the caramel begins to form, very carefully add the rum, chilli, bay, cinnamon and 50ml (1¾fl oz) of water to the pan. Be careful, the mixture will splutter. Add the pineapple and cook for 5–10 minutes, until the pineapple is tender and the sauce is thick and syrupy.

Cut the dough into 8 equally sized pieces. On a lightly floured surface, roll out each piece into rounds about 2mm ($^1/_{16}$in) thick.

To fry the buñuelos, heat 3cm (1¼in) of oil in a deep-sided frying pan over a high heat until the temperature reaches 180°C/350°F. (Use a digital thermometer to check the temperature, or test with a tiny piece of dough – it should sink, then rise to the surface in the hot oil, immediately frying crisp and puffed up.)

Working in batches of 3 at a time, fry the buñuelos for 2 minutes, or until crisp, puffed up and golden on both sides. Remove each batch using a slotted spoon and set aside to drain on paper towels. Toss the buñuelos in the remaining 3 tablespoons of caster (superfine) sugar to coat and serve with the spiced pineapple.

CHINESE DUMPLING FEAST

To drink: Cold, lager beer

Potsticker Pork & Chinese
Cabbage Dumplings

Pomelo and Ginger Sorbet

MAKES 40 DUMPLINGS,
SERVES 4

My stepmother Lily makes the best dumplings.
They are so good that I think she feels they are
pretty much a curse these days.

No longer living in China, nor in Uganda where she
met my dad, Lily now lives with him in Ludlow, in
Shropshire. When she telephones to ask the children
what they would like her to cook on our next visit,
my children's pupils take on a whirly, hypnotic,
monochrome pattern. 'DUMPLINGS!' all three shout,
giddy at the thought. I'm sorry Lily, I do try to
persuade them otherwise. You do also make a mean
mapu dofu, and noodles in many forms, and Beijing
duck pancakes (in truth, we are spoilt for choice), but
the girls are steadfast. It's the tower of dumplings
they crave from you.

Visiting Lily in Chengdu years ago, Matt and I sat in
her kitchen, along with her sister and mother. Matt
and I were single-minded, almost mercenary in our
mission to learn from three masters the trick to
making good dumplings. Lily's mum was a whiz, but
her sister was a complete pro. Li Ju masterfully rolled
and twisted the dough at breakneck speed. While
Lily's sister rolled better, more intricate dumplings,
it was always Lily who made the better and tastier
filling. We drank a lot of tea, the kitchen dreamy with
the scent of jasmine leaves, and the ladies all laughed
at our clumsy dumpling attempts: tsk, tsk! Chefs, the
pair of them and they can't pleat a dumpling skin! (At
least, that's what I imagine her mum was tutting – Lily
was too kind to elaborate in her translation!). My dad
played patience with a pack of cards and a cold beer
next door, drifting into the kitchen from time to time
to see how we were getting on. I love this memory.
Fifteen years on, Matt and I can both now pleat a
dumpling pretty well. Although Lily's, her mum's
and, of course, Li Ju's, are works of art.

The dumplings in this menu are potsticker dumplings,
so-called because of the dual cooking method used
to heat the dumplings through, first fried until they
stick a little to the pan, then steamed, then cooked
hot with the pan lid off to caramelize the skins.

We like to eat them dipped in a vinegar (an essential seasoning in Chinese cooking), soy, chilli and sesame dipping sauce. My kids like their dipping sauces to be strong with vinegar, mouth-puckering and refreshing. We especially like the very dark sort of vinegar known as Chinkiang, as it has a deep, mellow and malty flavour with a hint of sweetness.

For pudding I'm offering sorbet. Of the three fairly lengthy trips I've had to China over the years, I'm relatively confident when I say that pudding is not a customary Chinese habit to end a meal, although fresh fruit is. Sometimes you might be offered candied fruits and sweets, but these tend to be more for children or during festivals. But I have seen the odd ice cream and sorbet, and we did enjoy red bean ice lollies (and green tea ones, too) when we were last there. Just to be sure, I've run this menu past Lily and she approves. A British chef with a Chinese stepmother, I am relieved that my recipe for pomelo and ginger sorbet isn't too subversive. Lily even thinks her mother might like it! Buy pink-fleshed pomelo, which are like grapefruit, but without the bitterness. They are fragrant, sweet and ever-so slightly sour.

A final word on feasting Chinese-style: the Chinese like to serve multiple dishes, in a wave, never really delineated as starter, main course, then pudding. A Chinese table is laid for everyone to share all the dishes. With that in mind and because I think you'll have your work cut out making enough dumplings to feel it is a proper feast, I haven't included any other savoury recipes for this menu. If you like, though, you could steam some Chinese greens and dress them with some soy, sesame and chilli oil. Likewise, for ease, I have recommended you buy the dumpling wrappers, leaving you with just the filling to make. This is an industrious, although pretty simple meal, and one that everyone can get involved with (many hands and all that – although, of course, some of you will be more adept at dumpling pleating than others).

Potsticker Pork & Chinese Cabbage Dumplings

4 tbsp finely grated (shredded) fresh ginger

100g (3½oz) Chinese cabbage, very thinly sliced

big pinch of salt

300g (10½oz) minced (ground) pork with a high fat content, kept very cold

1 tbsp light soy sauce, plus more for the dipping sauce

1 bunch of spring onions (scallions), very finely sliced

40 round Chinese dumpling or wonton wrappers

Chinkiang or black Chinese vinegar (use rice vinegar if you can't find it), for the dipping sauce and to taste

Chinese chilli oil, for the dipping sauce and more to serve solo, both to taste

sesame oil, for the dipping sauce

sunflower oil, for frying

boiling water from a kettle

Soak the ginger in 150ml (5fl oz) of cold water for 5 minutes.

Rub the cabbage with the big pinch of salt and leave it in a colander to soften for a bit – 15 minutes or so – then finely chop and squeeze dry in a clean cloth.

Put the minced (ground) pork into a bowl. Strain the ginger water through a fine sieve into the mince, add the sliced cabbage, soy sauce and the spring onions (scallions). Mix gently until the water has emulsified into the pork, and the mixture feels very soft.

Lay the wrappers on a clean, dry work surface, keeping those you are not working with covered with a clean cloth. Take one wrapper and place 1 tablespoon of the filling in the centre without getting any filling on the edges (which would prevent the dumpling sealing properly). With your fingertip, paint the circumference of the wrapper with water. Fold the wrapper in half to form a half-moon shape and seal by pressing firmly between your fingers. If you want to pleat the dumpling in a classic shape, start at the centre and make two or three, or as many as necessary, pleats working toward the right corner of the dumpling seal. Repeat from the centre the other way, working toward the left. Holding the pleated edges gently, press the bottom of the dumpling on the work surface to flatten the base and to help the dumpling stand. Place the completed dumpling on a lightly oiled tray, then repeat with the remaining wrappers and filling.

To make the dipping sauce, combine two thirds soy sauce with one third Chinkiang or black Chinese vinegar. Add chilli oil to taste and a splash of sesame oil. Pour the dipping sauce into small dipping bowls and put to one side.

To cook the dumplings, work in batches – frying, steaming, then serving each batch for your guests to eat while you cook the next.

Heat a large non-stick or cast-iron frying pan (skillet) with a tight-fitting lid over a high heat, until very hot. Add enough sunflower oil to just cover the base of the pan and, working in batches of about 10 dumplings at a time, place the dumplings bottom-down in the oil. Don't overcrowd the pan. Reduce the heat to moderate and fry for about 1–2 minutes, until the bases of the dumplings are lightly browned.

Next, drizzle in 100ml (3½fl oz) boiling water from a kettle and cover the pan tightly with the lid. Steam the batch of dumplings for about 5–7 minutes, until most of the liquid has evaporated and the dumplings are sizzling in the pan with a good colour on their bases. Remove the lid, add a splash more oil, turn up the heat and fry, shuffling the pan a bit, for a further 1 minute, until bronzed and crisp in places. Remove from the heat and serve immediately with the dipping sauce. Repeat the cooking process for the next batch of dumplings, while your guests tuck in.

Pomelo & Ginger Sorbet

2 large ruby pomelos (or use about 5 pink grapefruits), peeled

40g (1½oz) caster (superfine) sugar, plus more to taste

2 tbsp stem ginger syrup

juice of 1 lime

Separate the flesh of the pomelos into pieces so that there is no filament nor any connective membranes. Place the peeled pieces of fruit in a bowl and sprinkle with the sugar, ginger syrup and lime juice and leave the mixture to sit for 30 minutes to macerate.

In a blender or food processor, purée the pomelo mixture until smooth, then strain through a fine mesh sieve, adding more sugar to taste, if necessary

Put the sieved mixture into an ice-cream or sorbet machine and churn until frozen. Alternatively, freeze as granita by pouring the mix into a metal tray about 2–3cm (1–1¼in) deep and forking the mixture through from the freezer every 45 minutes or so, disrupting the mix to freeze in shards until semi-solid. Transfer to a freezer-proof container and freeze until you're ready to serve.

Index

VEGETARIAN RECIPES

(see note on page 7)

QUICK AND EASY STORE-CUPBOARD RECIPES

SWEET TREATS

Acknowledgments

I admire the African proverb that it takes a village to raise a child, a prescient reminder that people bring different qualities and influences in life; the same can also be said about the writing and making of a book. So many people are involved in the different stages; from incubation, to me finally, months and months later, handing in the manuscript, then beyond, to making sure this book gets attention come publication. I am thankful to everyone and in particular:

KitchenAid: For bombproof kitchenware and a mixer that hardly ever gets switched off here at home.

TOAST: Source of handsome/beautiful/practical things with which to set the table and also to wear.

Netherton Foundry: From Shropshire and ironware like no other; that BBQ was insane, and your pans are my favourite.

Microplane: What did we all do before Microplane?

Savernake Knives: Dazzling knives.

Isle of Wight Tomatoes: For providing such ludicrously good-looking tomatoes; voluptuous doesn't even cover it.

Hugo's Greengrocer: A triumphant greengrocer; truffles, pink lettuces and leafy lemons, there wasn't anything you couldn't get us.

Anna Tasca Lanza Cookery School: I so enjoyed the week I spent in Sicily midway through writing this book. Such a tonic: bright-blue skies, lemon trees and bitter leaves, also a generosity of spirit in all you do at the school that sent me back to my desk charged with renewed brio.

Victoria Moore, for her frontline work in Piedmont at the time of my writing and fearlessly quizzing Italian waiters on my behalf about Barolo substitutes for the Brasato. 'There aren't any,' said one waiter, but I am prepared to brave it and give a little more wiggle room for this particular recipe.

Rachel Roddy: A favourite writer who writes with an elegant, also thrifty beauty, but whom I also call a friend – at the time, and snorting with laughter, that sausage focaccia (page 275) conversation will take some beating Rachel.

Jamey, Dan, Maya and Rui: Thank you not only for the space to shoot this book – yours is a wonderful, bright kitchen – but for embracing the commotion that went with us all taking it over at various times throughout this past year, and lastly too, for marching my children up to school on time.

Sarah Lavelle: a bit like Mary Poppins, all gentle persuasion with killer instinct. The best there is.

Nikki E: Design is everything (and something I know nothing about).

Judy Barratt: Your red pen makes everything sharper.

Sam Folan and Faye Wears: Photography and styling with such skill and precision, a joy to work with you both. Your jokes though, Sam, seriously?

My Mum: For swooping the children off and out of the house when I felt too inundated with words to write. Superhero skills.

Matt: Unfailing teamwork in books, children, home, life and always.

Grace, Ivy and Dorothy: Troopers, all three. Can you imagine life any other way? The kitchen table swamped with food to cook, recipes to test; *try this, eat that*. Quite often there is a cake, but more often, some colossal collection of vegetables, and while you have all been known to roll your eyes from time to time, you are steadfast in your loyalty and love. I will always be here for you.